AF560816

Managing E-Business

Managing E-Business

Amitendu Anand

RANDOM PUBLICATIONS
NEW DELHI (INDIA)

Managing E-Business

ISBN 978-93-5111-639-4

Published in 2015 in India by

RANDOM PUBLICATIONS

4376-A/4B, Gali Murari Lal, Ansari Road
New Delhi-110 002
Phone : +9111-43580356, 011-23289044, 011-43142548
e-mail: sales@randompublications.com,
info@randompublications.com, randomexports@gmail.com

Reprinted 2022

Type Setting by : Friends Media, Delhi-110089
Digitally Printed at : Replika Press Pvt. Ltd.

Preface

E-business (electronic business), derived from such terms as "e-mail" and "e-commerce," is the conduct of business on the internet, not only buying and selling but also servicing customers and collaborating with business partners.

E-business infrastructure does not lend itself to this model: nonrepudiation and authentication have to be provided digitally. Digital signatures and encryption frame works have been developed.

Measuring the value of electronically mediated business has become an important activity in its own right. Fraught with difficulty, it is one which has to date produced wide divergences in terms of predictions, many of them prepared by those with a material interest in promoting e-Commerce and e-Business. It is also one where the danger of double counting is most frequently encountered.

e-Business enthusiasts will be well aware of the technical and financial advantages of e-Commerce. There are also ethical benefits. These include the potential to remove prejudice and barriers, as transactions are carried out via disembodied computer screens.

The lack of need for a physical presence in a particular place, as long as computer access is available, opens up all kinds of possibilities for freedom of mobility and inclusion of those with physical needs which make working in an office environment difficult (ranging from physical disability to a distinct preference for working on a beach!).

Internet-based business activities are opening up markets, improving information provision about different products, including non-corporate information. (For example, typing 'Nike' into a search engine finds company pages as well as sites about Nike products alleging human rights abuses by the company.) The Internet allows consumers much greater access to information, opening up the market and undermining monopolies. Such impacts are highly ethical according to a utilitarian perspective.

E-business strategy means more than just determining target markets and developing business plans describing the return on investment. It is a comprehensive view of your institution's e-business goals, expected outcomes, rationale, branding, marketing, and launch strategy.

The book is of utmost importance to students, teachers, businessmen, traders and general readers.

I would like to thank my team for standing beside me throughout my career and writing this book. My special thanks go to "Random Publications" who have published the book.

– Amitendu Anand

Contents

1

E-Business Today

CHALLENGES OF E-BUSINESS CHANGE

One of the first challenges companies face when attempting to develop online channels is to consider how such a strategy will impact upon their 'bricks and mortar' organization. Developing a 'clicks and mortar' operation may result in a more 'virtual' form of organization in which traditional ways of working are mixed with electronic communications.

It is here that a company encounters its first problem, which is usually one of technology. The particular difficulty relates to the attempt to evolve 'legacy' systems (*i.e.* the technical infrastructure that has accumulated to support the business over time) to an infrastructure that will support e-Business. Few businesses find themselves in the position where they can 'throw away' the old and introduce new, customized computer systems. Legacy systems often perform essential activities upon which daily business processes depend.

While start-up companies can leapfrog these problems, established ones face some difficult challenges. Effective e-Business solutions demand integrated front-and back-end systems, a process which may demand close co-operation between two groups (or even subcultures) with the organization. As Nigel Waterson of Gemini puts it, 'The front end has quite often been built by guys in ponytails, while the people who understand the back end are often grey haired'.

System integration means that when customers interact via the Web, placing orders and purchasing goods, the stock control and financial systems also speak the same language and carry out their part of the transactions. The problem is that many such back-end systems are unlikely to be based on open Internet protocols and may even have been custom built. Nonetheless, such systems may be critical to a company's business, and include such details as bank account data and stock rotation information. As Conway points out, IT managers are loath to replace them with something new and untested. They may not even fully understand how their legacies work any longer. The people who built the systems may well have left the company, leaving present IT experts reluctant to tinker.

Replacing or upgrading such systems also takes time, which may slow up Web developments critical to speedy e-Commerce innovation.Over and above the technological matters identified above, major *organizational* change issues must be recognized and addressed for online strategies to be realized successfully. This is because of the need to redesign business processes and structures, change organizational culture, and engage in education and training. A wide range of stakeholders may be affected, with many personnel needing to 'buy in' to the change.

There is only one way to do e-Business: fully committed. Everyone in the company must be dedicated to the effort. You can't have ten people for every thousand working on it. You can't delegate it.You have to encourage everyone to jump into the water and support them in teaching each other to swim. I'm asking for the biggest cultural change in your company's history. These issues will now be considered in turn.

RESISTANCE TO CHANGE

There are a number of reasons why people may be unwilling to accept organizational change, as summarized below:

- Stability and security are threatened.
- Coping strategies and comfort zones are affected.
- The uncertainty of change creates anxiety.
- Imposed change reduces perceived autonomy and control.
- Job content is changed and new skills are demanded.
- Authority structures and reporting lines are altered.
- Work groups and other relationships are disrupted.
- Established routines and practices are abandoned.
- An individual's power and authority is threatened.

According to Markus (1999), workers' reactions to change vary greatly. She suggests that while some workers readily embrace new technologies, some can be hostile, and the reason for this hostility can often be attributed to poor communication and shifts in organizational power. Effective internal marketing is important here in order to segment employees into 'supporters', 'neutrals' and 'opponents' of change, and then develop appropriately customized communications in order to deal with the differing priorities of each of these groups.

Implementation of change involves the disruptive transition from a current state to a future state, as a result individuals or groups can resist change. They claim that there are three types of problems encountered when an organization goes through a significant change:

- *Power*. Change can be viewed as a threat to existing power structures and it creates uncertainties, so the struggle for power escalates as individuals and groups attempt to control their environment by resisting change.

- *Uncertainty*. Anxiety is created as individuals are not sure where they stand and whether at the end of the change process they will still have a role within the organization. As a result, individuals can act irrationally, as they find it difficult to understand and interpret clearly information related to the change.
- *Control*. During the change period, it becomes difficult to maintain control because goals are changing, as are structures and roles, and certain control systems become irrelevant.

These authors also highlight the important point that within large organizations individuals usually do not openly resist change; instead, they 'subtly or passively' resist. The degree of employee involvement and participation can significantly affect the success of change. Markus claims that workers' reaction to change is dependent on whether they have had a say in selecting the technology or the way it is introduced and used, how the new technology is communicated, how much training and support are provided, and how carefully the roll out is planned and executed.

Involving employees fully means that they become responsible for the success of the change, becoming 'owners' of the change process. IBM Global Services recommends that in order to build a successful e-Business, organizations need to challenge their employees to:

identify the cultural changes that will also be needed and to shape the processes, the linked education, learning and competency development that will be required to deliver real value in the new ways of doing business that they are proposing.

Another critical point is that organizations are bound to encounter complications in asking individuals to make changes that they are incapable of implementing. Adequate investments in training and development programmes are therefore essential, particularly, for example, if new skills in Web design are required. If individuals do not possess the skills and capability necessary to introduced planned changes, the likelihood of success is significantly reduced.

According to Buchanan and Boddy (1992), the more radical change projects are, the more open they are to organizational disruption and failure. Badham *et al.* (1997) point out that there are two aspects to radical change. The first concerns the issue of 'breadth' - the degree to which change is central to the organization's strategy - and demands radical as opposed to incremental modifications throughout the organization.The second relates to the degree to which such modifications mark a significant departure from existing ways of doing things. Both of these certainly apply to e-Business. For example, such changes point to business process redesign, the development of cross-functional team working, and the move towards a customer-focused (instead of management-led) culture.

These changes are likely to be politically controversial and threaten the interests of a wide range of stakeholders. Unlike routine change, such initiatives are also likely to be highly complex. As Badham *et al.* note, there may be a high degree of uncertainty as to what to do and how to do it; objectives may be less clear, and resource requirements will be less well known.

In addition, it may be less easy to create shared perceptions of goals and build and maintain necessary commitment. For this reason, these authors suggest that more time will need to be spent ensuring effective communication to encourage flexibility, address perceptions, and generate and regenerate involvement. To illustrate the problems that can ensue in such a situation, the authors describe Merrill Lynch's move into online trading:

At the core of the change process was conflict at many levels within Merrill Lynch. There was conflict between the defenders of the brokers and their commissions and proponents of online investing. There was conflict between Merrill brokers who were concerned about losing customers to online brokers and Merrill brokers who were concerned about losing commissions. There was even conflict among Merrill executives between who favoured setting up a separate online unit to compete with the brokers and those who favoured keeping the online unit under the same executive.

LEADERSHIP

Leadership plays a crucial role in effective change management. Hunt (1998) claims that change is a learning process because people have to learn to behave differently, but in order for this process to work and for change to be successful, individuals need to be encouraged, and it is here that leadership becomes very important. Carnall also expresses the need for strong leadership; that is, 'the ability to maintain progress and a facilitative and supportive approach', and suggests that for this to happen, the leader needs to have knowledge of the change area and appropriate skills to encourage learning and change.

Some leaders use 'coercive persuasion' to force change; in other words, 'employees have no alternative but to accept the new reality because they have nowhere else to go'. Although individuals may not like the change, they have no choice, so will accept the change and accommodate the new ideas. He goes on to state that leaders need to be able to 'manipulate people's understandings of what is going on, and who are able to deliver the results quickly'. The role of the leader can be to create conditions under which success can visibly be achieved, even if only in a limited and partial way, and to rationalize and capitalize upon positive events after they have happened. Managers will instead need to be skilled in the art of leadership and corporate politics. The need to enrol and re-enrol support, neutralize dissent and resistance, and secure resources will demand networking skills and the ability to build consensus and support.

They must start by gaining buy-in at the top. As Siegel puts it, 'You can have the world's greatest web strategy, but it won't work unless managers have a stake in the outcome'.

To make sure they do, Siegel recommends the formation of a change team, headed by a Chief Net Officer (CNO). Furthermore, he suggests that businesses should 'Strengthen the team with managers who have good relationships with people in other divisions.

The CNO will need a lot of favours, so make sure the team is credible in the eyes of the rest of the company'. If leaders recognize the type of change they are faced with, and are familiar with the sort of skills and tactics that may be employed to deal with it, the management of change is more likely to be successful.

RELATIONSHIP-BUILDING AND COMMUNICATIONS

The importance of effective internal marketing to engage staff in the change process was emphasized. Increasingly, such communications are a critical aspect of external relationship building too.

According to Symonds (1999a), a crucial misconception is that any business is a 'free-standing entity'. For example, in order to participate in a new development such as e-Procurement or customer relationship management, it is essential that companies involve their suppliers, partners and customers in their processes and allow each party to become familiar with each other's processes. This degree of openness and transparency is new to most organizations, and it requires significant change and high levels of trust between participants.

A genuine e-Business strategy provides electronic links in order to 'foster conversations' with staff, customers and partners. Such 'customer-led' approaches involve listening to customers in a strategic way, deepening relationships and loyalty.

The importance of engaging in rich customer conversations is underpinned by a number of recent works on e-Business. The highly influential *Cluetrain Manifesto*, for instance, asserts in the first of its ninety-five theses on the new economy that 'markets are conversations'. Newell's *Loyalty.com* (2000) underlines this point, and highlights the way companies must 'leverage customer information' for the effective management of customer relationships on the Internet.Seybold's *Customers.com* (1998) makes similar points, again focusing on the need for customer-focused strategies that engage customers as parts of a community based around a company's products and personnel. Such strategies suggest something much more radical in terms of change than the mere 'bolton' approach of adding an online channel to market, which is often proposed as a straightforward and simple process.

It calls for a re-engineering of processes and structures focused around key customer groups, rather than product or service divisions. It also implies cross-functional, team-based working. As Siegel puts it, The customer-led company has a broad interface across which all employees can get to know their customers. Employees invite customers in to collaborate on new products, support systems, and methodologies. Facilitating those interactions will take new communication skills, new tools, and the ability to move people in and out of product teams easily.

At Dell Computers, for instance, customers are brought into the product planning and manufacturing processes, with all employees encouraged to have contact with customers. Through effective collaboration across boundaries, ideas can be shared about product designs and value propositions. The result is faster and more customer-focused product and service innovation. To produce the capacity for this, considerable attention must be placed on organizational structures, processes, skills and culture - elements that may need a radical overhaul in established companies.

ROLE OF THE CHANGE AGENT

Buchanan and Boddy emphasize the importance of having an appropriate 'change agent' or 'project champion' in the successful implementation of change. The change agent should be someone who is committed to the success of the project and prepared to 'go the extra mile' in order to motivate, bully or cajole other participants as required. There is a diverse range of skills associated with performing this role; for example:

- Influencing;
- Negotiating;
- Selling;
- Inspiring;
- Commanding respect;
- Political;
- Magic and miracle working!

It is a tall order for any one individual to have all of these skills, and some will be more important than others at different stages of the project. In practice, therefore, more than one change agent may be required.

ADAPTING ORGANIZATIONAL CULTURE

There are many ways in which the terms 'culture' and 'organizational culture' can be understood, but for our purposes we have chosen the following: the system of meanings which are shared by members of a human grouping and which define what is good and bad, right and wrong and what are the appropriate ways for members of that group to think and behave. The pattern of learned basic assumptions that has worked well enough to be considered valid and, therefore, to be taught to new members as the correct way to perceive, think, and feel in relation to the problems of survival and integration.

Schein suggested that employee acceptance of technological change required a change in organizational culture, because practices and values tend to be built around existing technologies that have contributed to the successful development and self image of the organization. One of the strongest elements of culture he identified was the status system attached to these traditions, and the possession by individuals of critical skills.

Schein claimed that innovation was a property of culture, and the potential of information technology as a competitive and strategic weapon would not be fulfilled unless innovative cultures were present or developed, enabling the organization to learn and adapt. This attitude was also noted, whose theory of 'flexible specialization' emerged from their observations that technological progress could be self-blocking, and new products were generally designed to fit existing equipment and procedures.

The importance of culture was also emphasized in a study of video disk development by Graham, who found that prevailing cultural values and attitudes in the firm, based upon past experience, were inadequate when it came to dealing with an innovative product in a new market.

Although these studies pre-date the Internet era, they illustrate quite clearly how a change in organizational culture is often necessary for full advantage to be taken of the opportunities presented by new technologies. A vast literature now exists on the subject of how to change culture. As early as 1952, Lewin identified three phases of culture change, namely 'unfreezing', 'change' and 'refreezing'. 'Unfreezing' results from the questioning of norms that have led to a specific failure, thereby sensitizing employees to the need for change, which is then consolidated into new procedures or behaviours during the 'refreezing' phase. This theory seems overly simplistic and linear in its classification of the technological change process, which in practice appears invariably to be a more dynamic and turbulent series of events. Mintzberg (1979) advocated the development of a culture of 'adhocracy' that is organic and decentralized in structure, thereby avoiding the pitfalls that are usually associated with bureaucracy. He claimed that in search of innovation, such organizations minimize planning, control and the division of labour.

In practice, however, while examples do exist of individual companies, such as British Airways, that have 'created' a new corporate culture, these success stories appear to be few and far between. March and Simon, in their revised edition of a seminal text that introduced the concept of 'bounded rationality' (referring to the limited cognition of organizational members), maintained that their theory still holds true today. Despite the vastly increased resources available to the modern organization, these authors believed that potential for change would always be constrained by the conflicting agendas of employees. Green also questioned the ability of organizations to manage culture in a prescriptive way: If culture could be levered into shape then, by now, someone would have discovered the method. The metaphors of fine-tuning and fit which abound in much of the literature on culture and strategy are altogether inappropriate for something as complex as human social systems.

He noted that while corporate cultures appear to be stable and static when studied at a particular point in time, applying a longitudinal perspective reveals that they are in fact too multidimensional and dynamic to be susceptible to manipulation by management. The key point about culture change, therefore, is that it is rarely as simple a process as is sometimes suggested when recommended as a tool for implementing projects involving new technology.

CHALLENGES OF MULTI-CHANNEL MARKETING

The usage of various Internet access mechanisms has developed over the past few years. At this early stage, companies need to address a number of challenges when considering the development of multi-channel strategies that allow customers to access online content from a range of devices:

- The extent to which they should invest in these relatively untried technologies, with little indication of likely customer demand or long-term prospects for making money.
- The need to 'repurpose' content for each tool. For example, trying to display a Web site on a WAP screen means that graphics and pictures are lost, and different coding is required. Smith and Chaffey also note that switching between PC and iDTV is problematic because Web sites are designed to be viewed in 'lean-forward mode' from two feet away, but iDTV in 'laid-back mode' from more like eight feet away. Navigating with a mouse is also very different from navigating with a remote control device.
- The unique properties of each medium in terms of the user experience delivered. For example, mobile transactions are likely to be for low-value or distress purchases, because the amount and quality of information that can be displayed to the customer on screen is limited. In contrast, the PC allows huge volumes of data to searched and displayed, and so is best suited to situations where the customer wants to carry out extensive research before making a purchase. Digital television offers yet another dynamic; although it is still in its infancy, early usage suggests that purchases may take place in a more collaborative, impulsive and social context than through the other channels.
- Whether they should offer all their products or services across each

medium (and if so, the extent to which customization is necessary and/or appropriate) or 'mix and match' according to the characteristics of each channel and the specific message to be delivered.

- The need for *integrated* online and offline marketing campaigns. Smith and Chaffey (2002) describe how MTV asked viewers to send in SMS text messages to provide comments and vote for their favourite video. MTV then played the winning video together with the comments live. The event was promoted through offline magazines read by the target audience, and the paper-based advertisement demonstrated a text message on a phone explaining how to take part.
- How to manage the necessary internal information processing that will allow the company to achieve a unified view of customer activity across all channels. For this to work, a central database is necessary to provide up-to-date customer details to all channel operators. Remember that customers' expectations are continually rising and they may expect to use a combination of channels to effect just one single purchase ...

It should be clear from this brief discussion that the technical ability to offer multi-channel access is just the starting point. Considerable investment needs to be made in the back-office computer systems and business process integration necessary to actually make it work in practice. The difficulties are even greater for small firms with limited financial resources, or those with legacy computer systems that cannot be easily integrated. However, for those that succeed, the potential for combine multi-channel offerings with *personalized* content provides an enormous marketing opportunity.

THE GENIE MOBILE INTERNET PORTAL

Genie was launched in 2001 as the world's first exclusively online mobile service. Genie's UK mobile service operates on the BT Cellnet network and is therefore now part of O2. BT Cellnet is one of the largest UK mobile networks, with over 8 million customers, and offers 99 per cent coverage of the UK population. Genie is the UK's leading mobile Internet company, with over 3 million registered users of the Genie Internet portal. It provides free text messaging and free access to WAP. The mobile Internet is the technology that allows users to view information, play games and manage personal e-mail via a WAP phone. WAP stands for Wireless Application Protocol and is the worldwide standard enabling WAP mobile phones to access the Mobile Internet. Genie Mobile Internet provides a number of services available on WAP phones:

- E-mail - the ability to read, reply and forward emails;
- M-Commerce - you can now buy books and CDs;
- Information - the latest sports scores, current news and gossip;
- Enquiries - flight times, cinema times;

- Entertainment - games, competitions and reviews.

Mobile phone and Internet services are integrated so that customers can access information on a PC or via mobile phone.

The Genie portal itself runs at significant loss, but its services appeal to the key market segment of early-adopter mobile phone users. Members of this group are predisposed to purchasing new gadgets, understand the rapidly developing terminology and issues surrounding mobile developments, and also happen to spend the most money on mobiles. Any mobile user can register on the site - they do not necessarily have to be using O2 networks. By permission-based marketing to these registered Genie visitors, special deals can be offered to get them to switch to the O2 network. At this stage of market development, the key selling points as far as users are concerned relate to content (in the form of information and alerts about share prices, skiing conditions, sports results, etc.) rather than transactional commerce.

The Genie brand has high awareness ratings despite low advertising spend. According to *Campaign's* dotcom weekly awareness survey, Genie is ranked tenth in the UK, with an awareness rating of 27 per cent, just behind the Easy Group on 32 per cent and ahead of Wellbeing on 20 per cent. Genie is promoted on the major portals such as Google, MSN and Yahoo!, and pays for prominent placements on search engines so that a banner is invoked should a surfer conduct a search for 'mobile phone', for example.

Genie aims to leverage value from its mobile services by offering customers special deals through partnerships with banks and ISPs as part of a 'closed' network. This business model is superior to many 'open' network portals because partner firms will either pay for preferential access to Genie customers or at least provide content for free. Genie customers who want to access services from companies outside the partner network have to pay extra for the privilege. To illustrate how this works, consider the example of mobile banking.Genie provides secure links to eight leading banks to enable customers to access their bank accounts via their mobile phones on the O2 network. Within the next twelve months, customers will also be able to trade stocks in this way. Hence there is scope for the major stockbrokers to be 'plumbed in' to the partnership to make the entire contact, share purchase and payment transaction from the bank account a seamless and immediate process for the customer. If such a service is available, why would a customer want to look elsewhere for a stockbroker? Stockbrokers, therefore, will pay for a preferential placing in the Genie portfolio, and indeed several may compete with each other - with the best positions on the listing commanding the highest fees.From the partner firms' perspective, there are three key drivers for associating with Genie:

- To obtain additional revenue from existing customers by offering an alternative channel to access the company;
- To expand the customer base by appealing to new market segments

(for example people who use their mobile phone to bet with Ladbrokes through the Genie gateway have a very different demographic profile from that of Ladbroke's traditional customer base relying upon the firm's network of betting shops);

- To reduce the costs of servicing their customer base. This is the key driver for banking partners, for example.

To illustrate the potential of mobile services to reduce costs (and in some cases change the partner firm's entire business model), consider the example of a recruitment agency for temporary staff. In the past, such a firm would rely upon a team of office-based employees to make telephone calls to perhaps hundreds of registered individuals to advise them of newly received employment opportunities and sign people up as required. This could be an expensive and time-consuming exercise if large numbers of staff were required. By sending a text message simultaneously to the entire labour pool database requesting those interested to call in and sign up for the job, the entire cost structure of the business is altered. The staff employed to recruit would only have to answer calls from people accepting the work, rather than make a large number of outgoing calls touting for business. In the near future, the acceptance procedure will also become Web based, thereby reducing the need for human intervention still further.

THE NEED FOR A POLICY FRAMEWORK TO SUPPORT E-BUSINESS

In a farsighted article, Graves, Jenkins, and Parker at the University of North Carolina described the development of an electronic information policy framework. As e-business drives the Internet and Web from an infrastructure for storing static information to one over which much of the institutional mission is delivered, the need for such a policy framework becomes overwhelming. Although sound information policies will not guarantee entry into the world of e-business, lack of these policies will bar the door. Colleges and universities will need to develop a cohesive and consistent set of policies to guide the members of their community in a number of areas, including the following:

- Digital identity and the access to institutional technology and information resources
- Use of the institution's name and trademarks
- Acquisition, retention, and disposition of information resources
- Ownership of information in institutional systems and the management of intellectual property rights

Each of these issues is enormously complex, and colleges and universities worldwide have struggled with them for years. Digital Identity and Access to Institutional Technology and Information Resources.

In the technical context, colleges and universities must develop the means to authenticate an individual as himself or herself, recognize the individual as a member of the institutional community, and confer on or deny this individual different rights and authorities as a community citizen. In physical reality, these activities are transacted in a variety of complex formal or informal ways. We can demand photo ID cards, check signature files, or wave to the familiar librarian who regulates access to the closed stacks.The regulation of access to institutional resources in the physical context is governed by a tapestry of policies, procedures, customs, norms, and historical happenstance that computers are not yet intelligent enough to deal with. Instead, computers depend on precise information that derives absolute answers to the following questions: (1) are you who you claim to be, and (2) are you allowed to ... [consume this service, enter this building, use this parking lot]?

Not only is this a technical challenge of enormous proportions, it is a policy quagmire that requires colleges and universities to make explicit and public distinctions about the rights and privileges that accrue to different members of the academy. What rights does the president's spouse really have? What rights do lecturers have, relative to career-ladder faculty? These policy issues will become more complex as colleges and universities move into distance education and implement cradle-to-grave strategies to create relationships with promising applicants, lifelong learners, and potential donors.Of course, it is important to note that for public institutions, managing access to institutional information must be situated in the context of public records laws, which themselves are hard to reduce to simple rules that can be automated.

USE OF THE INSTITUTION'S NAME AND TRADEMARKS

The Internet and the World Wide Web are, among other things, a publishing infrastructure. Web browser technology is relatively simple to programme as well as to use, allowing "a thousand flowers to bloom."

At nearly every college and university, a myriad of operational and dead Web pages make volumes of campus information and misinformation available to anyone with an Internet connection.

Many institutions provide incoming students with sufficient disk storage to encourage their development of personal Web sites. Of course, into every flower garden will come the occasional weed, snail, or other predator. From a policy perspective, the challenge posed by the Internet and the Web is the challenge of cultural integration. Colleges and universities must specify policies that regulate the appropriate use of these very public resources. At stake in this extraordinarily complex area to govern are a variety of serious legal and public relations issues, including these:

- Pornographic materials on official institutional sites
- Sale of advertising on pages containing campus trademarks

- Creation of fraudulent sites
- Commercial use of campus resources for personal gain
- Trademark infringement
- Neglect of sites that make inaccurate, anachronistic, and obsolete information available to legislators, trustees, donors, auditors, and others

All of these issues can and will emerge within the broader policy contexts that typically respect and encourage free expression by members of the institution's community. As Graves, Jenkins, and Parker advise, "Any policy will need to balance the institution's role in protecting access to sensitive or potentially objectionable information and its role in supporting an individual's right of free expression". This difficult balancing act is hardly new, but is complicated by the levels of integration anticipated by e-business applications.

ACQUISITION, RETENTION, AND DISPOSITION OF INFORMATION RESOURCES

E-business, in much of the popular literature, begins with something called "e-tailing": the marketing of the enterprise to its existing or prospective clients. In one context, higher education institutions have been doing this for years. Each year, colleges and universities acquire the files of high school students who achieve high scores on the PSAT and shower these college-bound tenth and eleventh graders with literature extolling the virtues of their campus. In an e-business context, smart and aggressive institutions will acquire more and more information in the competition for the "best" students. These institutions will likely develop robust profiles of students to match against the target profiles of successful applicants. Similarly, the pathologies of university hospital patients will be profiled for matching against promising experimental drugs and therapies for possible targeting of such patients for clinical trials.These practices are entrepreneurial, effective (relative to their goals), and probably beneficial; certainly college-bound students want to be discovered and patients want access to the best modes of treatment available. However, the unprecedented ability of institutions to acquire personal information, combine this information in unique ways, and store massive amounts of this information on individuals who may, or may not, be part of the institutional community will raise significant privacy and security issues.

New policies regarding what kind of information is to be collected, how this information is to be used, and how long it is to be retained will become increasingly important.

The failure to develop new standards of practice in this area will invite new regulation of this area of institutional activity. The issue of individual and institutional access to this kind of information will also rise in importance and must be dealt with explicitly in campus information policy.In addition to developing the technologies and policies to ensure privacy and secure and protect information under institutional management, colleges and universities will need to devise and implement new policies to describe, manage, and protect related classes of information. Such classes of information include confidential information (tenure and promotion files), proprietary information (patents, trademarks, copyrights), privileged information (attorneyclient communications, counseling files), and trade information (public and private research activities).

E-business, among other things, assumes an unprecedented level of interoperation among the systems and data resources of "trading partners." In the future, campus suppliers will have access to institutional procurement systems, as will publishers, high schools, consortium partners, and others. This integration of systems and information will demand that policies and contracts regulate the acquisition, use, retention, and disposition by others in the newly extending community.

This has already become a complex area of policy development at research universities, where the university values of open sharing of research findings clash with desires of private clinical research sponsors to protect information as proprietary.

A final area of concern under this broad umbrella is the management of licensed software and information resources. Campus information policy must respect the rights of authors and distributors. Evolving technologies and law will likely enhance authors' and distributors' ability to track the use of their licensed property and perhaps even to implement campuswide penalties when infringements are identified.

OWNERSHIP OF INFORMATION AND INTELLECTUAL PROPERTY RIGHTS

Information policy must seek to distinguish the ownership status of information embodied in institutionally owned digital storage and transport media from the responsibilities for managing this information. Information policies should strive to define the standards and care with which information resources must be managed, while recognizing the inherently decentralizing tendencies of networked information and resources.

Most information policy frameworks that address networked information define and articulate a concept of information stewardship that allows the web of campus-related information to evolve in a fashion that balances the needs of individuals and local campus units with those of the institution as a whole.

Perhaps the most complex aspect of preparing the campus information policy environment for e-business is the set of policy issues surrounding the ownership and management of intellectual property generated on the campus. Colleges and universities have developed robust policies for the ownership and management of intellectual property protected by patents, but the rights to intellectual property developed by faculty and protected by copyright have traditionally remained with individual faculty. In fact, the total economic value of published college and university intellectual property has been small historically, and the institutional investment in the creation of this property has also been small.

The application of Internet, Web, and other information technologies to the core educational mission of higher education is changing all of this. Today, pioneering faculty are investing considerable time and energy to Web-enable their courses.Institutions in many cases are partnering with these faculty by providing grants to purchase release time from other obligations and by placing a variety of technical tools at the faculty's disposal. For the first time, faculty course materials organized in this fashion can reach beyond the confines of the classroom, hence changing simultaneously the cost structure, the investment model, and the economic value of traditional course materials. Courses created in this fashion become courseware and begin to accrue many of the attributes of books, which also are evolving to become more interactive.

As the e-learning aspect of the e-business revolution evolves, institutions, their faculty, and publishers are looking at course materials as scalable economic goods that can be modularized. New pedagogical standards are evolving in concert with new neuroscientific findings about the learning process. Institutions such as the University of Phoenix and Great Britain's Open University are investing millions of dollars in curricula for networked delivery. Faculty course notes on the Web are being reportedly pirated and repackaged for distribution by new proprietary e-business enterprises. Clearly the new potentials posed by the integrated technologies of e-business suggest the need for new policies regarding the ownership and management of rights to faculty course materials.Such changes are, however, countercultural and could also lead to new divisions on the campus. e-business is likely to change the way institutions operate. It is a mission-critical undertaking that will challenge longstanding institutional policies and will therefore demand the careful application of change management techniques and processes.

ELEMENTS OF AN INTEGRATED POLICY FRAMEWORK

Although each institution will develop a policy that best reflects its priorities, strategies, values, and history, a framework should contain some common elements. The list that follows is offered as a starting point.

CRITICAL ASSUMPTIONS

The institution will balance the rights of individuals with the institution's responsibility to make information available to support the mission. The role of the central campus is to articulate the standards of data access and integrity and to differentiate user rights and privileges so as to achieve such balance.

The following key assumption will need to be articulated:

- Under what conditions (responsibilities of resource users) and for what members of the community are access to the network, network-based services, and networked information a basic right of the campus community?

OPERATING PRINCIPLES

Policies are by definition value laden. Institutions can be well served by considering bounding the framework by principles.

At the University of North Carolina (UNC), information policy is bounded by principles that do the following:

- Identify the responsibility for making information available
- Limit the institution's regulatory responsibility for information for which it is not responsible
- Assume institutional responsibility for defining access privileges to its information for classes of users

The UNC policy framework and those of other leading institutions also outline in broad terms legal, ethical, technical, governance, and economic issues for the purpose of acculturating the policy reader to the complexity of the issues and the basic values of the institution.

INFORMATION ACCESS AND SECURITY

It will be important to establish the notion that institutional electronic information resources—including data, applications, systems, "We don't want just anyone coming in here and making toast. Type in your password." hardware, software, and networks—are valuable. Institutional assets, including electronic information resources, must be protected according to the nature of the risk and to the sensitivity and criticality of the resource being protected.

Information policy should endeavor to identify major classes of information assets requiring protection and assigning to them differential levels of protection. Information classes might include privileged information, personal information, personnel information, and public records.Areas in which security-related policies need to be addressed include the following, paraphrased from the University of California's "Business and Finance Bulletin IS-3: Electronic Information Security":

- Logical security. The policy should identify security measures to be enforced through software, network, or procedural controls (version management, and so forth), as well as communications security and reduction of risk from intrusive computer software. Various measures include end-user access controls, system administration access controls, applications software development and change control, and controls on data backup, retention, data privacy, and data transfers and downloads. Encryption policies will also need to be developed as these capabilities become ubiquitous, as will policies that specify which applications and resources must be protected by firewalls.

- Physical security. Even in an e-business environment, there are physical disaster controls and access controls (for example, check stock and other financial instruments) that must be covered by institutional policy.
- Managerial security. Although there are unique risks inherent in the management of electronic and particularly networked information resources, many of the risks remain people related. An information policy framework should attempt to integrate institutional policy related to bonding and background checking for personnel with access to sensitive and critical information. Procedures to implement such policies should also identify the processes for altering authorities when changes in duties or employment status occur.
- Responsibilities. An information policy framework must identify both those responsible for maintaining the policy and those responsible for its implementation. Ideally, policy compliance escalation procedures should be specified.
- Definitions and authorities. A policy framework should define key terms such as authorized user, disaster, and security. Information management roles such as stewardship and proprietorship should also be defined. Regulations and laws that govern an institution's access and security policies should be referenced, including public records law.
- Digital certificates. An emerging technology to meet the needs of electronic security in the networked context is the use of public key infrastructure and digital certificates. Institutions that implement certificate authorities and digital certificates also will need to develop congruent policies that identify processes for approving authorities, standards for certificates, and identification of certificates. Policies will have to be enacted that govern whether certificates are issued to individuals, servers, or certificate authorities; what the responsibilities of these authorities
- Are; and what the expiry dates of these certificates will be. Finally, policy in this evolving arena will need to describe the processes for registering and issuing certificates, maintaining a repository of certificates and public keys, revoking or renewing certificates, and managing the certificate authority's private key.

DISASTER PROTECTION

The information policy framework should describe the institution's plans, policies, and procedures for ensuring business continuity, including plans for testing critical systems periodically.The disaster recovery plan should identify emergency response procedures and specify teams of personnel responsible for responding to emergency situations.

E-MAIL

Although e-mail is not specifically a tool of e-business, its governance as a critical element of the overall campus information policy framework is critical. Institutions are advised to develop specific policies related to e-mail that establish the following elements:

- E-mail accounts as institutional property
- The institution's service commitments regarding e-mail
- The ownership of information produced and received using institutional mail accounts
- Institutional access to information in mail accounts under normal or extraordinary (emergency, investigative, and so forth) conditions
- Allowable use, including use for individual commercial gain, representations, and false identity
- Security and confidentiality of information in institutional mail accounts
- Individual and institutional responsibilities and authorities for ensuring compliance with policy

INTELLECTUAL PROPERTY

Policy related to the management and ownership of intellectual property is highly complex. For intellectual property not developed on campus and covered by copyrights, patents, licenses, or other contracts, the policy parameters tend to be straightforward:

- Software resident on institutional hardware must be used according to the terms specified under the appropriate software license agreement.
- The institution is responsible for compliance with licenses entered into by the institution on behalf of members of its community. It should maintain the right to revoke licensed privileges in cases where violations have been identified. Substantial violations of license conditions should be specified under policy, as should the process for investigating alleged misuse and for implementing remedial action.
- Information resources such as databases, books, and journal articles are governed by copyright law or by license agreements with their publisher. Institutional policy should affirm the rights of authors, publishers, and distributors to their intellectual property; define what constitutes fair use in the context of law and licenses; and identify

the processes for investigating alleged misuse and for implementing remedial action. For intellectual property developed on campus, the institution must distinguish between so-called works for hire and other works produced in the discharge of an employee's work-related roles:

- The ownership of a work for hire is generally assumed to be the property of the institution. The information policy framework should make explicit reference to the institution's assumptions about what works are considered to be works for hire and what ownership rights the institution wishes to assert. This policy should also specify what rights individuals who are creating works for hire may have (publication of a work report in a professional journal) and what the process is for securing individual access to such works.
- The ownership of other intellectual property produced by members of the campus community is more likely to fall under an institution's faculty handbook, or in policy covering patents, or even conflict of interest and commitment. As the boundaries between course materials and published materials begin to blur, institutions will need to revisit the ownership issues as part of an integrated information policy framework.

Policy by its nature is soft, squishy, and difficult. Policy development and the policy environment are inherently value laden, and therefore there are no detailed instructions for policy formulation. Policies are for the most part context specific. A Bible college's definition of appropriate use of technology will likely differ from that of a public research university.

Policy can be integrative, and integration is the mandate that looms ahead for institutions seeking to implement e-business solutions. Colleges and universities anticipating the move to e-business must recall that e-business in many areas is not merely the application of new technology to old processes. E-business applications will open new vistas and create new risks.

Extending the name and reach of your college and university can and will swell the ranks of members of your communities. As communities grow, opportunities grow. And along with opportunities come fraud, abuse, and misuse. An integrated information policy framework will be hard to institute. On the other hand, an integrated, e-business environment without a supporting policy framework will be nearly impossible to manage.

E-BUSINESS DRIVERS

Will e-business applications become widespread in higher education? Although these applications are being used primarily among early adopters, it is clear, when one examines the drivers, that e-business will garner more than ephemeral attention. According to some, the adoption of such applications in higher education will become pervasive as students and prospective students look to these applications for convenience and institutions seek to expand markets, lower costs, and provide improved customer service. Among the drivers for higher education institutions to develop an e-business strategy are these:

- The rising popularity of the Internet
- Increasingly demanding customers and unrelenting expectations for expedited services
- Continuing cost constraints
- Opportunities for new revenues

2

Electronic Commerce and Electronic Business Management

E-COMMERCE SYSTEMS

The buying and selling of products and services over the Internet is termed 'online trading'. Online trading or e-Commerce is important to businesses because it provides a flexible source of trading with customers, and with business partners.

To enable online trading, companies need to combine existing computerized transaction processing systems and information systems with Internet and Web technology. Existing computerized systems, databases, and Internet and Web technology are the basic components of online trading and form the architecture of e-Commerce systems. Computer system architecture consists of hardware and software components that are configured in terms of the needs of organizations.

Companies connect computers to a LAN, WAN and the Internet, using TCP/ IP, based on client-server architecture, to share computer software, printers or scanners. Basic Internet tools such as e-mail, browsers, search engines and protocols such as file transfer protocol (FTP) and Telnet are combined to form the system architecture for e-Commerce.

The systems architecture for a company will depend on its trading activities. A retail company will have a different architecture from a manufacturing company or a service company. As a company changes and evolves its mission or objectives, its e-Commerce system architecture will need to change too. Alternatively, the stimulus to change may come from competitors who use the most modern e-Commerce technology.

INTERNET, E-COMMERCE SYSTEMS AND INFORMATION SYSTEMS

Some of the terms used to describe a company's involvement with the Internet are that it has 'an online presence' or it has 'a Web site'. Such terms hide the complex IT and IS that form the infrastructure that underpin e-

Commerce systems.An information system is the application of a computer to capture and process data to provide information for managers and executives for the purposes of decision making and management. A company will normally have various information systems, such as an airline reservation system or an inventory control system. These systems will be linked to a corporate database that stores relevant data, like product or customer details. A company's Web site is connected to such information systems and databases to provide the essential product or service information for customer and employee use.

Companies' existing client-server technology and its IS/IT infrastructure is connected to the Internet to form part of an e-Commerce architecture. The e-Commerce architecture is based on a company's business model, consisting of the basic logic of what it wants to produce or sell, how it will market it, how it defines its customers and other fundamental business issues. IT is combined with Internet technology to enable a company to personalize its service to a customer.

DATABASES

A computer database consists of records on specific items of interest, for example customers' contact details or the products they have bought. It is a collection of data that can be queried for specific purposes such as targeting a particular customer for certain products. Databases are used to market products and services.This is termed *database marketing*. Databases are used to store data on the purchasing habits of customers and enable a company to develop a tailored relationship with its customers.The data are then processed to provide tailored information on individual customers' preferences that are then sent information about products or services relevant to their current buying habits. Data-mining techniques are used to reprocess existing data in databases to extract previously unrealized information of potential commercial use.

E-COMMERCE SYSTEMS AND THE CUSTOMER

e-Commerce systems that interface with the customer need to be pragmatic. The selection and evaluation of Internet technology need to be appropriate to both the company's needs and the customer's ability to use the system. A good business model will assume that the customer has little interest in technology and avoid the technology trap.*Avoiding the technology trap.*It is not user-friendly to use over-complex Internet and Web technology in e-Commerce systems. The technology needs to be appropriate to prevent prolonging the time it takes for customers' commands to be executed by the system.

WEB SITE EVALUATION SOFTWARE

It is possible to measure the popularity of a company's Web site using evaluation software that generates log files. Such log files record the number of visitors to the site or page impressions.They record which parts of the Web site are most popular, the times of the day people visit, record which search engines are being used by visitors and how long they spend on the site, known as the 'stickiness' of the site.

These log files can subsequently be used to evaluate the performance of the site from a business perspective and the information can be used to make it easier for customers to make transactions.

INTERNET SERVICE PROVIDERS

A company wanting to trade over the Internet has to agree a contract with an Internet service provider (ISP). ISPs provide communication and hosting services for individuals and companies wanting to access the Internet. ISPs provide access to the Internet and enable Internet commerce by connecting individuals and companies to the Internet.There are thousands of ISPs that a company can choose from, all of them providing domain name services and electronic mail. The two most popular ISPs are UUNET Technologies and AT&T World Net. Other organizations, like a bank with mainframe computers, may also act as an ISP.

ISPs also provide hosting services for Web sites by installing and operating the server computers and software for a company. The computers and software are located at the ISP's site. Transaction services such as payment systems or order capture and fulfilment are also provided by ISPs.

EXAMPLE OF E-COMMERCE ARCHITECTURE

The important considerations for designing e-Commerce architecture are the customer, the company, the company's existing information systems and how payment will be made. For example, a company with a Web site that includes an order form would need a Web server that can provide a catalogue, whose details would be retrieved from a catalogue database, and order form. It would need to interface with an existing database to collect and record the order details entered by the customer.

The payment might be transacted with a credit card whose details would be captured on the order form utilizing standard security features available on the Web.This example shows that an e-Commerce system is composed of existing information systems, databases and Internet technology.

Other sophisticated e-Commerce architectures are possible for companies that need distributed transaction processing. For example, the Open Buying Consortium (OBI) has proposed a system architecture consisting of six fundamental system components split into buy-side, the customer and sell-side activities. These components are: Browse, Request, Approve, Fill, Receive and Pay.

E-COMMERCE SECURITY TECHNOLOGY

The success of e-Commerce depends on the security of data like personal details and credit card numbers transmitted over the Internet. The domain name system Internet protocol that makes IP addresses readable by humans is insecure. Security measures need to be taken in e-Commerce systems to prevent compromising the systems. Some of these measures include building firewalls, incorporating cryptography and authentication, and using secure connections.

FIREWALL

A firewall is hardware and software that are used to secure a private computer network system from uninvited intruders. A firewall is used to control whether a client is permitted to connect to the private network it protects.

CRYPTOGRAPHY

Cryptography is a science that provides secure communication over vulnerable channels. Cryptography is fundamental to the success of the Internet and e-Commerce. Governments regulate cryptographic technology because of its importance to national security.

In cryptography a message, like a credit card number, is encrypted using a key and the encrypted message is transmitted. The receiver uses the key to decrypt the message and convert it back to its original form.

The basic elements of a cryptographic system are algorithms, protocols and key management. An example of key management is the secret-key encryption algorithms. These algorithms are 'secret' because only the receiver and sender know the secret key.

Cryptography is used to provide secure transmission of data over the Internet. Private data like credit card details or digital signatures are encrypted and then transmitted over the Internet.

Cryptography can keep a message secret and act as a gateway for identifying senders and receivers. It provides the secure electronic transaction technology for credit card transactions on the Internet.

AUTHENTICATION

Authentication procedures are used to establish the identity of an individual or another computer system. Authentication procedures can be hardware-or software-based. Authentication procedures make use of personal items of knowledge or possession such as secret names or birth dates. Good authentication systems make use of two-factor authentication, such as a place name and memorable date known to the user. Some banking systems make use of three-factor authentication before allowing customers to make online account transfers.

SECURE SOCKET LAYER

The secure socket layer (SSL) is a layer of security between the application and the transport protocol. The purpose of SSL is to enable secure and reliable data transmission and communication over the Internet. The SSL provides private connection, making use of encryption and secret-key cryptography.

Authentication in SSL is achieved using public-key cryptography, which consists of a private key that is never made public chosen by one participant in the data exchange, and a public key chosen by the other participant in the exchange. Either key may be used for encryption.

Reliability of data transmission is achieved by using secure hash functions like SHA or MD5. Secure hash functions check the integrity of a message. SSL is commonly used in e-Commerce systems.

E-COMMERCE GLOBAL STRATEGIES

The organizations practising in the area of e-Commerce are facing a number of d ecisions regarding their global activities. Having analysed the characteristics of the target foreign market, they now face the next stage of developing an international marketing programme.

This would include defining and selecting target segments, positioning the product or service and making the decision to modify the elements of the marketing mix to suit the conditions of the foreign market. For physical goods, the marketing mix is composed of four elements: product, price, place (distribution) and promotion. For services, the marketing mix extends to seven elements with the addition of people, processes and physical evidence.

Given the diversity of the global environment, with differing cultures, customs and competition, the decision facing the e-Commerce marketer is the degree of change necessary within the elements of the marketing mix. There are a number of pressures affecting this decision, which can be summarized as (1) staying local versus going global, (2) standardization or adaptation.

LOCAL VERSUS GLOBAL

Ten years ago 'pan-European' advertising was all the rage among direct marketing companies in the United Kingdom. A precursor of global communication, it was based on a simple idea, namely that consumers in various countries fall into the same socio-demographic categories, with similar if not identical buying habits and tastes brought about by low-cost cross-border travel. It uses the same imagery, messages, product and brand positioning across all campaigns and all markets. Economies of scale could be achieved and global brands built up, as campaigns could be extended from one country to another.

More recently, globalization has received a few hard knocks, due to changes in customer tastes and timing. Some products achieved global status because they required very little effort in terms of product development in order to be successful in new markets. Others needed extensive redevelopment in order to localize their marketing mix.A good example is basic office software such as Microsoft Word, which works equally well in most countries, once it has been localized for language characteristics. Other examples are soft drinks like Coca-Cola or imaging products like Kodak, which need only minimal changes of their global campaigns to adapt to local taste. Alternatively, cars are more of a 'lifestyle' purchase.Consumer tastes in cars vary more widely between the United States, Germany, Japan, Italy, the United Kingdom and India. Achieving substantial economies of scale either in product development or in advertising is more difficult. Ford has been one of the manufacturers most successful in using a modular approach to car manufacturing and marketing. Recognizing that there are strong differences in consumer preferences, Ford has reduced the number of components - and thereby has achieved economies of scale - without affecting the number of options available to customers in each of the seventy-five different national markets in which Ford sells cars.

Ford manages to use a modular approach also in its advertising messages, emphasizing safety in Scandinavia, performance in Italy, design in France and handling in Germany. The Ford brand may be global, but the product and its supporting marketing effort are very much local.

For e-Commerce marketers with global ambitions, the requirements are to find out if the product or service they represent and the way of doing business can be exported in their 'domestic' forms or they will encounter consumer resistance and will need substantial adaptation to suit consumer tastes.

THE RISKS OF GLOBAL WEB MARKETING

For companies that have an established global distribution system the decision to exploit the Internet as a marketing tool needs to be considered with care. Once a Web site is established which has an online purchase facility, there is the risk that overseas customers will cut out the local distributor, place orders electronically and expect price discounts.

This was the case of Millipore Corporation of Bedford, Massachusetts, a company with annual sales of $600 million specializing in filtration products for water purification for laboratories and the detection of contaminants in semiconductor manufacturing. With a 'blue chip' list of customers worldwide the Internet clearly offered an effective medium to both communicate information and provide the customer with a purchasing mechanism.

However, Millipore faced a massive complication in that, similar to many other multinationals, it charges higher prices overseas in order to cover the additional cost of support services. Having faced the potential dilemma associated with inter-country pricing differentials, Millipore decided to postpone offering an online ordering facility and instead restrict its Web site to providing information with supporting pre- and post-purchase service activities.

STANDARDIZATION VERSUS ADAPTATION

The decision whether to standardize or adapt the marketing mix elements is a major one for any organization operating outside its home environment. Standardization allows the organization to maintain a consistent image and identity throughout the world.

It provides economies of scale and is particularly valuable for maximizing impact with the internationally mobile customer. It works best within an identified international segment and with a product of well defined complexity. Global branding and the transfer of new product ideas across boundaries are both possible with standardization.

Standardization has been used successfully in running global promotional campaigns. Transferring campaigns from one country to another is almost impossible, owing to language and cultural differences. Nevertheless, the clever use of pop music as a universal language has allowed Levi's advertising to be successful where others have failed.

Coca-Cola has also succeeded with its 'one sound, one sight, one appeal' philosophy which brings it closer to a full standardization position. Benetton is still running their 'United Colours of Benetton' global campaign based on multi-cultural, universal images that appeal globally.

Adaptation is nevertheless necessary if the organization is under pressure to satisfy the multiplicity of needs of the global customer to the extent to which it will have to change the elements of the marketing mix.

CHANGING PATTERNS IN GLOBAL DISTRIBUTION

Distribution is the process by which all consumer and industrial goods are transferred from the producers to the end users. The process includes not only the physical handling and distribution of goods and the transfer of ownership from producer to consumer, but also the whole range of buying and selling negotiations between producers and intermediaries, and between intermediaries and consumers. Distribution channels are the ways and means by which goods are distributed from the producer to the end user. The traditional distribution model has been linear.

The producer is the originator of the products, which it builds or manufactures. Wholesalers and distributors bring together the products from a number of manufacturers, then divide them and transport them in small lots to resellers or retailers who deal directly with the consumers. The value added of the distribution chain has been in the dispatch, warehousing and delivering of products.

Sometimes distributors undertake the repackaging and marketing of the products. The chain of intermediaries, who are the wholesalers, distributors and retailers, adds substantial costs to the value chain, which can make the prices to the end user significantly higher than those of the producers. The

Internet has been unique in its potential to revolutionize the value chain, as it enables producers to reach the end users directly.As e-Commerce firms are developing, they will be choosing their entry and distribution modes on the basis of reducing their transaction costs even to the point of internalizing certain activities which have been traditionally performed by intermediaries. The Internet has raised expectations that, in time, producers will sell directly to end users and, in turn, end users will prefer buying direct from the producers. What is actually happening is that value chains are being deconstructed, reconstructed and transformed into value webs, giving rise to a new class of intermediaries, which are the collecting and distributing of information.For example, companies like Yahoo! or Netscape act as information collectors and disseminators, offering e-Commerce new possibilities of doing business.

E-COMMERCE DISTRIBUTION SYSTEM

For Web-based businesses focused on competing in global markets, there is every indication that representatives in the field are necessary in order to facilitate dispatch, the handling of returns and servicing. Companies that deal with consumer goods and have relatively low international volumes that require little service assistance may be able to dispense with any on-the-spot distribution requirements and rely on a global integrated carrier.

GLOBAL EXPORTING

The European Union in its present form has a larger population than the United States. Nevertheless, most of its producers and consumers live and work in a radius of 800 km, equivalent to 12 per cent of the land area of the United States, and for historical and economic reasons, transport in the European countries has been burdened with rules and regulations. For example, a trucker transporting goods from Glasgow to Athens used to spend 30 per cent of his time at border crossings, waiting and filling in up to 200 forms.

These inefficiencies are mercifully now a thing of the past. In order to move goods between EU member states only one simplified transit document is required and many of the custom formalities have been eliminated. However, consignment to countries outside the European Union is still burdened with an array of obstacles, cultural and linguistic, which lead to many companies failing to exploit the opportunities offered by overseas markets. The SME sector is affected in particular, as such companies do not have the resources to spend on overseas sales teams and trade-related computer systems.

E-COMMERCE SUCCESS

CIOs often suggest that better measures of the payoffs of e-commerce operational and capital investments are necessary to demonstrate the value creation of e-commerce initiatives and to obtain additional resources for critical e-commerce projects. The measures are essential to monitor the key performance drivers (inputs and processes) and assess whether the e-commerce initiative is achieving its stated objectives (outputs) and thus contributing to the long-term success of the corporation (outcomes).

Companies often waste resources on e-commerce initiatives or do not invest when they should because they cannot effectively evaluate the potential payoffs of e-commerce investments.Measuring returns on e-commerce projects can be a daunting challenge.

Predicting customer behaviour is difficult, because using the Web to do business is still relatively new to many businesses and thus forecasting sales and profits is typically imprecise. There is not much historical data and experience for managers to draw upon when developing or applying metrics, and many economic benefits of e-commerce projects are seen as difficult to measure.

Further, the pace of change in e-business and Web-based technologies has been so rapid that precise measurements are often difficult.Many senior managers have come to believe that further investment in new technology and e-commerce is an imperative that is required to maintain or develop a competitive position. They often make expenditures without completing a rigorous analysis.However, today's more stringent economic environment and the widely publicized negative impacts of many e-commerce initiatives has caused many senior managers to question the payoffs of e-commerce investments. As companies assess the choice of appropriate measures to evaluate e-commerce initiatives, numerous potential issues arise.

Since the choices are different for each company, because the strategies, structures, and systems are different, substantial customization is necessary. Senior managers should consider six initial questions that can lead to the development of appropriate measures for e-commerce operations:

- What measurement systems are currently in place and being utilized within the organization?
- What are the important criteria to the company and its constituencies and stakeholders?
- What does the company desire to accomplish with the e-commerce initiative?
- What is the anticipated time frame associated with the e-commerce programme?
- Who are the parties involved in implementing the e-commerce project, and who will be affected by the results?
- What critical processes are associated with the successful execution of the e-commerce project?

To address these questions, it is imperative that companies not only specifically tailor their e-commerce measurement approach but also utilize multiple measures to fully analyse their situations. Different measurement criteria are important for companies that have different strategies or may be in a different stage of their life cycle or their e-commerce development. The multiple measures will typically include both financial and nonfinancial measures that are leading and lagging indicators of performance.

They may be used in a balanced-scorecard, shareholder-value-added, or other approach and can be developed specificallyf or IT or e-commerce or as a part of an overall corporate performance measurement system. Companies can also use a weighted scoring system to evaluate investments related to overall IT, e-commerce, or business strategy.

There are many obstacles to implementing a successful measurement system, whether a lack of focus, a low priority, or just difficulty. It is the responsibility of senior managers to evaluate the e-commerce initiatives and decide on the right measures for their organization and ensure that the measures are captured and responded to properly.

To obtain adequate resources for e-commerce and to effectively manage e-commerce initiatives, the payoffs of e-commerce investments must be calculated and integrated into management decision-making systems.

DEVELOPING APPROPRIATE METRICS

To closely monitor the cause and effect relationships evidenced in the e-commerce causal linkage model, appropriate metrics must be developed. These metrics must be consistent with and support the objectives and drivers and key success factors already defined. The selected metrics will likely include a combination of input, processes, output, and outcome metrics to effectively measure performance.

Senior managers involved in the e-commerce decision-making process should develop metrics appropriate to the strategy and objectives of the e-commerce initiative, the company, and its stakeholders. During the measure selection process, it is useful for the involved individuals to choose just a few measures, to focus those senior managers involved in the e-commerce initiative on the critical performance indicators.

The list of metrics presented here is not meant to be a comprehensive set of e-commerce performance measures. Rather, it is a selection and example of some metrics that may be appropriate. Managers must select those that most closely fit their strategy and adapt or develop others. There is no rule for the right number of metrics to include in a measurement system; however, including too many tends to distract managers from pursuing a focused strategy. Generally, a complete measurement system includes perhaps three to six measures for each element being evaluated and no more than twenty measures in total.

For each key success factor, a specific target should be identified and results should be measured against these targets. These results should be widely communicated among not only those senior managers directly involved in the e-commerce initiative, but also other individuals within the organization upon whom the initiative will have an impact.

One of the important contributions that e-commerce can make to an organization is an expanded communication and informational capability. Any e-commerce measurement system will have little impact if the results are not fully discussed. Results should be monitored regularly and used to identify areas of weakness, address the plans and systems in place, and establish new initiatives to improve deficiencies.

The measures chosen should be quantifiable, in either absolute or percentage terms, as well as complete and controllable. They should be complete in that the measure sums up in one number the contribution of all elements of performance that matter; for example, profitability is a summary measure of revenue generation and cost control. They should be controllable in that employees in the organization can actually influence improvement in the factor measured.

Some of the metrics shown here are evaluations of overall firm performance. Others are indicators of e-commerce performance that are derived through an aggregation of measures of individual business units and functions. It is important to evaluate the performance of both overall e-commerce performance and the specific aspects of e-commerce that lead to revenue enhancement or cost savings to determine the success of various operations and corrective action that can be taken to make improvements.

The measures should be of use to both senior and middle managers in the business units and functions. Thus, they must be disaggregated so each unit can examine its contribution to the achievement of the company's e-commerce strategy.

These analyses ensure that each unit is making a contribution to the e-commerce initiative and improving corporate profitability. Additionally, these metrics can be used to provide a gap analysis that permits managers to determine what other inputs or processes are required to meet the company's e-commerce project objectives. Different tools and techniques are available to measure the different aspects of e-commerce performance.

For example, online surveys and polls are powerful tools to help e-commerce enabled companies to better understand the benefit of Internet usage for increasing revenue or decreasing costs related to their customers, thus providing valuable information regarding opportunities to improve overall profitability. Internally, surveys, focus groups, and other techniques are increasingly being used to measure and monitor employee, personnel, and stakeholder reactions and provide valuable feedback.

Once metrics have been developed, data on these indicators must be collected and statistical analysis, such as multiple regression, should be performed to analyse and test the validity of the customized e-commerce measurement system and causal relationships hypothesized by the company.

As companies evaluate the initial measurement system's performance, they will typically add some metrics and drop others because of a lack of evidence of a strong relationship. It is here that a final measurement system emerges, and the focus then shifts to applying the model to support improved decision making.

Outputs and outcomes: Overall-firm and e-commerce-specific performance. If the e-commerce initiatives are well designed and executed and the model of causal relationships properly specified, the identified inputs and processes should lead to improved performance. This should include increasing the success of the e-commerce initiative (outputs) and ultimately to improve corporate performance either through increased revenues or decreased costs (outcomes). To properly evaluate e-commerce performance, input, process, output, and outcome measures are all necessary and should be clearly linked in a causal relationship.

These performance indicators empower senior managers with the information to evaluate whether the e-commerce programme is achieving its stated objectives and contributing to overall corporate profitability.

For example, metrics such as the percentage of customer attrition are indicators of the e-commerce customer service provided by the company and the related level of customer satisfaction. Since the goals relate to increasing corporate profits, not just improving customer satisfaction, both output and outcome measures are necessary.

A weak performance on the output metrics should signal a need to examine the inputs and processes and determine whether they have been misspecified or just poorly executed. It also can provide an opportunity to identify potential benefits to organizational effectiveness and profitability from e-commerce that may have been overlooked.

This is an opportunity to examine how well e-commerce Programmes are contributing to corporate profits and should unveil specific opportunities, directions for improvements, and standards of performance. The e-commerce measurement system should highlight the specific contributions of the e-commerce activities, in addition to providing valuable feedback that can lead to future e-commerce programme and corporate improvements.

Results from the e-commerce evaluation and measurement process should be widely communicated throughout the organization. In a well-executed e-commerce venture, all units of the company will have some involvement in the e-commerce initiative.The evaluation and measurement of the e-commerce programme will have little impact if the results are not disseminated throughout the organization to the many disparate areas that both affect and are affected by it. Results should be monitored regularly and used to identify areas of weakness, challenge the plans and systems in place, and present new initiatives to improve deficiencies.

THE BUSINESS ENVIRONMENT FOR E-COMMERCE

By the middle of 2001 the business revolution promised by the 'new economy' and the functions of the Internet had come to naught. The promise of a new business model based on e-Commerce or e-Business failed to deliver as the dotcom phenomenon imploded into that of the dot-bomb. Simon Caulkin, management correspondent for the *Observer*, described it as follows:

So, farewell then death of the business cycle, the end of inflation and above all the myth of the New Economy: slain by revisions to US figures that show that, far from lifting the economy permanently to the sunny uplands of unending productivity growth, the great Internet binge has given us levels of improvement that haven't been seen since, er, the 1930s. This quotation brings to mind the cultural revolution promised by punk in the mid-1970s. According to the then manager of the infamous Sex Pistols, Malcolm McClaren, punk would sweep away all hitherto popular culture into the dustbin of history as it represented a new Situationist adventure. In reality, punk was a speeded-up version of good old rock 'n' roll and ironically corresponds to the Pistols' most famous album, *Never Mind the Bollocks.*

Similarly, the Internet, instead of promising a business revolution, speeds up the rate of transactions rather than their primary nature. *Never Mind the Bollocks* seems to be making a comeback, nearly thirty years on, but in a different guise.Where did it all go wrong? Why hasn't the move 'from capitalism to knowledge society', as in the essay title by the management theorist Peter Drucker, become our everyday reality? According to Drucker, economic history can be divided into three eras:

- The *industrial revolution.* From the late eighteenth century onwards, knowledge was applied to tools, processes and products.
- The *productivity revolution.* From 1880 until World War II knowledge was applied to work.
- The *management revolution.* From World War II onwards, knowledge applied to knowledge itself.

For Drucker, we now effectively live in a 'knowledge society'. For other contemporary theorists we inhabit 'the information society' in which the 'spirit of informationalism' drives all economic and social transactions. There are concepts derived from the same root: the 'weightless economy', the 'thin economy' and the 'weightless society' and the 'death of distance'. The factor common to all these conceptions is the role of technology. In fact, all these accounts can be said to be technologically determinist. That is, it is the technology that is transforming economy and society, rather than the business processes to which technology is put to use. In Drucker's account, technology and the invention of calculating machines, in particular the computer, are central to the progress of society through the three revolutions outlined above. Traditional factors of production - land, capital and labour - have become secondary to knowledge.

As long as there is specialized knowledge these factors can be obtained. In this view, company transactions become weightless. For example, the value of Coca-cola is tied not to the value of production of a fizzy drink, but the power the brand exercises in the market place.

A more salutary account is given by Robert Schiller in his book *Irrational Exuberance* on stock market volatility. He compares the building of the interstate highway system in the United States between 1956 and 1976 and the Internet as innovations. He argues that the Internet is 'notable for its visibility and vividness, and not unprecedented prospects for promoting economic growth and profits'. The interstate and Internet are both network innovations.

The former transformed the economic geography of the United States, promoting lower transport costs, greater market access, outward mobility into the suburbs and the rise of the local shopping mall. Schiller notes that while the Internet offers a wider selection and a greater ability to search, the delivery of goods is not immediate. Consequently, Internet marketing may not be superior to the marketing of the conventional shopping malls. The Internet remains part of the long march of creating innovations, but like all technology it is the nature of human inventiveness that makes them beneficial. The period of building the interstate system coincides with an annual average 1.6 per cent growth in real earnings on the Standard and Poor's 500 index of the financial performance of the top 500 US companies. Despite the enormous impact of the interstate on the economic geography of the United States why were these earnings not higher?

The answer according to Schiller was that the interstate system was just another innovation along the path of inventiveness. Similarly, evidence from McKinsey and Co., the international consultancy, shows that the impact of new technology, including the Internet, on productivity in the United States in the late 1990s was much less than was believed at the time.

The relationship between technological change, economic growth, increased productivity and profits is much more complex and indirect than the easy direct relationship suggested by some popular commentators. In the past decade the service sector has been in the forefront of investment in new technologies in the advanced economies. The benefits of these investments, however, have been decidedly uncertain:

Over the past decade senior managers in banking, insurance, health care, and other services have invested billions of dollars in computers and communications equipment - technology investments that promise to hone operations into an acute competitive weapon. But executives have been deluded: the payoffs have not been fully realized.

The primary reason is that technology alone does not determine corporate performance and profitability. Employee skills and capabilities play a large role, as do the structure of day-to-day operations and the company's policies and procedures. In addition, the organisation must be flexible enough to respond to an increasingly dynamic environment. And products must meet customer requirements.

These observations act as a health warning to the business environment for e-Commerce. This warning is not posted to suggest that Internet-based transactions will fail to deliver *material* benefits to producers and consumers alike. Rather, they act to signpost the difficulties associated with claims that we now live in a new business, economic and social order. The context in which e-Commerce has developed and the difficulty faced by companies that believe the Internet is the universal solution to all business problems.

First, we examine some definitions and models of e-Commerce, and highlight some of the problems that exist to derive an adequate taxonomy for this emerging area. Next comes an examination of the technological underpinnings of the Internet, and its child, the Web. Following this assessment comes a discussion of issues of trust and governance associated with the Internet, and the fact that there is considerable disquiet in some quarters on leadership. A brief examination of how to measure the Internet economy is followed by an identification of the drivers and barriers to e-Commerce take-up. We conclude by looking at some of the issues that have arisen from the implosion of the dotcom phenomena into the dot-bomb outcome. By doing so, we suggest that the business environment for e-Commerce has not destroyed the possibilities of a new economy, but is one in which the realities of the business cycle and the role of technological innovation are reasserted.

DEFINITIONS AND MODELS

There are many definitions of e-Commerce, but they all imply some manner of electronic mediation for business transactions. The UK Department of Trade and Industry (DTI) defines e-Commerce as:

The exchange of information across electronic networks, at any stage in the supply chain, whether within an organisation, between businesses, between businesses and consumers, or between the public and private sectors, whether paid or unpaid.

Though the word *commerce* carries with it a sense of activities being undertaken for payment, this definition gives the term *e-Commerce* a broad informational scope to also include activities for which no direct payment is made within a supply chain. A supply chain describes the distribution of goods, services and information flows between market participants within or between industries. For example, a vehicle manufacturer is at the heart of a variety of supply chains, including parts, raw materials, services, etc., supplied to it by other firms. The optimal management of a supply chain reduces transaction costs. As a result, the competitive advantage of the vehicle manufacturer is enhanced. This explains why many prefer the term *e-Business* rather than *e-Commerce* to describe such electronically mediated activities. The DTI definition does not just place the scope of e-Commerce as being Internet- or Web-mediated, but includes electronically mediated activities undertaken outside the Internet and/or which pre-date the Internet.Earlier forms of e-Commerce, prior to the term being coined, include Electronic Data Interchange (EDI). This is the exchange of information by trading partners, for example orders, using technically defined templates whose origins go back to 1969. The succeeding decades have seen many large corporations taking up EDI based on value-added networks. Value added is the process whereby each successive stage of production adds more value than the previous stage. Examples include private sector organizations such as IBM and GEIS (part of the US giant General Electric). Another major sphere is that of Electronic Funds Transfer (EFT) through which the banking system facilitates financial settlements. Prominent amongst EFT systems is SWIFT (Society for Worldwide Interbank Financial Telecommunication), which has handled international inter-bank settlements since the 1960s. The BACS system is one such that handles inter-bank settlement for the UK banking sector. Finally other industries have created their own forms of EDI such as the airline reservation system, SABRE.There is a distinct difference between the Internet and these other forms of electronic transactions:

- The Internet uses protocols that are *open* and *non-proprietary*. That is, these protocols are published so that theoretically any user can use them to hook up to the Internet
- EDI systems are *closed* or *proprietary* systems, which are open only to paying participants.

The fact that systems are closed means a greater guarantee of security for all transactors. Open systems are by definition open to potential fraudulent activity. So though the economic transactions may be alluring, the potential threat to the integrity of global payment systems is too great at present for the major international banks to shift towards Web-enabled systems. One of the major challenges to examining, analysing and explaining the business environment for e-Commerce is the confusion of terms. Perhaps more importantly, the lack of appropriate models by which to examine, analyse and explain it inhibits clarity of thought and interpretation.

Central to any market transaction, whether in a geographical or virtual location, is the exchange of information. In a market economy, prices signal information about transactions between consumers and producers and between producers themselves. The equivalent in e-Commerce is Business-to-Consumers (B2C) and Business-to-Business (B2B). The advantage of e-Commerce to consumers is greater access to fuller information on prices of goods and services. The advantage to producers is they can directly access a greater market potential for their goods and services.

TO:		
Consumer	B2C Organization sites (Dell, Amazon) Consumer market Places (Kelkoo.com, Shopsmart.com)	C2C Auctions (QXL, Ebay) Consumer reviews (Bizarre.com)
Business	B2B Organization sites (Dell) Business markets places (commerce One, Vertical Net)	C2C Customer bids (Lets Buyit.com, Price Line.com)
From:	Business	Consumer

Fig. Taxonomy of Transactions Between Businesses and Consumers

However, e-Commerce does not overcome the problem of transaction costs (particularly transport costs) and immediacy in purchasing goods and services at designated locations, although it may reduce search costs in some general instances and shift them from producers to consumers in others. Essentially, e-Commerce does not alter the nature of exchange and transactions in a market economy.

Moreover, given the relatively low level of Internet commerce in most advanced economies, the heroic assumption that the Internet is now the universal market transactor is not vindicated by evidence. Given the United States had first-mover advantage, and the size of its economy (which is only slightly less than the whole of the European Union), it may come as no surprise that e-Commerce revenue in the United States in 2000 was twenty-three times that of the United Kingdom, thirty-three times that of France and seventeen times that of Germany. The ratio of B2B to B2C for the same year in the United Kingdom, France and Germany was 7.04, 7.06 and 7.09 respectively, compared with 7.07 for the United States. If one looks at the contribution of total e-Commerce to national income, measured by Gross Domestic Product (GDP), the results do not stand up to many of the hyped claims.

Notwithstanding the rise and then fall in e-Commerce revenues in 2000 and 2001, and allowing for the size of the US economy, e-Commerce represents a small proportion of all economic transactions.

The essential issue is that the dominant virtual medium is television and is likely to remain so for a long time, so that adaptations of this technology to the demands of e-Commerce are more likely to generate longer-term benefits and greater market access. There is also a tendency to conflate goods and services that can be downloaded via a modem, for example software and music, with more physical goods that have to be delivered to the home or pick-up point. In other words, there is as much variability in e-Commerce transactions as there is in conventional ones.

Examples of B2C include Amazon.com, the on-line retailer of books, music and games. Amazon started achieving profitability ($5 million) only in the last quarter of 2001 after having invested $3 billion in its short life, much of which has been spent establishing itself as an on-line brand and creating a fulfilment system. The disadvantage for many B2C companies dealing in tangible goods is the lack of a distribution system that is reliable and economically efficient. These firms to date have difficulty obtaining the economies of scale and scope derived by large retail outlets in conventional shopping malls.

Much of B2B activity is associated with the operation and management of supply chains. Advances in information and communications technology (ICT) have facilitated the development of real-time supply chains, that is, orders for goods and services that are activated immediately. For example, the Ford Motor Company had proposed to link its suppliers of car parts to Ford's production sites through their Web sites so that adjustments in demand for parts could occur instantaneously. However, rather like Just-in-Time (JIT) inventory systems, instantaneous delivery of large items of inventory from anywhere in the globe was not realizable owing to size and cost restraints. The technology does speed up the turnover time of production through instant receipt and processing of orders. What these changes produce is an electronic continuum along which supply chains find themselves in terms of the two types of flow:

- Those which use electronic mediation to organize their supply chains, but whose tangible goods require physical transportation, and whose payment is handled using traditional inter-company means.
- Products whose entire supply chain can be mediated by electronic means, in terms of product, payment and its mediation. So digital artefacts, for example computer Programmes can be developed, and then searched for, ordered, invoiced, paid for and delivered to customers using wholly electronic means.

Chaffey's taxonomy includes other less well cited e-Commerce models such as C2C and C2B. Consumer-to-Consumer (C2C) implies the sale of goods and services between individuals, often via auction sites such as eBay. Consumer-to-Business (C2B) implies individuals selling goods and services to companies. Examples include the sale of cars by individuals to companies. Conceptually in these cases, it is difficult to define who is the consumer and who is the producer. By definition, a consumer does not sell. Such models persist even though the semantic irregularities demand otherwise, partly because no better descriptions currently exist, and that these are part of marketing strategies and ploys by particular companies.

A more concrete model is Business-to-Public Institution, or, more commonly in the United Kingdom, Business-to-Government (B2G). This relates to the trade in goods and services between the private sector and the different forms of government, whether local, regional or national. This particular description is gaining greater resonance as governments in the advanced economies seek to promote the concept of e-Government. A final model is the User-to-User or Peer-to-Peer, which is styled P2P. This implies a relationship between two individuals that is electronically mediated but not via any central body. Freenet is an example of a network that promotes the digital exchange of music artefacts on a P2P basis.

THE TECHNICAL ENVIRONMENT FOR E-COMMERCE

Many of the claims for a significant break with the past stem from the more sceptical accounts of post-industrialism and the information-based economy, for example by the sociologist Daniel Bell. Other more enthusiastic and technologically determinist accounts include those of the futurologist Alvin Toffler, who coined the phrase 'Third Wave' to imply an impending information revolution. What they share is the prediction and formulation of the concept of an 'information society'. The problem for commentators like Bell and Toffler (in common with almost everybody else) was an inability to predict the physical agency that would bring the 'information society' to fruition. This agency was the Internet.

The Internet began life in 1969 as a demonstration project linking up four university campuses in the United States. It showed how a primitive file-sharing system worked. Today the Internet boasts in excess of 300 million users, offering the most rapid take-up of any technology in history. For a relatively small outlay on a computer, a suitable telecommunications link (*e.g.* via a phone line and modem) and an on-line account provided by an internet service provider, individuals located across the globe can access this massive network which has grown at an exponential rate. The network - the Internet - hooks up the physical infrastructure of computers via cable and wireless links so that users can access rich informational sources (*e.g.* via the Web) and use interactive forms of communication (*e.g.* e-mail). However, though the population of Internet users across the globe has grown exponentially, their dispersal is not uniform internationally. The relative density of hosts across the globe is variable. It may be unsurprising to note that the higher concentrations of users are in North America and Europe.

Levels of computers and data services can be shown by measuring Internet access. Network Wizards provide a longitudinal study of the growth of Internet nodes (computers with unique 'Internet Protocol' (IP) addresses) from the network's earliest days. Growth between 1980 and 1987 shows numbers of hosts in the tens of thousands. After 1987, when the US funding body NSF (National Science Foundation) started to work with the Internet, the growth leapt into the hundreds of thousands: many non-US academic sites and scientific and research bodies linked up at this point. The next pulse of acceleration of this growth came when the World Wide Web appeared in 1990. Rapid growth rates ensued, especially after 1993, when the graphical browser called Mosaic appeared, and the scale of change moved into the millions. From an almost unknown medium at the beginning of the 1990s, the Internet by the year 2000 was heading for 100 million *hosts* (*i.e.* unique computers linked up) across the world. Gartzen (2001) estimates that in broad terms the number of users is due to grow from around 300 million in 2001 to around 1 billion in 2005.

In addition to these *fixed* hosts that link individual desktop computers to the Internet there will be *mobile* hosts linking up mobile phones to it using wireless technology. In predictions offered in May 2001, phones labelled as 'Third Generation' (3G) in Gartzen's 'ball park' are due to amount to 1 billion by 2005. This potential rapidity of the Internet's growth creates problems for its continued deployment. Notwithstanding the assumptions underlying these forecasts, even the current global downturn does not detract from the problems associated with the growth of Internet usage. This issue will become sharper if the 'digital divide' is not overcome. That is, between countries that are hardly wired, as in the developing world, and those with maturing virtual infrastructure, for example in the advanced economies.

The Internet - an *inter*connected series of *net*works - began life as a project supported by the US Department of Defense's Advanced Research Project Agency (ARPA). Based on an original concept (the use of a multi-nodal network) developed by the Rand Corporation in the early 1960s and added to by bodies such as the UK National Physical Laboratory (which had developed packet switching ideas), the objective of the research was to provide the United States with a communications network that would survive in the event of a nuclear conflagration. This product of the Cold War was a network purposely designed to offer resilience during a hot war of massive destruction such that it would continue to function whilst 'in tatters'. Up to this time, network paradigms had offered a central node by which messages could be routed (on a circuit-switched basis). A paradigm is defined as a set of theories, concepts, methodologies and practices usually associated with particular forms of knowledge. For example, the natural sciences and social sciences have complementary but sometimes opposing paradigms. So the implication was that if this one central node were to be destroyed, then communications on a continent-wide US basis would have been impossible. In order to circumvent such an emergency, the need was established for a network whose technical architecture was based on multiple nodes, and whose messages could be distributed as packets of data.

As long as every computer linked to the network could be uniquely identified, then messages broken up into packets (each with a header detailing message destination and source) could be routed across the network via diverse nodes and could be reassembled at the destination computer. In-built system resilience meant that if elements of a message were not present for reassembly (identified through gaps in packet sequences), an automatic request would be generated for retransmission. The events of 11 September demonstrated the robust nature of the Internet: where fixed and mobile telephony failed to function in parts of Manhattan after the deadly attacks on the World Trade Centre, e-mail continued to get through.

One notable feature of the Internet's tremendous growth is based on the fact that core software elements were given away by suppliers for free. Mosaic - the first graphical browser - was distributed via the Internet and magazine CD-ROMs to all who wanted to use it at no charge. Its authors (who worked at a university department in Illinois) received no royalties for this work. In the same manner, the underlying software operating system of the Internet - TCP/IP - was also available free to anybody who could hook up to the Internet. TCP/IP is a set of protocols or technical definitions, developed by Vinton Cerf, which, when rolled out across a number of networks in 1983, allowed their inter-linkage and the coining of the term 'Internet'. TCP (Transfer Control Protocol) and IP (Internet Protocol) handle packet disassembly/reassembly and computer addressing respectively.

Central to the development of the Internet is the root democracy. The ARPAnet was developed for operation under cataclysmic conditions. Whatever remnant nodes that existed on a network were required to function. One way of helping to maximize success was to keep any processing tasks as simple as possible. So once the interrogation of a packet's destination is adduced, a routing computer does little more than pass it on. At root, therefore, the Internet evinces 'packet switching democracy': all packets are equal under TCP/IP. In the event of a network disruption, therefore, all packets would be delayed equally.

This inherent lack of packet prioritization has significance for any time-critical or contiguous operations, and thus the efficacy of the Internet can be called into question, not least by commercial interests. This treatment of message packets is defined by the IP protocol in its fourth version (known as IPv4). Though a new version, IPv6, allows packet prioritization, it is not yet pervasive. For some commercial interests, delay in introducing this prioritization will be significant, and ultimately have an impact on the growth of e-Commerce.

While TCP/IP has provided the 'glue'of the Internet, until 1993 it was mainly the preserve of a 'high priesthood' of academics and scientists who used detailed knowledge of protocols to exploit Internet applications. Only with the emergence of the World Wide Web - or 'the Web' - did individuals with little knowledge of such protocols manage to participate in this electronic medium. Initially the Web was text-based only.

The relative simplicity with which new users can hook up to the Internet, given telecoms access, has meant its vast and dispersed take-up, such that demand peaks can lead to network congestion and the so-called 'World Wide Wait'. Innate human perception of delays in response times means that 'waiting' for more than a second can be intolerable for some. Nevertheless, the response of suppliers has not been slow, as the vast investments in Internet connectivity make clear. However, the very success that the Internet enjoyed in its rapid take-up led to so much conceptual and financial hyperbole during the late 1990s that speculative activities intended to reap vast profits from vast investments reaped vast losses instead.

On so much technical configuration does human response lie. If nothing else, the dotcom crash had the effect of sharpening the eye for the detail of the Internet's case. In a fundamental degree that case is shaped by technical protocols. Where once the examination of such arcane documents may have been the preserve of technical departments, now they are examined in boardrooms. Many are aware that technical protocols govern the way they undertake business, and that tiny changes to protocols, for example, can have disproportionate effects on business prospects. The ability to influence the technical standards of Internet technologies is therefore to permit some control over financial destinies.

TRUST AND GOVERNANCE: WHO GOVERNS THE INTERNET?

Trust and governance are seen as key concepts in the contemporary business environment. Trust is crucial in businesses that act as intermediaries. For example, when we write or receive a cheque, we take it on trust that the intermediary between the issuer and the recipient of the cheque will honour the payment. In this case, the intermediary is a commercial bank. Similarly, when we buy goods or a service via the Internet, we take it on trust that the goods or service will be delivered at the price quoted. *Governance* is a slippery concept that has become current in a number of fields. Essentially, governance refers to the manner in which activities are governed through a set of institutions, practices and procedures. For example, corporate governance refers to the way in which companies are governed in respect of fulfilling obligations to the various stakeholders. Governance will often include legal obligations, but can be distinguished from *government*, which is the formal organization of legally binding functions operated on the behalf of a population, be it local, regional or national. Government includes legally imposed regulations, practices and procedures.

The governance of the Web and the Internet started from the view that it should be a universally available and free resource. However, as the Internet has developed, there is an implication that its governance will shift towards more formal regulation as large corporations come to dominate its activities. No single entity owns the Internet or is wholly responsible for its functioning. It is a decentralized network, whose operation is influenced by a number of bodies and forces, not least large commercial interests such as Cisco and Microsoft which help drive ICT standards and innovation in the market place itself, and as members or otherwise of the various bodies.

Between 1987 and 1995, however, one of the most dominant influences on the Internet and Web was the US National Science Foundation (NSF), which subsidized its use, along with scientific and academic institutions that paid for servers and created Web content. The ethos underpinning the Internet at this point was one of not-for-profit, and the lack of packet prioritization underpinned an essentially democratic spirit amongst its user communities.

However, with the 'Boucher amendment' of 1992 the US Congress permitted this not-for-profit medium to extend its remit to include for-profit activity. This had an impact in 1995 when the publicly funded NSFNET (whose 'charter' precluded direct commercial activity) withdrew from network backbone responsibilities in the United States to be replaced by private and commercial funding. In the same year Netscape, which had launched its Navigator browser the previous year, sought share capital through an Initial Public Offering (IPO) and staggered the markets with a 'Day 1' capitalization in excess of $2 billion. It is the year 1995 therefore that can claim to be the birth date of e-Commerce - at least in popular imagination - and from this point the rapid colonization of the network by commercial interests began.

The operation of the Internet in hardware and software terms is based on technical standards produced by a plethora of bodies. Telecommunication standards and other technical specifications have been set by the International Telegraphic Union (ITU) and OSI (representing the French for 'International Standards Organization') for a number of decades. Principal among the bodies that have a prescribed influence on the development of the Internet and the Web are IETF, W3C and ICANN.

The IETF (Internet Engineering Task Force) was created in 1986 to be responsible for drawing up the technical standards for the Internet and comes under the aegis of the Internet Society (ISOC) - created in 1992 - which assumes overall responsibility for the organization of its development. The World Wide Web Consortium (W3C) focuses on the development of the Web (a subset of the Internet) and was created in 1994. It is chaired by the Web's original creator, Tim Berners-Lee. The Internet Corporation for Assigned Names and Numbers (ICANN), created in 1998, controls the accreditation of domain name registrars that undertake the business of registering Web sites. Decisions made by these bodies determine how Internet and WWW operations take place, and by definition what products and/or services are to be successful in the market.

Indicative of the self-view of these organizations is a statement from ICANN:

ICANN has no statutory or other governmental power: its authority is entirely a consequence of voluntary contracts and compliance with its consensus policies by the global Internet community. It has no power to force any individual or entity to do anything; its 'authority' is nothing more than the reflection of the willingness of the members of the Internet community to use ICANN as a consensus development vehicle. Other than in their own terms, no major legal statutes charter these bodies or determine their membership or procedures. ISOC, IETF, ICANN and W3C are bodies that determine their own existence, their own charters and their own procedures, and tend to have memberships composed of established figures in the Internet world, whether from academia or from industry. The claimed ethos of these groups is to further the development of the Internet on the basis of consensus.

ICANN, however, has attracted conflicting views since its incorporation in 1998, when it took responsibility for the Domain Name System (DNS), IP address space allocation and the Internet root server. The significance of this is high-lighted by David Post, who observes:

Any entity responsible for, and exercising control over, the root server data-bases possesses immense power over the future development of the Internet itself, and will, accordingly, be subject to immense pressure to act in ways that may be contrary to the best interests of the Internet community as a whole. Devising ways to prevent arbitrary, oppressive, or self-interested actions by this entity is a task of deep, of truly constitutional importance to that community.Whilst the technology creates the physical mechanism by which the Internet functions, the determining of domain names (*e.g.* www.abc.com) along with their unique numerical identities (*e.g.* 234.5678.901.234) gives ICANN the power to create definitive and addressable electronic spaces, central to the establishment of Internet and Web entities. Without them commercial enterprises would be unable to establish any Web presence.

The issue of trust and governance is central to the business environment for e-Commerce. From a system of governance that was essentially self-regulating we are moving towards a market structure in which a few large firms are starting to dominate. From economic theory, this is akin to market structures that are oligopolistic - markets dominated by a few large firms that formally or informally collude - and monopolistic - markets dominated by one large firm. Despite the low cost of entering Internet-based markets, the resources and infrastructure needed to sustain larger volumes of business suggest that firm size and market consolidation in the form of mergers and take-overs will become characteristic features. In this scenario, some form of government regulatory intervention is inevitable - the admirable roots of the Web as a free resource then being under-mined by the imperative of avoiding monopolistic dominance of the Web and the Internet by large corporations.

The other side of the regulatory governance coin is trust. Given that the Internet establishes a new set of intermediaries between consumers and producers, producers and producers, trust is essential for sustaining the basis of e-Commerce and e-Business. Consumers can inspect, check and then buy goods at their local mall at a given price instantaneously, whereas there is the virtual intermediary of purchasing on the Internet and the physical intermediary of getting goods delivered. There is also the issue of credit and payment card security, which at present is higher in conventional shopping outlets. The beauty of the Internet for the consumer is that it reduces search costs. One can search various outlets to compare the availability and prices of goods and then visit one local mall to purchase them. Similarly, for producers, transaction costs are transferred to the consumer as the latter provides details of preferences, tastes and prices he or she is willing to pay, thereby allowing producers to identify their markets more clearly. The issue of trust and governance is thus central to developments in the business environment for e-Commerce as the Internet and other media, particularly television, are increasingly adapted for B2B and B2C transactions.

MEASURING E-COMMERCE

Measuring the value of electronically mediated business has become an important activity in its own right. Fraught with difficulty, it is one which has to date produced wide divergences in terms of predictions, many of them prepared by those with a material interest in promoting e-Commerce and e-Business. It is also one where the danger of double counting is most frequently encountered. One source of data is the University of Texas at Austin, where Barua *et al.* identify four levels of the 'Internet economy'.

- *Layer 1: The Internet infrastructure layer.* This includes trade in products and services that provide for the electronic infrastructure. It encompasses Internet backbone providers (*e.g.* Nortel Networks), Internet service providers (*e.g.* AOL), networking hardware and software (*e.g.* Cisco), PC and server manufacturers (*e.g.* Dell), security vendors (*e.g.* Norton) and fibre optic manufacturers (*e.g.* Corning).

- *Layer 2: The Internet applications layer.* This includes products and services that build upon the infrastructure layer and make it technologically feasible to undertake business activities online. Categories include all software applications such as browser and server software (*e.g.* Netscape, Microsoft), multimedia (*e.g.* Macromedia), Web building (*e.g.* Adobe), search engines (*e.g.* Google), databases (*e.g.* Oracle), on-line training (*e.g.* Assymetrix, ilearn.to) and consultancy (*e.g.* Scient).
- *Layer 3: The Internet intermediary layer.* Internet intermediaries seek to increase the efficiency of electronic markets by facilitating the meeting of buyers and sellers and their interaction. Categories include Web portals (*e.g.* Yahoo), brokerages (*e.g.* Schwab), content aggregators (*e.g.* ZDNet), market makers (*e.g.* IFX) and online advertising brokers (*e.g.* Doubleclick).
- *Layer 4: The Internet commerce layer.* This layer concentrates on Web-based commerce transactions. It includes the new 'e-tailers' (*e.g.* Amazon.com), manufacturers (*e.g.* Dell), fee/subscription-based providers (*e.g.* Forrester) and online entertainment (*e.g.* AOL Time Warner) and professional services (*e.g.* KPMG).

This is a useful approach to measuring the Internet economy. The difficulty is untangling what is attributable to the 'new economy' and what is attributable to the 'old economy'. In fact, this example is as problematic as trying to separate out manufacturing from services: a common mistake among politicians and journalists. There is also the problem of double counting. In national income accounting, each successive stage of production adds value to the previous stage. For example, coal is mined and then sold to make steel. Steel is made from the combination of coal, iron ore and lime. Steel is used in the production of, say, beams for buildings, which are manufactured and then sold to construction companies to be used in buildings which are then sold or leased to clients. At each stage in the production value is added. The value of the coal, iron ore and lime is added to the net increase in value of the steel, what it is sold at less the cost of the material inputs. The value of the steel beams less the cost of the steel inputs is then added and finally the value of the buildings less the cost of the steel beams is added to produce final national income made up of the value added at each production stage. This method avoids double counting and it is this kind of approach that should be used in measuring the value of the Internet economy, notwithstanding the general problem of disentangling conventional economic transactions from those associated with the Internet. Although the taxonomy is a useful way to think about measuring the 'Internet economy', the necessary corrective. It shows that the contribution of B2B and B2C to national income was very small in 1999, just before the peak of the so-called productivity miracle in the United States.

The significant slowdown from the end of 2000 and subsequent recession in the United States, the fall-out from dot-bomb phenomena and events after 11 September 2001 show that the brave new world of the virtual economy was as susceptible to the business cycle and political shocks as the so-called old economy. In the words of Public Enemy, the US rap band, 'Don't believe the hype.'

DRIVERS AND BARRIERS FOR E-COMMERCE TAKE-UP

The principal driver for the take up of e-Commerce is economic. If we accept what corporate forecasters such as Forrester and IDC predict, then more than 80 per cent of the growth of electronically mediated trade in the period 1999-2004 will be via B2B e-Commerce. At root, this take-up is driven by transaction costs. As an example, banks feel that the cost of processing a financial transaction via the Web can be as little as 1 per cent of that performed at a branch using traditional paper methods. So once fixed costs such as equipment and telecommunication lines are found, the marginal cost of servicing transactions on the Web can be very low.

For a relatively small outlay, companies and individuals can hook up to the Web and access sites that are dispersed across the globe. This fact has contributed to an explosion of infrastructural and service provision on the Internet and prompted many commentators to enthuse about the potential it holds for the traditional economics of location. Frances Cairncross (1998), for example, asserts that the communications revolution removes geographical boundaries to trade. 'No longer will location be key to most business decisions. Companies will locate any screen-based activity anywhere on the Earth, wherever they can find the best bargain of skills and productivity.'

However, though the Internet can facilitate market growth for individual companies, commentators point to more complex factors at work in terms of location. Pratt cites New York's 'Silicon Alley' as a cluster of software developers that could locate in a disaggregated manner if they wished but choose to retain close physical proximity. Whatever the reasons for this and the nature of the particular business function, it suggests that commentators such as Cairncross are ignoring the potential value of social interaction and informal face-to-face networks that clustering might imply. In the case of the City of London, Europe's largest financial centre, large international financial institutions, law and accounting firms and business services providers seek to locate in close proximity.

The underlying logic is associated with external versions of economies of scale and scope. That is, the ability to explore large and different transactions in the same place. Other key factors are the ability to easily recruit specialist labour, access to informational and transport infrastructure and, perhaps more important, the development and sustaining of a powerful innovation environment in which new financial products are developed. Richard Sennett, the American sociologist, has pointed out that in an apparently global era, the leading international economic and business activities are still crowding into the world's major cities. Whatever the claims made for an imagined virtual future, place still matters to business and society.

The cost of computing power has declined over the past thirty years to such an extent that claims are made that the power of the multi-million-dollar mainframes supporting the Apollo mission to the moon at the end of the 1960s can now be contained within a desktop computer costing less than $1,000. The precipitous increase in the power of 'microchips' has followed a pattern first predicted by Gordon Moore, a co-founder of Intel, in 1965. 'Moore's law' reckoned that the power of chips would double at intervals of every eighteen months to two years.

The effect has been that, in relative terms, the cost of ICT is now so low and its power so great that companies have little financial reason to avoid taking up Web-mediated business if they so wish. Once installed, all that a user needs is an account with an Internet service provider (ISP). At the height of the dotcom boom, there were hundreds of ISPs on the UK market offering access to the Internet, and pricing reflected their relative quality of service.

Globalization and Competition

Globalization has engendered as much debate about the new economy. For some, it represents a cleavage with the past. For others, the hype does not measure up to the reality and is merely a different version of the past, this difference being due almost entirely to the evolution of information and communications technology (ICT) and the subsequent speeding up of economic transactions. Leaving aside the influences that pervade under the notion of 'global culture', economic globalization can be defined in the following way:

- The development of and access to markets, the organization of production, corporate decision making and consumer strategies on a global scale.
- Capital markets operating through electronic media twenty-four hours a day.
- The development of transnational corporations (TNCs) in which there is significant foreign ownership and whose board of directors has a large proportion of foreign members.

The reality is a little more mundane. The world appears to be made up of three large economic blocs, the Americas, Europe and East Asia, each accounting for around a third of the world's income, and the United States, Germany and Japan being the largest constituent national economies. If one looks at a mapping of Internet traffic, its volume and frequency tend to mirror telephone and airline traffic, the largest amounts being between the three largest economic blocs. Large parts of Asia, Africa, Latin America and Eastern Europe are bypassed. For these regions of the world, the 'digital divide' is more appropriate than the 'digital revolution'. It also suggests that the world's economy is characterized more by regionalism than by globalization.

What has afforded a more global perspective is the manner in which ICT developments, deregulation and liberalization have opened new markets and productions sites around the world. The general level of production costs has been lowered, and increased international take-overs and mergers by large corporations have generated large economies of scale and scope. As a result, there has been a tendency towards the over-supply of goods, partly rendering a low inflationary environment and a much more intensively competitive environment. In such an environment, new modes of market access with the possibility of lower transaction costs, such as the Internet, have been beneficial to firms' international strategic position, at least in the short term. The key issue for international firms' strategies is still the development of new business models arising from the development of technology rather than market change being driven by the technology itself. Like the proclamations of the new economy, globalization is long on promise and short on delivery.

Political Imperatives

The political imperatives that both drive and arise from the prospect of the Internet economy are relatively easy to understand. Political cycles and the longevity of politicians' careers tend to rest on achieving economic growth and full employment. Any prospect of short-cutting the achievement of these twin goals, for example by the evolution of the new or Internet economy, is often greeted with quasi-religious fervour. By also embracing the ideology of globalization the political elites can escape blame for any of the local social costs, whilst taking credit for the creation of local benefits in the form of inward investment, employment creation, innovation generation and so on.

Added to these aspects is the development of e-Government in which many of the public administration's operations could be transferred to online media.

In the United Kingdom, the government has set up the Office of the e-Envoy to encourage and develop e-Government activities. In the United States, the federal government's Office of Commerce has undertaken similar activities. In the European Union, politicians and business proponents have been arguing for the speeding up of further telecoms liberalization so that high-speed Internet access is provided directly to small and medium-size enterprises (SMEs) and individual subscribers. An EU summit held at Lisbon in March 2000 created an over-ambitious timetable when Member States demanded that incumbent telcos should allow access to rival service providers from 1January 2001. Incumbent telcos have been laggard in this. At the same summit, the UK Prime Minister,

Tony Blair, boasted of the United Kingdom becoming the leading knowledge economy in the European Union by the end of the decade. Apart from these examples, governments in general in the advanced economies account for about 40 per cent of national income. They are large purchasers of private goods and services, invest heavily in infrastructure and information systems and employ large numbers of people. They also initiate and underwrite big technology research and innovation programmes and projects under the rubric of building and sustaining the knowledge economy. Therefore, the political imperative driving the Internet economy is both concrete and abstract.

Barriers

Physically, before users can begin to address linking up to access the Internet via an internet service provider they must have a telephone line (or some other kind of communications link). In many economies, telecoms provision has increased significantly as the result of deregulatory policies that have seen competition introduced into telecom markets. Once physical connectivity is possible, you can begin to exchange electronic communications across a global network by virtue of an account with an ISP. Initial ISP hook-ups provided speeds of data transfer of nine kilobits per second (kbps) - or 9k - but successive jumps via 14k and 28k generations have seen the establishment of a 56k standard.

Computers work at a digital granularity with all messages and their modes of communication (text, audio, still and moving images) being decomposed into streams of noughts and ones. The telephone system though was originally designed for voice. So, for data transfer to take place, computers were obliged to communicate via the network using sound. Thus the 56k modem converts a digital signal from the computer (composed of noughts and ones) into an analogue signal - sound - for delivery along the telephone system as a stream of sounds of two discrete pitches. The fact that further modem standards have not been developed is indicative of the apparent physical limit of 'acoustic coupling'.

While the demands of asynchronous communications such as e-mail, on-line chat and simple Web pages can be accommodated satisfactorily within 56k, such data transfer rates are not sufficient for synchronous communications such as video-conferencing or 'video on demand'. Thus wholly digital transfer technologies such as ISDN (128k) and ADSL (from 500k) have come into focus and are seen as the means of opening up multimedia - and hence e-Commerce - delivery to domestic premises and small firms. Such bandwidth had only been available to large companies using leased lines before this.

Though deregulation of telecoms markets had seen the development of digital communications in trunk networks, their extension to the 'last mile' of telecom networks (*i.e.* from local exchange to domestic or small firm premises) occurred only in the late 1990s. For competition to prevail, two physical developments must occur. At the exchange the physical unbundling of copper wires is required. This 'unbundling the local loop' allows digital equipment to be hooked up to individual lines by alternative telecom providers. At the domestic or small firm premises, the installation of a digital adaptor is required. However, political imperative has not led to the desired opening up of the local loop market, with ex-monopolist telcos such as BT and France Télécom failing to act with the speed the regulators envisaged. As a result, high-speed services are not as prevalent as proponents of e-Commerce desired.

With 20:20 hindsight, it seems clear that incumbent telcos would not vote for reductions in their revenue streams with gusto. In the United States, however, where unbundling began in the mid-1990s, the liberalized telephony and data services regime was to allow regional telcos to enter long-distance markets and permit long-distance telcos to enter the local loop market, so long as access could be gained to individual subscribers by any service provider. Purton (2001) observes that while US service providers were allowed to enter each other's markets in exchange for giving up exclusive service provision in their own markets, in the European market there had been no such *quid quo pro*.

Further comparison of US *v.* European markets shows that in the United States, subscribers pay a flat fee to their telecoms provider for line rental. After paying this fixed cost, there are no further charges for calls using local exchanges. In Europe, on the other hand, local market practice saw the establishment of per-minute charging on local networks from the 1960s onwards. There is an impact on Internet use of 'unmetering' and 'metering'. Metering inhibits Internet use owing to the ongoing financial penalty of maintaining a presence on a line. An unmetered approach promotes potential Internet use owing to a user's indifference to the quantity of time spent maintaining a presence on a line - at least in financial terms.

Technical Problems

The Internet protocol IPv4 was not designed either to handle very large numbers of unique addresses or the different levels of 'Quality of Service' (QoS) that different forms of media and hence e-Commerce require. The Internet has become a victim of its own success, and it is assumed that all IPv4 addresses will be exhausted by the 2005-11 period (Pouffary 2001) if predictions about the total number of devices that will be attached become true. This includes extra fixed links such as printers, cookers and fridges and mobile links including 3G phones, vehicles, ships and planes. Whereas businesses with the necessary resources can avoid traffic problems on the public switched telephone network by leasing telecom lines to guarantee QoS levels, the Internet works on a 'one size fits all' approach. Mathy *et al.* (2000) note that it was originally designed primarily to move files between computers. For this there were no strict time requirements - termed *elastic* - and a 'best effort service' was adequate for the task of delivering e-mail and Web pages. However, applications such as video-conferencing are much more demanding and require on-demand, guaranteed and immediate delivery of data packets. These have *inelastic* service requirements, and imply a more complex set of service quality attributes than IPv4 can offer. IPv6 has been designed, however, to allow service discrimination, and data packets are forwarded depending on their prioritization.

E-COMMERCE MANAGEMENT AND SEPARATE E-COMMERCE BUSINESS UNITS

While the spin-offs were failing, companies looked for other creative ways of achieving "separation" without spinning the e-commerce venture off entirely. One method has been to create a separate business unit so divorced from company headquarters as to seem to be its own organization. This separation may be achieved by physical distance, radically different business unit structure, systems, rewards, and culture, or the selection of leadership to run the unit.

Some companies have elected to have entirely separate management structures. One concern is whether these structures can aid in the implementation of an effective e-commerce strategy that is focused on ultimate company-wide integration of e-commerce. For many companies, the preferred approach is to establish an e-commerce unit flexible enough to foster innovation but integrated enough to be consistent with a well-formulated e-commerce strategy.This type of unit should largely resemble the company's other business units, serving as a profit centre and reporting through normal channels and the existing hierarchy on issues ranging from the effectiveness of e-commerce initiatives to the integration of those initiatives within the overall structure of the company.

It may, however, have different management control systems from the rest of the company, especially in the areas of performance measures and incentive systems. It is these differences, not pretenses of geographic distance or office design, that can truly foster innovation.A successful separate business unit for e-commerce displays numerous attributes.

- The SBU should be well integrated into the traditional business management structure so that the goals of the SBU are aligned with those of the company.
- A primary function of the SBU should be to lead the company's integration effort to the point where the e-commerce initiative becomes a part of every level of the company, not just the original SBU, to both increase revenues and decrease costs.
- The SBU should be given enough freedom to utilize e-commerce in ways that were not possible for the traditional business of the company.

- The SBU should be charged with specific goals regarding the company's e-commerce strategy and integration efforts.

The e-commerce unit, however, may also take on some characteristics of a traditional functional unit. Depending on their breadth, these units are sometimes treated instead as cost centers to serve the business units rather than external customers.

In addition to integrating the Web channel with other channels and business units, the unit (whether functional or business unit) may also provide e-commerce solutions to other parts of the company and integrate the company's back-end systems. Some examples of separate business units and the forms they have taken include the following.

- UPS formed a wholly-owned subsidiary, e-Ventures, in 2000 to provide services for small and medium e-commerce companies. The unit operated semi-autonomously but used the same trucks and warehouses as the rest of the company. The unit boosted its capabilities by acquiring a number of smaller logistics firms.
- Tesco built its grocery internet unit out of Tesco Direct, a small unit that began direct retailing in the mid 1990s, and opened a Web site in 1996. Tesco.com was also a 100 percent-owned subsidiary, although at one point there was discussion of a possible spin-off. Internal investment in the unit was cautious, with an eye on gradual geographical expansion. The unit chose not to build inhouse warehouses, instead supplying customer orders directly from the physical stores' shelves. The Web site did, however, offer more heterogeneous product offerings, including music, small electronics, and dishware.
- Wells Fargo runs e-commerce from a very tightly integrated "total business unit" that treats the Internet as another delivery channel. There is strong integration on both the front end and back end, with offline customers automatically signed up for an online account, and aggressive cross-promotion. The unit does not separately track profitability for e-commerce, but it points to lower attrition rates and higher purchase rates as measures of success.

Some successful companies have chosen not to create a separate business unit for e-commerce, instead treating the Web as a co-equal with other sales channels and integrating it throughout the organization. Still others have created a hybrid business unit that combines e-commerce and other parts of the business, such as catalog sales, in a much more limited fashion than full integration.

The rationale is that catalog sales and Web sales have much in common, especially in contrast with a physical store channel. Moreover, because of the expenses associated with mailing catalogs and maintaining catalog call centers, an effort to shift catalog customers to the Internet is highly cost-effective. Nordstrom Direct, which evolved after Nordstrom.com was folded back into the parent company, is an example of this structure.

Keeping e-commerce management internal is vital to implementing e-commerce strategy, but the successful implementation of e-commerce must also allow for flexibility in the management structure. The IT backbone that implements back-end systems for e-commerce should also provide the basis for a highly networked organizational structure. As such, the company can reap the benefits of decentralization without incurring the high costs or loss of the advantages of a more centralized and integrated structure.

OUTSOURCING

Though typically not desirable, outsourcing of IT as a part of e-commerce is not always a harmful decision. In limited contexts, the benefits of outsourcing can outweigh the costs of contradicting the integration paradigm. Back-end capabilities should, however, be developed internally in cases where they are related to a core competence, represent a source of competitive advantage, or involve unique or idiosyncratic activities. To understand those proper contexts, one must examine the range of IT capabilities relevant to e-commerce.

- IT infrastructure is a first priority for a company seeking an integrated e-commerce effort, and speed is a strong consideration. Although a company's legacy systems may have their unique characteristics, the software and hardware in this area is highly imitable and does not represent a likely source of competitive advantage. Therefore, a company should feel equally comfortable outsourcing this task or acquiring the capabilities and handling it internally.
- In functional areas such as payroll and human resources, e-commerce can also provide ample opportunities for cost savings. Software packages in these areas are also commodities and an unlikely source of competitive advantage. If upgrading capabilities in these areas is a part of the overall integration of e-commerce and it is not a core organizational competency, outsourcing may be an acceptable approach. For smaller firms, these commoditized solutions can provide relatively similar, if not superior, capabilities in areas such as payroll and human resources at a fraction of the cost of an in-house approach.
- Logistics is a third area in which a company has a reasonable choice between internal fulfillment and outsourcing. If logistics has been a core competency in traditional commerce, such as was the case with Wal-Mart, it should continue to be handled internally for e-commerce. If, however, fulfillment capabilities cannot be quickly and cost-effectively developed from within, outsourcing may be an acceptable alternative, in that it is unlikely to matter to customers by whom the order is fulfilled.

Despite its spin-off model of e-commerce, Staples showed an understanding of this contrast through its model of IT development. Its IT department focused on solutions that directly impacted the customer, while it outsourced back-end operations to a single vendor. This single-vendor form of outsourcing sometimes increases costs in the short term, but it often saves costs related to future vendor competition and is a good alternative to internal development because of uniformity and clear lines of responsibility. It also facilitates a much easier integration if the company decides to bring the capabilities inside at a later date. When operational capabilities involve direct interaction with the customer, outsourcing becomes a generally undesirable choice. Web site design and customer service related to the Web site must be core competencies for any large company seeking success in e-commerce.

Failure to develop core competencies in these areas is an indication that a company has not made enough of a commitment or investment in e-commerce. Proceeding without developing these competencies is likely to do considerable damage to the brand name and future customer acquisition and retention efforts.

WEB SITE DESIGN AND INTERNET PLATFORM

Building a Web platform is an activity that should typically be handled internally. Web site design expertise is widely available and may be acquired if necessary. Though utilizing consultants and Web site design firms can provide some valuable needed guidance and experience, handing the task off completely to a consulting firm often prevents the company from imparting vital business-specific knowledge into building the site. It also lengthens the learning period for employees who will need to understand the site's design, while at the same time handicapping the company's future e-commerce development by not cultivating this knowledge internally.The design of the site is closely tied to the customer service and support capabilities of the site, which are among the most vital capabilities to develop from within.Many companies that have gone outside the company for Web site design have done so because of the service capabilities provided by their partner. The highest profile examples have been alliances between Amazon and Toys'R'Us, Borders, and Target, among others.

No one story describes the relationships with the companies that have partnered with Amazon:

- Toys 'R' Us partnered with Amazon because of its failure to develop internal e-commerce capabilities, especially in the area of fulfillment. Even as a venture capital-funded spinoff, the e-commerce venture of Toys 'R' Us was running out of money and had created too much damage to the company's reputation to grow revenue.
- Borders joined Amazon because they realized that Amazon's first-mover advantage within the bookstore industry prevented Borders from becoming an industry leader in e-commerce capabilities. This

union permitted Borders to have a relatively easy-to-maintain digital "storefront" for its traditional brick-and-mortar operations, without competing against Amazon on the electronic front.

- Target's agreement sought to capitalize on Amazon's unique customer-care capabilities while eliminating the need for separate fulfillment partners. Target had rejected the spin-off model of e-commerce initially attempted by competitors Wal-Mart and Kmart but determined that its brand-driven integration strategy would not work without stronger fulfillment capabilities.

These alliances notwithstanding, a company often sacrifices a substantial amount by turning its customer service capabilities over to a third party. Amazon's reputation and capabilities are unique online, and since not every company can hope to strike a similar alliance with Amazon, its example should not be viewed as a generalizable model for e-commerce success. The more reliable approach is to build and acquire the necessary resources to handle customer service from within and integrate both online and physical channels for maximum customer convenience.

PARTICULARS OF E-COMMERCE ALLIANCES

In the previous sections, we have provided a strong rationale for funding, managing, and providing IT solutions for e-commerce from within the organization. Selling part of the e-commerce venture or outsourcing operations to IT firms simply does not usually permit a company to reap the maximum benefits of e-commerce.

At times, however, it may be in a company's interest to go outside the firm and form strategic alliances with companies in the same or complementary industries.As is the case with outsourcing operations, such as the relationships with Amazon, alliances should not generally relate to the company's core competencies. They also should not typically relate to customer interaction activities such as customer service and fulfillment, unless there are clear advantages related to a company's capabilities. In two areas, however, alliances have been very successful in e-commerce: procurement and customer acquisition.For procurement, alliances can help overcome some of the unresolved issues on the B2B side of e-commerce.

Although e-commerce clearly provides a potential for vast savings in purchasing, not all industries have been able to realise these savings. Industry leaders such as Dell, GE, and Wal-Mart have been able to realise these savings, while at the same time sending their competitors scrambling to catch up, as detailed in the following.

- The union of HP and Compaq has provided many challenges and opportunities. However, a major obstacle in the company's competition with Dell has been its attempt to meet Dell's level of productivity by cultivating the type of supplier alliances that have given Dell such an advantage over others. The merged company is hoping that the union of the two companies will allow it to overcome its entrenched supplier methods and improve performance.

- Omnexus is an alliance of many of GE's competitors in the plastics industry. Facing competition from both GE's well-established

Polymerland and pure-play public market PlasticsNet, the founders of Omnexus tried to carve out a position by offering scale (founders included BASF, DuPont, Bayer, and Celanese) while maintaining GE's more private format and hosting value-added services. Omnexus' alliance partners, many of whom have their core competencies in chemicals rather than plastics, maintain some internal control over the venture while having the advantages of a collaboration that may lead to a less costly and more successful strategy.

- The Worldwide Retail Exchange (WWRE) is a large partnership that includes discount retailers Kmart and Target, pharmacies, and a host of specialty retailers. The WWRE allowed Kmart and Target to compete with Wal-Mart on the procurement side because of the sheer scale of the WWRE's buyers. Because the WWRE is integrated with each company's systems, these benefits are achieved without damaging the overall integration for the company, which is especially relevant for Target, which was one of the earliest advocates of full e-commerce integration.

Alliances have also been used to gain access to new customer bases through some of the sites that serve as portals for the Internet.

Viewed broadly, this category includes Internet service providers such as AOL, portals such as Yahoo, browser operators like Microsoft, and the increasingly ubiquitous Amazon.com and eBay.

Companies in a variety of industries have attempted to draw customers from these central locations to their businesses:

- Office Depot struck a deal with Amazon that allowed it access to the bookstore giant's huge customer base. Unlike deals with Toys 'R' Us and Borders, this deal did not entail Amazon taking over operations for Office Depot. Rather, it is only a complement to the originally successful OfficeDepot.com. The Amazon component of Office Depot is more targeted to the individual consumer than the B2B-friendly OfficeDepot.com.
- Bank One was the first company to partner with Microsoft and its new line of.NET services in 2002. The partnership allows BankOne's online customers easier access to a variety of online services, but it also calls for Microsoft to sell BankOne products through the widely used MSN.com and Hotmail.
- UPS entered a partnership with eBay to allow customers in the

consumer to consumer (C2C) transactions easier access to shipping options. The deal was more than simply a link to UPS.com; a special shipping function was integrated directly into eBay's site. UPS was able to access a new customer base in an industry that does not typically lend itself to online marketing.

In each of these deals, the company was able to benefit from an outside alliance without threatening an overall integration strategy. Some of the characteristics of successful e-commerce alliances are:

- Alliances should not be used to substitute for deficiencies in aspects of a company that are core competencies.
- Typically, alliances should not be used in ways directly related to customer interaction.
- Alliances can be used to reinforce B2B relationships for needs such as procurement and support systems.
- Sharing of information, ranging from customer information to production data, is essential in successful alliances.

3

E-Business Strategy

E-business strategy means more than just determining target markets and developing business plans describing the return on investment. It is a comprehensive view of your institution's e-business goals, expected outcomes, rationale, branding, marketing, and launch strategy.

The following sample diagnostic questions assess readiness:

- Do you have an electronic business strategy?
- Do key stakeholders buy in to the plan?
- Have you clearly defined the goal of your e-business strategy?
- Do you have a robust implementation plan for this strategy, including key milestones?
- Have you created a feedback loop and a time at which you will review the results and reevaluate the strategy? (Market conditions may change and may negate your strategy.)
- Have you developed strategic alliances or partnerships with any vendors for Web-based applications?
- Have you determined the return on investment of your strategy? Have you defined success and set clear milestones to gauge progress and considered your exit strategy should market conditions change?
- Have you developed your funding plan? Do you have a plan to recoup your initial investment?
- Have you developed your strategy based on information from current and prospective users? Are you building sites that meet their needs?
- Have you developed a brand for your institution and a corresponding process to maintain, protect, and strengthen this key asset?
- Have you developed a promotional campaign for your Web strategy?
- Have you adequately identified the downside risks? Do you have a plan to address them?

ORGANIZATION AND CAPABILITIES

E-business is far more than putting up a Web site and creating on-line processes. Each unit that implements e-business requires dramatic change.

Often referred to as e-engineering, e-business means that organization structures change, new positions are created, roles and responsibilities are altered dramatically, and new ventures are launched.

For many institutions, requisite skills are in short supply, and outsourcing arrangements are used to accelerate the transition to a new way of doing business.

The following sample diagnostic questions assess readiness:

- Do you have clearly identified business leaders and administrators responsible for e-business?
- Are the appropriate people in the organization responsible for electronic commerce?
- Have you appointed Web designers responsible for the appearance of your Internet applications?
- Have you communicated e-business roles and responsibilities across the entire institution?
- Can you be as entrepreneurial as you need to be?
- Can you move rapidly enough to achieve your goals within your stated time line?
- Have you appointed Web architects whose roles are to turn business requirements into a system design, capabilities for on-line transaction processing (for students, principle investigators, alumni, and vendors), and related services?
- Does the organization have access to appropriately qualified resources?
- Do you have a plan to retrain staff?
- Have you rethought your human resources performance and reward systems?

DELIVERY AND OPERATIONS

The IT support area in your organization will go through its own transformation as it supports your e-business initiatives. And not only will the roles of your IT professionals change, but new organizations will need to be developed to take on new quasi-IT tasks, such as converting content to on-line formats

.This area includes the following topics: backup and continuity planning, development of new content, content management, managing service providers, preventing systems failure, systems maintenance, Web site development and implementation, database administration, interfaces and messaging, network management, and service management.

The following sample diagnostic questions assess readiness:

- Have you put in place a process for creation, publication, evaluation, and quality assurance of all Web content on an ongoing basis?

- Have you defined a uniform set of Web design principles for use across the institution that have been communicated to all schools, divisions, and departments and are used by all Web applications?
- Has your institution put in place backup systems that automatically allow access to your Web site should the primary system fail?

PROCESSES

E-business means e-engineering your processes. You cannot simply put your existing forms on-line. To take full advantage of the promise of Web-enabling existing processes, the underlying process must be completely rethought and dramatically changed. Linkages among existing systems need to be developed, support desks need to be implemented, upgrades need to be planned and executed, and controls need to be in place.The following sample diagnostic questions assess readiness:

- If you plan to offer full Programmes (degree or nondegree) over the Internet, do you have the supporting processes in place?
- Has your institution developed Web-based applications to provide enabled services and transactions over the Internet (for example, on-line applications, on-line registration, and on-line alumni pledges)? If so, have you developed the plan to change the process?
- Have you linked your new processes to your existing systems? Do these Internet-based applications feed data directly into your core administration (for example, student, financials, human resources, research, or advancement) without manual intervention?
- Do you have on-line links with suppliers for functions such as ordering goods and services, remitting payment, and submission of proposals or quotes?
- Do you use off-line methods to promote your Web site?
- Do you offer a customer help line that is available twenty-four hours a day, seven days a week, to assist customers with technical problems encountered while using your Web-based applications?

SYSTEMS AND TECHNOLOGY

E-business depends on adequate systems and technology infrastructure to support your objectives. The systems and technology area includes backend systems, front-end systems, middleware, and transaction processing, as well as an overarching IT strategic plan to update capabilities continually to meet your e-business requirements.

The following sample diagnostic questions assess readiness:

- Does your institution use accepted Internet standards for both internal and external systems?
- Have you assessed the current suitability of IT technical resources for e-business?

- Has your institution implemented automatic systems to check the consistency and quality of Web sites?
- Are the technologies being used to support e-commerce suitable and scalable?
- Are the current electronic delivery channels appropriate based on user preferences?
- Is the organization able to respond to and capitalize on rapid changes in underlying technologies and delivery channels?
- Are the e-commerce services implemented to minimize additional investment and duplicated business logic?

PERFORMANCE MANAGEMENT

You will need to establish and monitor tailored criteria by which to judge e-business effectiveness and to manage and improve your e-business initiatives. These should be linked to institutional objectives and priorities. Measures can be strategic (for example, student satisfaction, impact on learning outcomes, impact on research productivity), financial (for example, revenues generated, impact on process costs), or transactional (for example, Web site availability, user profile and usage).

The following sample diagnostic questions assess readiness:

- Have you already considered how you will monitor the success of your Internet-based services and functionality (for example, improved services, increased enrollments, reduced costs, reduced queues or cycle time for registration and other transactions, increased revenues)?
- Do you have a plan to collect and analyse information and data regularly (for example, feedback from students and business partners, press coverage, traffic, matching of achievements with original objectives of the Web site, improved communication with all stakeholders, and image)?
- From a user perspective, is the e-commerce service providing satisfactory service levels?
- Are service levels and usage monitored on a regular basis?
- Does the organization have in place a means to monitor and report on key performance indicators and the realization of business benefits?

SECURITY

E-business exposes your campus to new security risks: cybercrime, loss of data, and privacy concerns. Identifying and addressing security risks can mitigate these concerns and instill confidence for all of your campus constituents.

The following sample diagnostic questions assess readiness:

- Has your institution appointed a security officer responsible for e-business security?

- Have you established a set of security standards that have been communicated institution-wide?
- Have you implemented some form of authentication (for example, log-on IDs and passwords) to control access to sensitive areas of your Web site?
- Have you created controls (for example, firewalls) to protect the underlying network infrastructure and Internet connections?
- Have e-commerce projects adequately considered and addressed the implementation of security that is appropriate for the e-commerce solution?
- Has the organization taken reasonable steps to minimize the potential for a security breach?
- Have you implemented confidentiality and process integrity controls over your e-business application?

TAX AND LEGAL

Tax and legal issues related to e-business abound. Involving your legal department and soliciting the advice of tax consultants is an important part of planning for e-business. Failure to do so can result in unfortunate and unforeseen circumstances, even stopping a strategy in its tracks.

The following sample diagnostic questions assess readiness:

- If your organization generates any revenue from sales over the Internet, have these revenue sources been reviewed for exposure to unrelated business income tax (UBIT)?
- If your organization receives fees for providing any type of services over the Internet (such as Internet access, e-mail, or search services), have these activities been reviewed for exposure to UBIT?
- If your organization has any publications that appear on-line that include any type of advertising (such as advertisements, placards, running banners, and so forth), have these activities been reviewed for potential exposure to UBIT?
- If your organization's Web site has a chat room where users can participate in electronic discussions, are discussions monitored for content that could jeopardize your tax-exempt status, such as the endorsement of political candidates?
- Does the e-commerce system keep adequate legal and audit trails to support e-commerce transactions?
- Has a policy on intellectual property been developed that stipulates ownership of content and revenue sharing procedures?

HOW TO USE THIS DIAGNOSTIC TOOL

To use this diagnostic tool effectively, your institution must undertake the following activities:

- Answer questions honestly by involving relevant constituents

- Identify gaps in e-business readiness (based on questions to which the answers are no)
- Determine the root causes of the identified deficiencies
- Develop a plan and timetable to address deficiencies based on institution-wide objectives and internal capabilities

Achieving the promises of e-business requires successful navigation of a multitude of challenges. The pervasiveness of these challenges necessitates an institution-wide approach to assessing e-business readiness, identifying deficiencies, developing a strategic plan, and proceeding with implementation.

FRAMEWORK FOR AN E-BUSINESS STRATEGY

At Pricewater house Coopers, we have identified four evolutionary stages for adopting an e-business strategy relevant for all industries, including higher education: presence, integration, transformation, and convergence.

PRESENCE

The first step to doing business on the Internet is to establish a presence there. Often called "electronic brochureware, " this presence usually describes your institution's basic Programmes, courses, and services, and gives contact information.

Examples include on-line descriptions of purchasing procedures, on-line catalogues of campus information, and on-line syllabi and course information. At this stage, risks are small, and so are the likely bottom-line benefits. Nonetheless, this is an essential stage for experimenting, learning, and building commitment. Virtually all colleges and universities have reached this first stage because it is relatively simple to create and maintain a read-only file of Programmes, courses, and faculty for interested parties.

INTEGRATION

In the integration stage, an institution connects with its wider network of suppliers and students by extending its reach beyond institutional walls. At this stage, your institution will enable business functions through the Web—for example, by allowing students to register for courses on-line. In addition, you will use business-tobusiness links with procurement vendors, the Department of Education (for financial aid eligibility verification), funding agencies, research subcontractors, benefit administration vendors, and financial institutions.

Opportunities exist at this stage to realise efficiency and revolutionize customer service. However, challenges exist to integrate Web-based applications with legacy administrative information systems, provide prompt customer service, compete with nimble new entrants, and allocate resources to significant IT investments. Also, tax, legal, risk management, and audit issues loom larger as you begin to conduct real business on-line.Typically in this stage, colleges and universities do the following:

- Begin offering on-line courses. The institution will experiment with technology-enabled and-mediated courses to test and improve processes for the development and delivery of on-line courses. The objectives will be to generate additional revenues, stay ahead of competitors, and gain feedback in an operational setting to test assumptions and help refine new process, organization, and technology designs prior to full-scale implementation.
- Provide on-line student services. Students will be able to go on-line to apply for admissions and financial aid, register for courses, monitor progress, check financial status and pay bills, select housing options, and e-mail faculty. Many institutions use packaged applications such as Campus Pipeline, MyBytes.com, or vendorprovided ERP system enhancements.
- Provide on-line alumni and development services. Webbased applications enable on-line pledge processing, payment processing (with an instantaneous e-mail receipt for acknowledgements), record updating, event registration and reply, and membership sign-up and renewal.
- Transform the procurement cycle. On-line market sites will dominate procurement, streamlining request-forproposal processes and ordering and payment procedures. Procurement processes will be radically shortened, thereby reducing costs amid plentiful choices and more and better services. For a majority of purchases, staff and faculty will order directly from a Web-based market site that is integrated with the administrative system of the institution and the vendor. Information regarding established contracts— products, prices, usage, and so forth—will be immediately accessible and verifiable.
- Develop intricate links throughout the entire research administration process. Research-intensive colleges and universities will seamlessly share information with principal investigators, funding agencies, corporations (funding research and establishing technology transfer arrangements), clinical trial sites, subcontractors, and other constituents. This process will reduce costs, shorten cycle time, improve service, and become a required core competency for competing for federal and industry research dollars.

TRANSFORMATION

Process specialization and disaggregation of the value chain drive the transformation stage. With the e-business infrastructure in place, executives can focus on the job of delineating their core and noncore competencies. E-business allows institutions to unbundle operations more easily, retaining only those components of the value chain where a competitive advantage exists.An institution in the industry transformation stage will outsource many of its noncore activities. Opportunities exist for your institution to identify and invest in activities that truly add value, exploit process excellence by selling to others, rebundle products and services, and create new entry barriers by developing superior knowledge of customer needs and wants. However, challenges exist since margins are squeezed and new entrants increase competition. And identifying and partnering with the best vendors may be impeded ultimately if the best vendors form exclusive arrangements with other institutions, leaving some institutions to choose among less-than-optimal partners.It is expected that at this stage, colleges and universities will do the following:

- Form strategic partnerships with vendors to complement expertise and resources. Although some institutions will develop and provide on-line services themselves, most institutions will select a partner for on-line procurement, student services, research administration, advancement, and distance learning. This disaggregation of the value chain will be met with some controversy and resistance on the part of various stakeholders, but the results—reduced costs, improved services, and heightened focus on core competencies—will prove beneficial to the higher education industry generally and to individual colleges and universities specifically. Narrowing margins and increasing competition will force even reluctant institutions to outsource many noncore processes.
- Develop a core competency in technology-mediated delivery of education. In many instances, distance education courses and Programmes will be developed and delivered by a separate organization (perhaps a for-profit entity in the form of a university.com subsidiary such as New York University, Columbia University, and the University of Nebraska have already done), freed from the confines of the traditional institution but supporting the institution-wide mission. Asynchronous options will allow students, not colleges, to determine the convenient time, place, and pace for education, ideal for lifelong learning. Students will be able to choose modules from a variety of providers, thereby enhancing consumer choice but intensifying competition.

CONVERGENCE

The fourth and final stage, convergence is about more than just the much-heralded coming together of consumer electronics, information technology, telecommunications, and e-business. Convergence leads to the blurring of market boundaries. For example, colleges and universities will soon be competing with training providers, publishers, software vendors, and entertainment providers as these industries converge into the learning industry.

Certainly opportunities exist to enter new markets with no baggage, exploit process skills (for example, superior customer skills), and exploit strong brand name, but challenges exist on how to maintain entry barriers for core businesses (that is, teaching and research) and where to focus the brand name. Colleges and universities will find themselves competing across industries and geography against the University of Phoenix, UNEXT.com, Harcourt Direct Learning, the Open University, and even the likes of Thomson Learning, Asymetrix, Microsoft U, and a multitude of accredited corporate universities.

THE PURPOSE OF A BUSINESS-LEVEL STRATEGY

The purpose of a business-level strategy is to create differences between the firm's position and those of its competitors. To position itself differently from competitors, a firm must decide whether it intends to *perform activities differently* or to *perform different activities*. In fact, "choosing to perform activities differently or to perform different activities than rivals" is the essence of business-level strategy. Thus, the firm's business-level strategy is a deliberate choice about how it will perform the value chain's primary and support activities in ways that create unique value.

Indeed, in the complex 21st-century competitive land-scape, successful use of a business-level strategy results only when the firm learns how to integrate the activities it performs in ways that create competitive advantages that can be used to create value for customers. Firms develop an activity map to show how they integrate the activities they perform. We show Southwest Airlines' activity map in Figure. The manner in which Southwest has integrated its activities is the foundation for the successful use of its inte-grated cost leadership/differentiation strategy. We describe how Southwest Airlines is *killing* its competitors. The tight integration among Southwest's activities is a key source of the firm's ability to operate more profitably than its competitors.

Southwest Airlines has configured the activities it performs such that there are six strategic themes—limited passenger service; frequent, reliable departures; lean, highly productive ground and gate crews; high aircraft utilization; very low ticket prices; and short-haul, point-to-point routes between midsized cities and secondary airports.

Individual clusters of tightly linked activities make it possible for the outcome of a strategic theme to be achieved. For example, no meals, no seat assignments, and no baggage transfers form a cluster of individual activities that support the strategic theme of limited passenger service. Southwest's tightly integrated activities make it difficult for competitors to imitate the firm's integrated cost leadership/differentiation strategy.

The firm's culture influences these activities and their integration and contributes to the firm's ability to continuously identify additional ways to differentiate Southwest's service from its competitors' as well as to lower its costs. In fact, the firm's unique culture and customer service, both of which are sources of differentiated customer features, are competitive advantages rivals have not been able to imitate, although some have tried.

US Airways' Metro- Jet subsidiary, United Airlines' United Shuttle, and Continental Airlines' Continental Lite all failed in attempts to imitate Southwest's strategy. Hindsight shows that these competitors offered low prices to customers, but weren't able to operate at costs close to those of Southwest or to provide customers with any notable sources of differentiation, such as a unique experience while in the air. Fit among activities is a key to the sustainability of competitive advantage for all firms, including Southwest Airlines.

As Michael Porter comments, "Strategic fit among many activities is fundamental not only to competitive advantage but also to the sustainability of that advantage. It is harder for a rival to match an array of interlocked activities than it is merely to imitate a particular sales-force approach, match a process technology, or replicate a set of product features. Positions built on systems of activities are far more sustainable than those built on individual activities."

TYPES OF BUSINESS-LEVEL STRATEGIES

Firms choose from among five business-level strategies to establish and defend their desired strategic position against competitors: *cost leadership, differentiation, focused cost leadership, focused differentiation,* and *integrated cost leadership/differentiate*. Each business-level strategy helps the firm to establish and exploit a particular *competitive advantage* within a particular *competitive scope.* How firms integrate the activities they perform within each different business-level strategy demonstrates how they differ from one another. Thus, firms have different activity maps, meaning, for example, that Southwest Airlines' activity map differs from those of competitors Jet- Blue, Continental, American Airlines, and so forth.

Superior integration of activities increases the likelihood of being able to outperform competitors and to earn aboveaverage returns as a result of doing so. When selecting a business-level strategy, firms evaluate two types of potential competitive advantage: "lower cost than rivals, or the ability to differentiate and command a premium price that exceeds the extra cost of doing so." Having lower cost derives from the firm's ability to perform activities differently than rivals; being able to differentiate indicates the firm's capacity to perform different activities.

Thus, based on the nature and quality of its internal resources, capabilities, and core competencies, a firm seeks to form either a cost competitive advantage or a uniqueness competitive advantage as the basis for implementing a particular business-level strategy. There are two types of competitive scope—broad target and narrow target. Firms serving a broad target market seek to use their competitive advantage on an industry-wide basis. A narrow competitive scope means that the firm intends to serve the needs of a narrow target customer group. With focus strategies, the firm "selects a segment or group of segments in the industry and tailors its strategy to serving them to the exclusion of others." Buyers with particular needs and buyers located in specific geographic regions are examples of narrow target customer groups.

A firm could also strive to develop a combined cost/uniqueness competitive advantage as the foundation for serving a target customer group that is larger than a narrow segment but not as comprehensive as a broad customer group. In this instance, the firm uses the integrated cost leadership/differentiation strategy. None of the five business-level strategies is inherently or universally superior to the others.

The effectiveness of each strategy is contingent both on the opportunities and threats in a firm's external environment and on the possibilities provided by the firm's unique resources, capabilities, and core competencies. It is critical, therefore, for the firm to select a business-level strategy that is based on a match between the opportunities and threats in its external environment and the strengths of its internal environ-ment as shown by its core competencies.

COST LEADERSHIP STRATEGY

The cost leadership strategy is an integrated set of actions taken to produce goods or services with features that are acceptable to customers at the lowest cost, relative to that of competitors. Firms using the cost leadership strategy sell no-frills, standardized goods or services to the industry's most typical customers.

Cost leaders' goods and services must have competitive levels of differentiation in terms of features that create value for customers. Indeed, emphasizing cost reductions while ignoring competitive levels of differentiation is ineffective. At the extreme, concentrating only on reducing costs could find the firm very efficiently producing products that no customer wants to purchase. The firm using the cost leadership strategy targets a broad customer segment or group. Cost leaders concentrate on finding ways to lower their costs relative to those of their competitors by constantly rethinking how to complete their primary and support activities to reduce costs still further while maintaining competitive levels of differentiation. Cost leader Greyhound Lines Inc. , for example, continuously seeks ways to reduce the costs it incurs to provide bus service while offering customers an acceptable experience.

Recently Greyhound sought to improve the quality of the experience customers have when paying the firm's low prices for its services by "refurbishing buses, updating terminals, adding greeters and improving customer service training." As primary activities, inbound logistics and outbound logistics often account for significant portions of the total cost to produce some goods and services. Research suggests that having a competitive advantage in terms of logistics creates more value when using the cost leadership strategy than when using the differentiation strategy. Thus, cost leaders seeking competitively valuable ways to reduce costs may want to concentrate on the primary activities of inbound logistics and outbound logistics.

Cost leaders also carefully examine all support activities to find additional sources of potential cost reductions. Developing new systems for finding the optimal combination of low cost and acceptable quality in the raw materials required to produce the firm's goods or services is an example of how the procurement support activity can facilitate successful use of the cost leadership strategy.

Big Lots Inc. uses the cost leadership strategy. With its vision of being "The World's Best Bargain Place, " Big Lots is the largest broadline closeout discount chain in the United States. Operating under the format names of Big Lots, Big Lots Furniture, Wisconsin Toy, Consolidated International, Big Lots Capital, and Big Lots Wholesale, the firm strives constantly to drive its costs lower by relying on what some analysts see as a highly disciplined merchandise cost and inventory management system. The firm's stores sell name-brand products at prices that are 15 to 35 per cent below those of discount retailers and roughly 70 per cent below those of traditional retailers. Big Lots' buyers travel the country looking through manufacturer overruns and discontinued styles, finding goods priced well below wholesale prices. In addition, the firm buys from overseas suppliers. Big Lots thinks of itself as the undertaker of the retailing business, purchasing merchandise that others can't sell or don't want.

The target customer is one seeking what Big Lots calls the "closeout moment, " which is the feeling customers have after they recognize their significant savings from buying a brand name item at a steeply discounted price.

The customer need that Big Lots satisfies is to access the differentiated features and capabilities of brand-name products, but at a fraction of their initial cost. The tight integration of purchasing and inventory management activities across its full set of stores is the main core competence Big Lots uses to satisfy its customers' needs. Firms use value-chain analysis to determine the parts of the company's operations that create value and those that do not.

Figure demonstrates the primary and support activities that allow a firm to create value through the cost leadership strategy. Companies unable to link the activities shown in this figure through the activity map they form typically lack the core competencies needed to successfully use the cost leadership strategy. Effective use of the cost leadership strategy allows a firm to earn above-average returns in spite of the presence of strong competitive forces.

Rivalry with Existing Competitors

Having the low-cost position is a valuable defence against rivals. Because of the cost leader's advantageous position, rivals hesitate to compete on the basis of price, especially before evaluating the potential outcomes of such competition. Wal-Mart is known for its ability to both control and reduce costs, making it difficult for firms to compete against it on the basis of costs. The discount retailer achieves strict cost control in several ways: "Wal-Mart's 660, 000-square-foot main headquarters, with its drab gray interiors and frayed carpets, looks more like a government building than the home of one of the world's largest corporations. Business often is done in the no-frills cafeteria, and suppliers meet with managers in stark, cramped rooms. Employees have to throw out their own garbage at the end of the day and double up in hotel rooms on business trips."

The former Kmart's decision to compete against Wal-Mart on the basis of cost contributed to the firm's failure and subsequent bankruptcy filing. Its competitively inferior distribution system—an inefficient and high-cost system compared with Wal-Mart's— is one of the factors that prevented Kmart from having a competitive cost structure. Although Wal-Mart is favorably positioned in terms of rivalry with its competitors, there are actions firms can take to successfully compete against this retailing giant. We discuss these actions in the Strategic Focus. Notice that in each instance, competitors able to outperform Wal-Mart complete one or more activities that create value for customers better or differently than Wal-Mart.

Bargaining Power of Buyers

Powerful customers can force a cost leader to reduce its prices, but not below the level at which the cost leader's next-most-efficient industry competitor can earn average returns. Although powerful customers might be able to force the cost leader to reduce prices even below this level, they probably would not choose to do so. Prices that are low enough to prevent the next-most-efficient competitor from earning average returns would force that firm to exit the market, leaving the cost leader with less competition and in an even stronger position.

Customers would thus lose their power and pay higher prices if they were forced to purchase from a single firm operating in an industry without rivals. Consider Wal-Mart in this regard. Part of the reason this firm's prices continue to be the lowest available is that to successfully compete against competitors that are also trying to implement a cost leadership strategy, Wal-Mart continuously searches for ways to reduce its costs relative to competitors'. Thus, customers benefit by Wal -Mart having to compete against others trying to use the cost leadership strategy and lowering its prices in the course of engaging in competitive battles.

Bargaining Power of Suppliers

The cost leader operates with margins greater than those of competitors. Among other benefits, higher margins relative to those of competitors make it possible for the cost leader to absorb its suppliers' price increases. When an industry faces substantial increases in the cost of its supplies, only the cost leader may be able to pay the higher prices and continue to earn either average or above-average returns. Alternatively, a powerful cost leader may be able to force its suppliers to hold down their prices, which would reduce the suppliers' margins in the process. Wal-Mart uses its power with suppliers to extract lower prices from them. These savings are then passed on to customers in the form of lower prices, which further strengthens Wal-Mart's position relative to competitors lacking the power to extract lower prices from suppliers.

Potential Entrants

Through continuous efforts to reduce costs to levels that are lower than competitors', a cost leader becomes highly efficient. Because ever-improving levels of efficiency enhance profit margins, they serve as a significant entry barrier to potential competitors. New entrants must be willing and able to accept no-better-than-average returns until they gain the experience required to approach the cost leader's efficiency. To earn even average returns, new entrants must have the competencies required to match the cost levels of competitors other than the cost leader. The low profit margins make it necessary for the cost leader to sell large volumes of its product to earn above-average returns. However, firms striving to be the cost leader must avoid pricing their products so low that their ability to operate profitably is reduced, even though volume increases.

Product Substitutes

Compared with its industry rivals, the cost leader also holds an attractive position in terms of product substitutes. A product substitute becomes an issue for the cost leader when its features and characteristics, in terms of cost and differentiated features, are potentially attractive to the firm's customers. When faced with possible substitutes, the cost leader has more flexibility than its competitors. To retain customers, it can reduce the price of its good or service. With still lower prices and competitive levels of differentiation, the cost leader increases the probability that customers will prefer its product rather than a substitute.

Competitive Risks of the Cost Leadership Strategy

The cost leadership strategy is not risk free. One risk is that the processes used by the cost leader to produce and distribute its good or service could become obsolete because of competitors' innovations. These innovations may allow rivals to produce at costs lower than those of the original cost leader, or to provide additional differentiated features without increasing the product's price to customers.

A second risk is that too much focus by the cost leader on cost reductions may occur at the expense of trying to understand customers' perceptions of "competitive levels of differentiation." As noted earlier, Wal-Mart is well known for constantly and aggressively reducing its costs. At the same time, however, the firm must understand when a cost-reducing decision to eliminate differentiated features would create a loss of value for customers.

A final risk of the cost leadership strategy concerns imitation. Using their own core competencies, competitors sometimes learn how to successfully imitate the cost leader's strategy. When this occurs, the cost leader must increase the value that its good or service provides to customers. Commonly, value is increased by selling the current product at an even lower price or by adding differentiated features that customers value while maintaining price.

DIFFERENTIATION STRATEGY

The differentiation strategy is an integrated set of actions taken to produce goods or services that customers perceive as being different in ways that are important to them. While cost leaders serve an industry's typical customer, differentiators target customers who perceive that value is created for them by the manner in which the firm's products differ from those produced and marketed by competitors.

Firms must be able to produce differentiated products at competitive costs to reduce upward pressure on the price customers pay for them. When a product's differentiated features are produced with noncompetitive costs, the price for the product can exceed what the firm's target customers are willing to pay. When the firm has a thorough understanding of what its target customers value, the relative importance they attach to the satisfaction of different needs, and for what they are willing to pay a premium, the differentiation strategy can be successfully used.

Through the differentiation strategy, the firm produces nonstandardized products for customers who value differentiated features more than they value low cost. For example, superior product reliability and durability and high-performance sound systems are among the differentiated features of Toyota Motor Corporation's Lexus products. The Lexus promotional statement—"We pursue perfection, so you can pursue living"—suggests a strong commitment to overall product quality as a source of differentiation. However, Lexus offers its vehicles to customers at a competitive purchase price.

As with Lexus products, a good's or service's unique attributes, rather than its purchase price, provide the value for which customers are willing to pay. Although it is currently experiencing difficulties, including ongoing investigations of the firm's finances, specialty retailer Krispy Kreme uses a differentiation strategy to produce premium-quality doughnuts. A unique recipe to produce its products and The Doughnut Theatre are sources of differentiation for Krispy Kreme. Continuous success with the differentiation strategy results when the firm consistently upgrades differentiated features that customers value, without significant cost increases. Because a differentiated product satisfies customers' unique needs, firms following the differentiation strategy are able to charge premium prices.

For customers to be willing to pay a premium price, however, a "firm must truly be unique at something or be perceived as unique." The ability to sell a good or service at a price that substantially exceeds the cost of creating its differentiated features allows the firm to outperform rivals and earn above-average returns. For example, shirt and neckwear manufacturer Robert Talbott follows stringent standards of craftsmanship and pays meticulous attention to every detail of production.

The firm imports exclusive fabrics from the world's finest mills to make men's dress shirts and neckwear. Single-needle tailoring is used, and precise collar cuts are made to produce shirts. According to the company, customers purchasing one of its products can be assured that they are being provided with the finest fabrics available. Thus, Robert Talbott's success rests on the firm's ability to produce and sell its differentiated products at a price significantly higher than the costs of imported fabrics and its unique manufacturing processes. Rather than costs, a firm using the differentiation strategy always concentrates on investing in and developing features that differentiate a good or service in ways that customers value. Robert Talbott, for example, uses the finest silks from Europe and Asia to produce its "Best of Class" collection of ties. Overall, a firm using the differentiation strategy seeks to be different from its competitors on as many dimensions as possible. The less similarity between a firm's goods or services and those of competitors, the more buffered it is from rivals' actions. Commonly recognized differentiated goods include Toyota's Lexus, Ralph Lauren's wide array of product lines, and Caterpillar's heavy-duty earth-moving equipment. Thought by some to be the world's most expensive and prestigious consulting firm, McKinsey and Co. is a well-known example of a firm that offers differentiated services.

A good or service can be differentiated in many ways. Unusual features, responsive customer service, rapid product innovations and technological leadership, perceived prestige and status, different tastes, and engineering design and performance are examples of approaches to differentiation. There may be a limited number of ways to reduce costs. In contrast, virtually anything a firm can do to create real or perceived value is a basis for differentiation.

Consider product design as a case in point. Because it can create a positive experience for customers, design is becoming an increasingly important source of differentiation and hopefully for firms emphasizing it, of competitive advantage. Indeed, product design may be a competitive dimension that will help GM get out of the 1970s mind-set in which the firm appears to remain grounded. Some analysts believe that newly formed, interactive collaborations between GM designers and engineers are contributing to the development of car designs that are more stylish and visually appealing. Firms using a differentiation strategy should remember that the work being completed in terms of all competitive dimensions should be oriented to satisfying customers' needs. A firm's value chain can be Analysed to determine whether the firm is able to link the activities required to create value by using the differentiation strategy. Examples of primary and support activities that are commonly used to differentiate a good or service are shown in Figure.

Companies without the skills needed to link these activities cannot expect to successfully use the differentiation strategy. Next, we explain how firms using the differentiation strategy can successfully position themselves in terms of the five forces of competition to earn above-average returns.

Rivalry with Existing Competitors

Customers tend to be loyal purchasers of products that are differentiated in ways that are meaningful to them. As their loyalty to a brand increases, customers' sensitivity to price increases is reduced.

The relationship between brand loyalty and price sensitivity insulates a firm from competitive rivalry. Thus, Robert Talbott's "Best of Class" neckwear line is insulated from competition, even on the basis of price, as long as the company continues to satisfy the differentiated needs of its customer group. Likewise, Bose is insulated from intense rivalry as long as customers continue to perceive that its stereo equipment offers superior sound quality at a competitive purchase price.

Bargaining Power of Buyers

The uniqueness of differentiated goods or services reduces customers' sensitivity to price increases. Customers are willing to accept a price increase when a product still satisfies their perceived unique needs better than a competitor's offering can. Thus, the golfer whose needs are uniquely satisfied by Callaway golf clubs will likely continue buying those products even if their cost increases. Similarly, the customer who has been highly satisfied with a 10-year-old Louis Vuitton wallet will probably replace that wallet with another one made by the same company even though the purchase price is higher than the original one.

Purchasers of brand-name food items will accept price increases in those products as long as they continue to perceive that the product satisfies their unique needs at an acceptable cost. Loyal customers of Abercrombie and Fitch

Co. 's "preppy but edgy casual clothing at high prices" continue to buy the products even as they become more expensive. In all of these instances, the customers are relatively insensitive to price increases because they do not think that an acceptable product alternative exists.

Bargaining Power of Suppliers

Because the firm using the differentiation strategy charges a premium price for its products, suppliers must provide high-quality components, driving up the firm's costs. However, the high margins the firm earns in these cases partially insulate it from the influence of suppliers in that higher supplier costs can be paid through these margins. Alternatively, because of buyers' relative insensitivity to price increases, the differen-tiated firm might choose to pass the additional cost of supplies on to the customer by increasing the price of its unique product.

Potential Entrants

Customer loyalty and the need to overcome the uniqueness of a differentiated product present substantial barriers to potential entrants. Entering an industry under these conditions typically demands significant investments of resources and patience while seeking customers' loyalty.

Product Substitutes

Firms selling brand-name goods and services to loyal customers are positioned effectively against product substitutes. In contrast, companies without brand loyalty face a higher probability of their customers switching either to products that offer differentiated features that serve the same function or to products that offer more features and perform more attractive functions.

Competitive Risks of the Differentiation Strategy

As with the other business-level strategies, the differentiation strategy is not risk free. One risk is that customers might decide that the price differential between the differentiator's product and the cost leader's product is too large. In this instance, a firm may be offering differentiated features that exceed target customers' needs. The firm then becomes vulnerable to competitors that are able to offer customers a combination of features and price that is more consistent with their needs. Another risk of the differentiation strategy is that a firm's means of differentiation may cease to provide value for which customers are willing to pay.

A differentiated product becomes less valuable if imitation by rivals causes customers to perceive that competitors offer essentially the same good or service, but at a lower price. For example, Walt Disney Company operates different theme parks, including The Magic Kingdom, Epcot Center, and the newly developed Animal Kingdom. Each park offers entertainment and educational opportunities. However, Disney's competitors, such as Six Flags Corporation, also offer entertainment and educational experiences similar to those available at Disney's locations. To ensure that its facilities create value for which customers will be willing to pay, Disney continuously reinvests in its operations to more crisply differentiate them from those of its rivals.

A third risk of the differentiation strategy is that experience can narrow customers' perceptions of the value of a product's differentiated features. For example, customers having positive experiences with generic tissues may decide that the differentiated features of the Kleenex product are not worth the extra cost. Similarly, while a customer may be impressed with the quality of a Robert Talbott "Best of Class" tie, positive experiences with less expensive ties may lead to a conclusion that the price of the "Best of Class" tie exceeds the benefit. To counter this risk, firms must continue to meaningfully differentiate their product for customers at a price they are willing to pay.

Counterfeiting is the differentiation strategy's fourth risk. Makers of counterfeit goods—products that attempt to convey a firm's differentiated features to customers at significantly reduced prices—are a concern for many firms using the differentiation strategy. For example, Callaway Golf Company's success at producing differentiated products that create value, coupled with golf 's increasing global popularity, has created great demand for counterfeited Callaway equipment. Through the U. S. Customs Service's "Project Teed Off " programme, agents seized over 110 shipments with a total of more than 100, 000 counterfeit Callaway golf club components over a three-year period. Altria Group's domestic tobacco division, Philip Morris USA, files lawsuits against retailers selling counterfeit versions of its cigarettes, such as Marlboro. Judgments Philip Morris has won in these suits include immediate discontinuance of selling the counterfeit products as well as significant financial penalties for any future violations. Pfizer is placing radio tags on bottles of Viagra. The small computer-like chips allow Pfizer to track each bottle of Viagra and confirm its legitimacy.

THE CONCEPT OF BUSINESS ETHICS

Ethics is about understanding right and wrong. Business ethics is an increasingly acknowledged part of business life, and this is no less true for e-Business. The concept of business ethics and looks particularly at how they relate to e-Business. It will discuss the extent to which ethical e-Business issues are distinctive, how they result in particularly challenging dilemmas because of the need to rely on computers and evolving debates about ethics in cyberspace. In theoretical perspectives on business decision making, the dominant discourse is often focused on maximizing profit for company shareholders alone.

This perspective is increasingly proving to be inadequate. In practice, profit maximization in the long term may best be achieved by making sustainable decisions that take the consequences for trust between stakeholders (including employees, competitors, suppliers, customers, the local community and shareholders) into account. This is called 'enlightened self-interest' - where business managers take 'ethical' decisions because of the positive impact on the financial bottom line. It is far from being the only reason for the increasing acknowledgement of business ethics. Some business people see the primary role of business as being other than profit maximization. Owner-managers of small firms, for example, have been found to be particularly concerned about the financial and personal welfare of their employees. Business and managers have increasing power as a result of their activities, and with it comes responsibility for their actions.

While there are common understandings of right and wrong in business life which we use every day and see in newspaper headlines, a detailed consideration of ethics in business cannot rely on shallow statements of how we ought to behave. It is necessary to draw on well established theories of ethics. Here the briefest of introductions will be given to some of the key ethical perspectives. Further reading on ethics is strongly recommended.

Ethical theories offer frameworks by which individuals can reflect on the acceptability of actions taken and evaluate moral judgements and moral character. The theories are normative, and outline ways of assessing good and bad behaviour, usually on the basis that decisions about moral practices can be cognitively arrived at. The purpose of the application of ethical theory is *not* to make blanket judgements about the rights or wrongs of the actions observed. The theory enables a systematic analysis using established structures for analysing behaviour from the perspective of moral philosophy. Ethical egoism, utilitarianism, Kantianism, discourse ethics theory and virtue theory.

Ethical egoism and utilitarianism are consequentialist theories. This means that, when considering whether an act is right or wrong, the actor considers the likely outcome of that act. Both theories suffer from the fact that outcomes can be difficult to predict and they also ignore the individual rights of others.The ethical egoist acts in a way which furthers his or her own self-interest (although it may be 'enlightened' self-interest). Faced with the possibility, for example, of copying a competitor's Web page design, the ethical egoist will weigh up what the likely outcomes will be if he or she does so.

If caught out and labelled with a bad reputation by employers, possibly even facing legal charges of violating copyright, the ethical egoist will not copy other people's work. If the egoist will not be found out and will save him or herself time and trouble while still fulfilling work obligations, then the outcome is positive for the egoist and he or she should act in order to further their own self-interest. The theory suffers from inconsistency, since the egoist simultaneously must expect that everyone else will further their own self-interests too, which may well conflict with their own advancement.Utilitarianism promotes the notion of achieving maximum happiness for society (or avoidance of pain and pursuit of pleasure). The person acting ethically according to utilitarianism will weigh up carefully which act will result in the most positive outcomes for those individuals who will be affected by it, a kind of cost-benefit analysis for happiness. When deciding, for example, whether to undercut the prices of high-street booksellers, an Internet-based business that bases the ethics of its activities on utilitarianism would consider all the positive and negative impacts on individuals of not making their books cheaper, and all the positive and negative impacts on individuals of undercutting.

In such an example, although a price cut might result in some job losses and reduced dividends for shareholders, the weight of advantage for many customers is likely to be widespread, hence utilitarianism might see price undercutting on the Web as ethical.Kantianism is a very important ethical theory. Kant argued that every individual must seek to do his or her duty. He defined 'duty' very precisely as obedience to the 'categorical imperative', which is what an individual would consider to be the rational, universal, ethical action. The act is the focus of attention in Kantian ethics and an ethical act is one which complies with the categorical imperative, *i.e.*:

- It is universalizable - if it is right in one situation for one person, it must be right in every situation for everyone.
- It respects other people and never uses them as a means to the actor's end.

Table. Summary of Ethical Theories

Theory	Basis	Characteristics
Ethical egoism	Consequence-based: maximize own selfinterest	Promote own well-being above everyone else's
Utilitarianism	Consequence-based: maximize utility	Greatest good of the greatest number
Kantianism	Act-based	Act in a way which is universalizable Treat people as ends in themselves, never means to ends
Discourse ethics theory	Process-based	Consensus by full, open discussion
Virtue theory	Character-based	What sort of person should I be?

This approach is clearly quite different from the consequentialist perspectives. For Kant the consequences of an act do not matter. It follows that it is our ethical duty not to lie, cheat or steal, to keep promises and not to use others.Discourse ethics theory focuses on the process by which a decision is reached. Ethical actions are those which are reached by full, open discussion including all those who are connected in any way with a decision. For a business this means including all stakeholders actively in decision making. This is impracticable in some instances, and is not always culturally readily achievable, since some groups are more disposed to work towards consensus than others.

The Chinese government, for example, seeks to block access by its citizens to Web sites containing material deemed inimical to the Chinese Communist Party. They do so by blocking access to two Californian search engines, Google and Altavista, via Chinese internet service providers. This action, while no doubt well intentioned, also blocks the autonomy and free choice of the citizens. They have no opportunity to voice their preference, negotiate or discuss the issue. Power is held by one party, unless individuals have the technical ability to overcome the restrictions, for example by using a numerical address.

Virtue theory considers the character of the individual who acts. A virtuous person is one who classically possesses characteristics of justice, wisdom, temperance and courage. Modern-day virtues include co-operation, loyalty, friendliness and trustworthiness. However, there is no definitive list of virtues, and they may be culturally distinctive.

In the realms of e-Business, many of the issues are still finding legal precedent. Most of the ethical theories incorporate reference to legal perspectives, for example Kantians will on the whole follow the law, as will ethical egoists, since it is likely to be in their own self-interest so to do. In the global context of e-Commerce, the law simply does not provide sufficient, worldwide guidance on how e-Business managers should behave. Ethics can help fill that gap.

ARE THERE DISTINCT ETHICAL ISSUES IN E-BUSINESS?

e-Business enthusiasts will be well aware of the technical and financial advantages of e-Commerce. There are also ethical benefits. These include the potential to remove prejudice and barriers, as transactions are carried out via disembodied computer screens.

The lack of need for a physical presence in a particular place, as long as computer access is available, opens up all kinds of possibilities for freedom of mobility and inclusion of those with physical needs which make working in an office environment difficult (ranging from physical disability to a distinct preference for working on a beach!).

Internet-based business activities are opening up markets, improving information provision about different products, including non-corporate information. (For example, typing 'Nike' into a search engine finds company pages as well as sites about Nike products alleging human rights abuses by the company.) The Internet allows consumers much greater access to information, opening up the market and undermining monopolies. Such impacts are highly ethical according to a utilitarian perspective.

Freedom of speech is often cited as one of the benefits of cyberspace. Freedom of speech is a fundamental human right, yet it is not enjoyed by all. The Internet can be a means of increasing freedom of speech. Technology and law have been unsuccessful as a means of controlling what is on the Web. This means, at one extreme, that abhorrent pornography is available and that inaccurate claims made in relation to e-Business products or services are equally difficult to control.

We generally become aware of ethical issues through dilemmas, conflicts and discomfort with situations, behaviours and acts. The more challenging aspects of e-Business, particularly the implications for workplaces reliant on ICTs and the new issues prevalent to cyberspace.

COMPUTERS IN THE WORKPLACE

The expansion of e-Business goes hand in hand with reliance on computers in the workplace. Organizations have become information technology-intensive in their operations, and this in itself has significant implications for employees.

Advantages and Changes

Anyone who works in an office will have noticed some of the great advantages of workplace computerization. Among other advantages, the new communication medium eases the sharing of information. For instance, UK customers of www. Amazon.co.uk will find that they are 'known' to the German www. Amazon.de Web site when they log on there for the first time. There is no need to re-register even though a new retail Web site has been accessed. Customer records kept on an electronic database mean that more and more data can be gathered and marketing targeted at individuals. The computerization of many activities results in at least the potential for reducing paper files and archives. In fact the 'paperless office' turns out to be mythical, as some aspects of computerization result in an increase of paper production (for example, the ease of producing several edited versions of a report rather than one completed one), and individuals do not have sufficient confidence that an electronic file can be held with the same security as a paper one. Despite the evident advantages of computers, the fallibility of computers and computer systems and the fragility of electronic data do not lend credibility to reliance on strictly electronic records.

Disadvantages

Prolonged computer use without a break can result in eyestrain and serious problems from repetitive strain injury (RSI), for example from constant use of the same muscles in manipulating the mouse. Back problems are increasingly common in the workplace as individuals maintain constant, inappropriate positions while sitting at a desk to use a computer. Ergonomic solutions to these problems are available but not widely used.

Damage to the environment as a result of computer use is unknown, but the speed of technological updates results in a very short life cycle of computers as two- or three-year-old' machines are discarded as being out of date. In addition of course, computers require constant electricity supply. Some suggest that teleworking and the reduced need for face-to-face interaction may have negative psychological effects on individuals, who experience isolation and the loss of 'social glue'. Others argue that computerization enables social freedom for the shy and the removal of potential prejudice, as race, age and disability cannot be seen through a computer screen of text.

COMPUTER-MEDIATED COMMUNICATION

One of the key questions confronted by business ethicists is whether computer-mediated communication (CMC) requires fundamentally different ethical considerations than have gone before. Those who argue that there is a difference cite areas such as the following for their reasoning: the changed relationship between humans, the fragility and ownership of electronic data, use and abuse of workplace facilities, and monitoring and privacy. While none of these factors is in itself unique, the combination of new perspectives, and the rapidity with which new technologies are becoming the norm in the workplace, do establish a heightening of certain issues in a unique combination in relation to ethical use. Here the focus is particularly on electronic mail and Internet technology and use.

The Changing Nature of Human Relationships

A key characteristic of the computerized workplace is the changing nature of relationships between humans that ICTs have enabled. There can be a lack of 'social glue' in a highly computerized world, where there is no natural space for casual conversation.

The extent to which e-mails are really different from previous technologies such as communication by fax machine or disembodied telephone is unclear. There *is* a difference: we say things in e-mail that we might never say in hard copy or verbally, and different rules of grammar, punctuation, and even honest representation and use of crude language, seem to apply.

In a UK context, personal relationships are an important bond in managing business and organizations. This is achieved even where communication technologies enable increased personal distance between those communicating. Just as a 'business' telephone call may begin with some social conversation, an e-mail too can combine the social and strictly functional business for which it is composed. Electronic communication may even support 'social glue' by enabling naturally shy people to take part in communication fully without the psychological pressure of face-to-face contact.

The removal of the immediate proximity of sender and receiver of messages may have Equal Opportunity implications. While telephone helps prevent some prejudicial judgements such as those based on skin colour, age or dress, dialect and manner of speaking may still be discerned. The typewritten script of an e-mail, although not guaranteeing grammatical accuracy, offers everyone the opportunity of an equally professional status. Interestingly some interpret this as 'coldness' and use symbols to convey emotions such as happiness (), thereby personalizing their message. CMC also allows the leaving of messages for respondents to pick up as and when is convenient for the respondent, and potentially avoids the need for individuals to waste time chasing up absent colleagues. Telephone answer machines can operate on the same principle, but an e-mail can cope with a rather more complex message. This sophistication does not prevent individuals ignoring their messages, but that is a human rather than electronic frailty! CMC commonly allows asynchronous 'discussion', where there is a time gap between normally text-based messages being sent and responses received.

Finally, a key point here must be the combination of communication media. Where a sensitive point is being made about which the response of the receiver cannot be predicted, the messenger may choose face-to-face or telephone communication in order that the response can be read *as the message is delivered,* and the tone of delivery adjusted simultaneously. In fact, just as with other communications methods, there is still a need for 'interpersonal skills' in choosing the medium and the mode of delivery. CMC can be seen as a liberating social force, offering an additional means of communication, and empowering those who are less comfortable with other methods. While it might be a mistake to consider it as a replacement for other means of communication, it can certainly act as a complement and, used sensibly, enables communication rather than disabling it.

Fragility and Ownership of Electronic Data

The apparent fragility of electronic data, for example the fact that important data tables can be altered with almost no trace, adds additional responsibility to the conveyors of electronic information. Issues of responsibility for accuracy and the protection of information become paramount. This, it could be argued, is one of the distinctive features of electronic communication, since systems of protection for intellectual works (such as patenting and copyright) were designed for tangible products. At the moment there is neither clear protection for electronic data nor understanding of the limits of ownership and responsibility for accuracy. Such issues are compounded by the potential for mass dissemination via the Internet and by means of electronic mail. Given that even accidental inaccuracy by experienced keyboard operators occurs at a rate of one inaccurate keystroke per 100, the potential for incorrect information dissemination is great. Similarly the ownership of electronic data, accurate or otherwise, is unclear and could have critical implications for the user and subject of information.

Even if we accept that employers own the data that is sent on their systems (that is, e-mail content sent by employees), interpretation of the data may be incorrectly handled by employers, particularly since e-mails are commonly written in shorthand and abbreviated form.

Use, Dual use and Abuse

The increasing prevalence of computer-mediated communication in the work-place has focused the minds of employers on the use of organizational equipment for non-organizational tasks. This is not of course a new phenomenon. The blurred lines between work and personal life are to be found in the use of work stationery for personal tasks, the use of private telephones for 'work' calls, the use of work telephones for 'private' calls, the reading of newspapers in work time, unpaid overtime, and so on. Such issues are particularly relevant in office environments. Some occupations, such as factory production line work and call centre operators, are indeed more strictly controlled and delineated in the timing of their activities. There are no clear lines to be drawn in any of these cases. The introduction of widely available ICTs has again broadened the spectrum of possibilities by offering a powerful tool of information access and distribution to many employees. A distinction can be made here between use, dual use and abuse of ICTs in the workplace. Brown (1996) distinguishes between the realms of business necessity and of individual personhood and suggests that their intersection covers the domain of workplace privacy. A link has been made between Brown's notions of 'business necessity', 'workplace privacy' and 'individual personhood' and the employment of ICTs for 'business use', 'dual use' and 'abuse'. The associations in the diagram are not absolute but they may provide a useful framework for considering the issues of the use of workplace CMC, such as e-mail and Internet access, common to any e-business.

Using the available CMC resources for business necessity is the easiest to identify. Where e-mail or the Internet are employed for purposes directly related to the functional role of the individual in the organization, there is no immediate problem.

Where e-mail or the Internet is used for purposes which have nothing whatsoever to do with the organizational business, or the well-being of the individual in doing his or her task, it might be said that there has been an abuse of the access to CMC facilities. 'Abuse' of a firm's resources can be defined as the use of e-mail by the employee to further personal rather than organizational objectives. This might include illegal activities such as hacking into national security databases, but is not restricted to them. Examples might be the circulation of offensive materials, the setting up of a personal private business on work equipment or the accessing of indecent Web sites. With few exceptions such actions amount to abuse of the organization's resources.

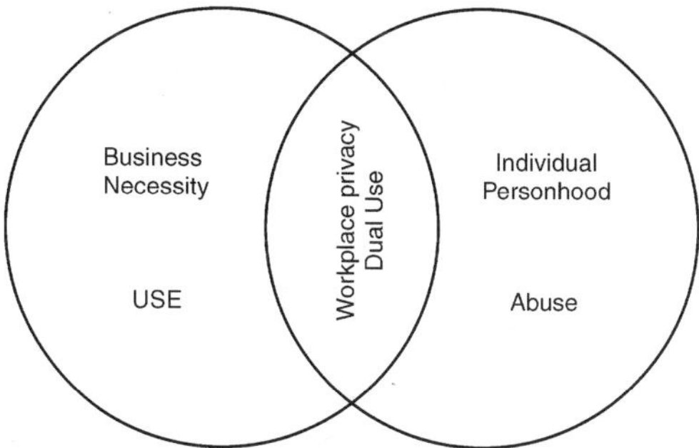

Fig. Locating the use and Abuse of ICTs in the Workplace

The most difficult area to discern is the intersection between use and abuse, the area where personal use may have some positive workplace implications, and work use may benefit the individual personally. Internet surfing for hobby interests will hone the IT skills of employees who use those same skills for work tasks. Non-work friends may enable problem solving that would otherwise cost time and resources in-house, whether they be through the resolving of ICT queries or personal counselling. The ability of employees to resolve individual issues such as the renewal of car insurance over the Internet allows them to concentrate on work tasks. Furthermore it is natural, even desirable, that employees become friendly with colleagues, and the combining of social and work discussions within e-mails is a clear example of 'dual use'. Individuals do not leave their personal lives at home entirely, and employers should not expect them to do so. Employers might keep in mind that employees will often take work home with them, either literally or mentally.

It seems a fair reciprocal exchange to be tolerant of home life making an appearance in the workplace. Accepting employees as whole human beings, with all the benefits and some of the drawbacks this may bring, is likely to be beneficial to all in the longer term. No differentiation has been made in the discussion so far between use of workplace CMC and use of work time. This, again, is a difficult distinction. On the one hand utilization of organizational software and hardware may not in itself be considered problematic by employers. The equipment has been purchased for work reasons and once installed the incremental costs of its use are likely to be negligible. However, the work time which employees use in the pursuit of personal goals may well be an issue. Surfing the Internet proves to be a surprisingly time-consuming activity,and responding to personal e-mails may well distract individuals from their work tasks. The relevance of time lost must to some extent depend on the type of work done. Where individuals are doing tasks strictly limited to particular hours, or even paid by the hour, time lost during the working day will be of significance. On the other hand, for professionals who are measured by their output rather than their (intellectual or actual) presence nine to five, time lost might be considered as merely a reallocation of time use.

The management of household matters in work time is inevitable in a social environment in which workdays are longer and household management responsibilities are shared between multiple earners with careers. Important in the consideration of the use and abuse of work time is the fact that the technology is readily available to monitor Internet and e-mail use of networked employees remotely.

Monitoring and Privacy

enormous potential for infringing the privacy of employees and customers. ICT archiving and particularly computer-mediated communication mean that employees in the workplace can be monitored to unprecedented levels. Electronic monitoring can be defined as the capture and analysis of 'data' to measure the work (not) performed by employees. These data may show Web sites accessed, e-mail traffic, e-mail content or the use of video and audio facilities.

Electronic monitoring is sometimes seen as a sinister 'Big Brother is watching you' perspective on our lives. Reasons put forward to defend the use of electronic monitoring in the workplace include the following:

- *Security.* Closed Circuit Television (CCTV) can protect against theft and violence.
- Employers pay employees to do a particular job. It could be argued that employers have a *contractual right* to check that employees are doing what they are paid to do.
- Monitoring of employees stops abuse of work time and *increases productivity*.
- Electronic monitoring is simply an electronic version of *'managing by walking about'*, which saves management time.
- Electronic means of measurement mean that performance appraisal of employees is backed up by precise statistics and is *unbiased*.
- Electronic monitoring provides data *quickly and frequently.*
- It ensures *realistic targets* are set.

Electronic monitoring may be used as a deterrent to stop inappropriate work-place behaviour, rather than being used to penalize those caught not working 100 per cent of the time. This can be likened to Jeremy Bentham's Panopticon. The Panopticon was a circular prison with no bars. All the cells were arranged around a tower with a single guard in it. From the tower the guard could see into all the cells. However, the prisoners could not see whether they were being observed. Their behaviour was thus controlled by the fact that they *might* be being monitored. In the same way that a speed camera without a film in it can still influence motorists to keep to the legal speed limit, the fact that employees or customers know that they may be being watched means that they act as they would if they *were* being watched.On the other hand, like watching rats in a cage, constant monitoring can have uneasy effects on individuals. Those against electronic monitoring argue that:

- It constitutes an *invasion of privacy.* Being paid by an organization does not mean that it owns you.
- Monitoring implies suspicion of misbehaviour. This *undermines the trust, goodwill and loyalty* of employees toward the employer.
- Monitoring results in the setting of *unrealistic targets,* because employees cannot keep up the fastest rate constantly. The result is increasing stress, absenteeism and ultimately employee turnover.
- In a climate of increasing empowerment, monitoring erodes the independence of the individual to work in a way which suits him or her (*e.g.* chat to a friend between 9:30 and 10:00 but work over lunchtime) and *disempowers* the individual's control.
- Electronic monitoring is more suited to *measuring quantitative* factors than qualitative ones, hence number of phone calls rather than relationship building with potential clients is most likely to be measured in a call centre.

In most countries, legally there is generally no reason why employers should not monitor employee e-mails, yet it is unlikely to be in the employer's self-interest to exercise the right. Monitoring employees to check whether they are abusing company resources may be justified if the system is being overloaded, although setting limits would achieve the same ends. Being an employer does not mean having the right to monitor private conversations.

THEORETICAL ISSUES IN BUSINESS ETHICS

CONFLICTING INTERESTS

Business ethics can be examined from various new perspectives, including the perspective of the employee, the commercial enterprise, and society as a whole. Very often, situations arise in which there is conflict between one or more of the parties, such that serving the interest of one party is a detriment to the other(s). For example, a particular outcome might be good for the employee, whereas, it would be bad for the company, society, or vice versa. Some ethicists (*e.g.*, Henry Sidgwick) see the principal role of ethics as the harmonization and reconciliation of conflicting interests.

ETHICAL ISSUES AND APPROACHES

Philosophers and others disagree about the purpose of a business ethic in society. For example, some suggest that the principal purpose of a business is to maximize returns to its owners, or in the case of a publicly-traded concern, its shareholders. Thus, under this view, only those activities that increase profitability and shareholder value should be encouraged, because any others function as a tax on profits. Some believe that the only companies that are likely to survive in a competitive marketplace are those that place profit maximization above everything else. However, some point out that self-interest would still require a business to obey the law and adhere to basic moral rules, because the consequences of failing to do so could be very costly in fines, loss of licensure, or company reputation. The noted economist Milton Friedman was a leading proponent of this view.

Some take the position that organizations are not capable of moral agency. Under this, ethical behaviour is required of individual human beings, but not of the business or corporation.Other theorists contend that a business has moral duties that extend well beyond serving the interests of its owners or stockholders, and that these duties consist of more than simply obeying the law. They believe a business has moral responsibilities to so-called stakeholders, people who have an interest in the conduct of the business, which might include employees, customers, vendors, the local community, or even society as a whole. Stakeholders can also be broken down into primary and secondary stakeholders. Primary stakeholders are people that are affected directly such as stockholders, where secondary stakeholders are people who are not affected directly such as the government. They would say that stakeholders have certain rights with regard to how the business operates, and some would suggest that this includes even rights of governance.

Some theorists have adapted social contract theory to business, whereby companies become quasi-democratic associations, and employees and other stakeholders are given voice over a company's operations. This approach has become especially popular subsequent to the revival of contract theory in political philosophy, which is largely due to John Rawls' *A Theory of Justice*, and the advent of the consensus-oriented approach to solving business problems, an aspect of the "quality movement" that emerged in the 1980s. Professors Thomas Donaldson and Thomas Dunfee proposed a version of contract theory for business, which they call Integrative Social Contracts Theory. They posit that conflicting interests are best resolved by formulating a "fair agreement" between the parties, using a combination of i) macro-principles that all rational people would agree upon as universal principles, and, ii) micro-principles formulated by actual agreements among the interested parties. Critics say the proponents of contract theories miss a central point, namely, that a business is someone's property and not a mini-state or a means of distributing social justice.

Ethical issues can arise when companies must comply with multiple and sometimes conflicting legal or cultural standards, as in the case of multinational companies that operate in countries with varying practices. The question arises, for example, ought a company to obey the laws of its home country, or should it follow the less stringent laws of the developing country in which it does business? To illustrate, United States law forbids companies from paying bribes either domestically or overseas; however, in other parts of the world, bribery is a customary, accepted way of doing business. Similar problems can occur with regard to child labour, employee safety, work hours, wages, discrimination, and environmental protection laws.

It is sometimes claimed that a Gresham's law of ethics applies in which bad ethical practices drive out good ethical practices. It is claimed that in a competitive business environment, those companies that survive are the ones that recognize that their only role is to maximize profits.

CORPORATE ETHICS POLICIES

As part of more comprehensive compliance and ethics Programmes, many companies have formulated internal policies pertaining to the ethical conduct of employees. These policies can be simple exhortations in broad, highly-generalized language (typically called a corporate ethics statement), or they can be more detailed policies, containing specific behavioural requirements (typically called corporate ethics codes). They are generally meant to identify the company's expectations of workers and to offer guidance on handling some of the more common ethical problems that might arise in the course of doing business. It is hoped that having such a policy will lead to greater ethical awareness, consistency in application, and the avoidance of ethical disasters.

An increasing number of companies also requires employees to attend seminars regarding business conduct, which often include discussion of the company's policies, specific case studies, and legal requirements. Some companies even require their employees to sign agreements stating that they will abide by the company's rules of conduct. Many companies are assessing the environmental factors that can lead employees to engage in unethical conduct. A competitive business environment may call for unethical behaviour. Lying has become expected in fields such as trading.

An example of this are the issues surrounding the unethical actions of the Saloman Brothers.

Not everyone supports corporate policies that govern ethical conduct. Some claim that ethical problems are better dealt with by depending upon employees to use their own Judgement.

Others believe that corporate ethics policies are primarily rooted in utilitarian concerns, and that they are mainly to limit the company's legal liability, or to curry public favour by giving the appearance of being a good corporate citizen. Ideally, the company will avoid a lawsuit because its employees will follow the rules. Should a lawsuit occur, the company can claim that the problem would not have arisen if the employee had only followed the code properly.Sometimes there is disconnection between the company's code of ethics and the company's actual practices. Thus, whether or not such conduct is explicitly sanctioned by management, at worst, this makes the policy duplicitous, and, at best, it is merely a marketing tool. To be successful, most ethicists would suggest that an ethics policy should be:

- Given the unequivocal support of top management, by both word and example.
- Explained in writing and orally, with periodic reinforcement.
- Doable....something employees can both understand and perform.
- Monitored by top management, with routine inspections for compliance and improvement.
- Backed up by clearly stated consequences in the case of disobedience.
- Remain neutral and nonsexist.

Ethics Officers

Ethics officers (sometimes called "compliance" or "business conduct officers") have been appointed formally by organizations since the mid-1980s. One of the catalysts for the creation of this new role was a series of fraud, corruption and abuse scandals that afflicted the U.S. defence industry at that time. This led to the creation of the Defence Industry Initiative (DII), a pan-industry initiative to promote and ensure ethical business practices. The DII set an early benchmark for ethics management in corporations. In 1991, the Ethics and Compliance Officer Association (ECOA) — originally the Ethics Officer Association (EOA)— was founded at the Centre for Business Ethics (at Bentley College, Waltham, MA) as a professional association for those responsible for managing organizations' efforts to achieve ethical best practices. The membership grew rapidly (the ECOA now has over 1,100 members) and was soon established as an independent organization.

Another critical factor in the decisions of companies to appoint ethics/ compliance officers was the passing of the Federal Sentencing Guidelines for Organizations in 1991, which set standards that organizations (large or small, commercial and non-commercial) had to follow to obtain a reduction in sentence if they should be convicted of a federal offence. Although intended to assist judges with sentencing, the influence in helping to establish best practices has been far-reaching.

In the wake of numerous corporate scandals between 2001-04 (affecting large corporations like Enron, WorldCom and Tyco), even small and medium-sized companies have begun to appoint ethics officers. They often report to the Chief Executive Officer and are responsible for assessing the ethical implications of the company's activities, making recommendations regarding the company's ethical policies, and disseminating information to employees. They are particularly interested in uncovering or preventing unethical and illegal actions. This trend is partly due to the Sarbanes-Oxley Act in the United States, which was enacted in reaction to the above scandals. A related trend is the introduction of risk assessment officers that monitor how shareholders' investments might be affected by the company's decisions.

The effectiveness of ethics officers in the marketplace is not clear. If the appointment is made primarily as a reaction to legislative requirements, one might expect the efficacy to be minimal, at least, over the short term. In part, this is because ethical business practices result from a corporate culture that consistently places value on ethical behaviour, a culture and climate that usually emanates from the top of the organization. The mere establishment of a position to oversee ethics will most likely be insufficient to inculcate ethical behaviour: a more systemic programme with consistent support from general management will be necessary. The foundation for ethical behaviour goes well beyond corporate culture and the policies of any given company, for it also depends greatly upon an individual's early moral training, the other institutions that affect an individual, the competitive business environment the company is in and, indeed, society as a whole.

BUSINESS ETHICS AS AN ACADEMIC DISCIPLINE

As an academic discipline, business ethics emerged in the 1970s. Since no academic business ethics journals or conferences existed, researchers published their papers in general management outlets, and attended general conferences, such as the Academy of Management. Over time, several peer-reviewed journals appeared, and more researchers entered the field. Especially, higher interest in business topics among academics was observed after several corporate scandals in the earlier 2000s. As of 2009, sixteen academic journals devoted to various business ethics issues existed, with Journal of Business Ethics and Business Ethics Quarterly being considered the leading A+ outlets.

RELIGIOUS VIEWS ON BUSINESS ETHICS

The historical and global importance of religious views on business ethics is sometimes underestimated in standard introductions to business ethics. Particularly in Asia and the Middle East, religious and cultural perspectives have a strong influence on the conduct of business and the creation of business values.

Examples include:

- Islamic banking, associated with the avoidance of charging interest on loans.
- Traditional Confucian disapproval of the profit-seeking motive.
- Quaker testimony on fair dealing.

Related Disciplines

Business ethics should be distinguished from the philosophy of business, the branch of philosophy that deals with the philosophical, political, and ethical underpinnings of business and economics. Business ethics operates on the premise, for example, that the ethical operation of a private business is possible — those who dispute that premise, such as libertarian socialists, (who contend that "business ethics" is an oxymoron) do so by definition outside of the domain of business ethics proper.The philosophy of business also deals with questions such as what, if any, are the social responsibilities of a business; management theory; theories of individualism vs. collectivism; free will among participants in the marketplace; the role of self interest; invisible hand theories; the requirements of social justice; and natural rights, especially property rights, in relation to the business enterprise. Business ethics is also related to political economy, which is economic analysis from political and historical perspectives. Political economy deals with the distributive consequences of economic actions. It asks who gains and who loses from economic activity, and is the resultant distribution fair or just, which are central ethical issues.

Multinational Corporation

A multinational corporation (MNC) or transnational corporation (TNC), also called multinational enterprise (MNE), is a corporation or enterprise that manages production or delivers services in more than one country. It can also be referred to as an *international corporation*.

The first modern MNC is generally thought to be the Poor Knights of Christ and the Temple of Solomon, first endorsed by the pope in 1129. The key element of transnational corporations was present even back then: the British East India Company and Dutch East India Company were operating in different countries than the ones where they had their headquarters.

Nowadays many corporations have offices, branches or manufacturing plants in different countries than where their original and main headquarter is located. This is the very definition of a transnational corporation. Having multiple operation points that all respond to one headquarter.

This often results in very powerful corporations that have budgets that exceed some national GDPs. Multinational corporations can have a powerful influence in local economies as well as the world economy and play an important role in international relations and globalization. The presence of such powerful players in the world economy is reason for much controversy.

Market Imperfections

It may seem strange that a corporation can decide to do business in a different country, where it doesn't know the laws, local customs or business practices. Why is it not more efficient to combine assets of value overseas with local factors of production at lower costs by renting or selling them to local investors? One reason is that the use of the market for coordinating the behaviour of agents located in different countries is less efficient than coordinating them by a multinational enterprise as an institution The additional costs caused by the entrance in foreign markets are of less interest for the local enterprise. According to Hymer, Kindleberger and Caves, the existence of MNEs is reasoned by structural market imperfections for final products. In Hymer's example, there are considered two firms as monopolists in their own market and isolated from competition by transportation costs and other tariff and non-tariff barriers. If these costs decrease, both are forced to competition; which will reduce their profits. The firms can maximize their joint income by a merger or acquisition which will lower the competition in the shared market. Due to the transformation of two separated companies into one MNE the pecuniary externalities are going to be internalized. However, this doesn't mean that there is an improvement for the society.

This could also be the case if there are few substitutes or limited licenses in a foreign market. The consolidation is often established by acquisition, merger or the vertical integration of the potential licensee into overseas manufacturing. This makes it easy for the MNE to enforce price discrimination schemes in various countries. Therefore Humyer considered the emergence of multinational firms as "an (negative) instrument for restraining competition between firms of different nations".

Market imperfections had been considered by Hymer as structural and caused by the deviations from perfect competition in the final product markets. Further reasons are originated from the control of proprietary technology and distribution systems, scale economies, privileged access to inputs and product differentiation.

In the absence of these factors, market are fully efficient. The transaction costs theories of MNEs had been developed simultaneously and independently by McManus (1972), Buckley and Casson (1976) Brown (1976) and Hennart (1977, 1982). All these authors claimed that market imperfections are inherent conditions in markets and MNEs are institutions which try to bypass these imperfections. The imperfections in markets are natural as the neoclassical assumptions like full knowledge and enforcement don't exist in real markets.

BUSINESSES AND STAKEHOLDERS

A business is owned by its shareholders. A traditional view is that the behaviour of the business is nobody's business but the owners', the shareholders who are interested in profit.

A more modern view is to consider all the groups of people that are affected by a business' behaviour – employees, customers, suppliers, the local community – and not just the shareholders.The word 'stakeholders' is used to describe this wider community of interests. Some investment funds and pension companies refuse to invest in businesses whose behaviour they disapprove of eg arms manufacturers.

BUSINESS AND ETHICS

Ethical behaviour is morally 'good' behaviour. Businesses have always been ethical to the extent that their owners and managers have been interested in ethical behaviour (sometimes very little). There is now a new and strong interest from a growing number of businesses in ethical behaviour, especially in large MNCs which operate in different societies with different ethical standards. Some businesses even employ professional philosophers to help them understand the ethical consequences of their behaviour.

The main reason for this is that society at large takes more of an interest in ethical behaviour, and society has much bigger expectations of businesses. There are Different Reasons Given for This Development.

1. Employees (including managers) are better educated than they used to be, and so understand these issues better than they used to.
2. We have a less deferential society where 'ordinary' people are more willing to questions and challenge the decisions of their 'elders and betters'.
3. Competition for customers is fiercer, and any possible reason for losing customers has to be taken seriously.
4. The same issue is developing in employment, with employers increasingly dependent on attracting high quality staff who, with more choice than they used to have, are less willing to work for morally 'iffy' businesses.
5. The media have become very good at exposing questionable behaviour. Allied to this is that information is now so easy to get hold of, and the Internet makes it easier again.
6. Business decisions can be much more complex than they used to be., especially where very advanced technology is involved, and not all the consequences are known.
7. Businesses are entering new and morally more debatable areas. A good example of this is medical businesses where new knowledge about eg genes raises the possibility of products that pose fundamental moral questions; these were simply irrelevant until recently because no-one knew how to do it.

External environment of a business refers to all those factors that directly influence the working of the business. However, these factors are outside the control of the business. External environment shapes the kind of business activity you can have. That is why it is extremely important for business. The factors that constitute the external environment include:

- Political and Legal factors
- Economic factors
- Social and Cultural Factors
- Technological Factors
- Competitors
- Demographics of consumers.

Now whatever the business might do, it can not control all the above factors. It can only plan its business by studying the trends in these factors closely. The Political and Legal factors define the government policies. These policies determine what kind of relaxation the business has. The Economy defines that kind of economic or business activity it can have. The Social and cultural factors along with the demographics of the society defines the acceptability and sales of that product. The technological factors define the technology and its affects on business. Lastly, competitors are also one of the influential factors.

All businesses and organisations operate in a changing world and are subject to forces which are more powerful than they are, and which are beyond their control. No business can survive without continued interaction with the external environment, just as a ship at sea is subject to powerful natural forces of which it needs to be aware and deal with, organisations are influenced by forces in their external business environment. Any business strategy needs to take account of all these forces so that opportunities and threats can be identified and the organisation can navigate its way to success by matching its internal strengths to external opportunities. (A SWOT Analysis can help here.) As an aid to identifying all these external forces, a couple of acronyms come in handy.

IMPORTANCE OF GOING GLOBAL

Globalization involves the transfer of an existing business system to other countries or the management of another business system in other countries. The terms 'international', 'multinational', 'global' and 'transnational' have been used to describe different stages in the globalization ladder of business development. The decision of nationally based e-Commerce to go global will depend on factors such as demography, entry modes, socio-cultural diversity, as well as the approach and management style to be used when entering new markets. The United States today represents the largest national market in the world, with roughly 25 per cent of the total world market for all products and services. The fact that 75 per cent of the world market potential is outside their national territory has been the force driving many US companies to 'go international' and even to extend further and 'go global'. With three-quarters of its revenue generated by its soft drink business outside the United States, Coca-Cola, acknowledged as the most successful global company, has driven the message of globalization further than anybody else. For non-US companies the incentive is even stronger. The two wealthiest countries after the United

States, Japan and Germany, have 85 per cent and 94 per cent respectively of the world market potential.Today there are only seven countries where English is the primary language spoken, by about half a billion people or 8 per cent of the total population, their combined economies representing only 30 per cent of the total world economy. e-Commerce companies that will continue to target this small percentage of the world market will miss out on capturing a much larger potential market.

The total global e-Commerce market is forecast to reach $1.6 trillion by 2003, a very powerful incentive for companies entering this arena. If present e-businesses have been able to achieve year-upon-year growth in visitors, sales or members using only domestic focused Web sites, then in order to sustain or increase this growth it will be almost impossible to do so without entering and servicing new markets. Almost 10 per cent of the world's population has access to the Internet.

The global Internet audience had grown to 580.78 million people by the end of May 2002. The survey indicated that, for the first time ever, Europe has the highest number of Internet users in the world, with 185.83 million Europeans online, compared with 182.83 million in the United States and Canada, and 167.86 million in Asia-Pacific. The survey's findings also indicate that the digital divide between developed and developing nations is as wide as ever. While Europeans account for 32 per cent of global Internet users, only 6 per cent of the world's Net users are based in Latin America. The Middle East and Africa combined account for just 2 per cent of global Internet users; the lack of telecommunications infrastructures in those regions means that most citizens remain unconnected.

Methods of Entry

Until recently a traditional business has had the options of entering new geographical markets through direct or indirect exporting, new start-ups, franchising, joint ventures, acquisitions, concessions or licensing, depending on the degrees of risk and the level of involvement they were prepared to accept.

To these alternatives can be added now the virtual business via the Internet. The nationally based business will start with cautious testing of new markets, often selected with a similar culture, having a focus that is culturally and managerially 'ethnocentric' or centred around the home market. A multinational business will have a 'polycentric' orientation, *i.e.* a focus based on the understanding and appreciation of different operating contexts.

The global or transnational business will have a fully global strategy, focusing on maximizing the benefits obtained from economies of scale in sourcing, product standardization and marketing. Typical of global operators is their adaptable, geocentric approach, which allows them to 'think globally but act locally'.

Opportunities and Threat

The Internet has already made a big difference in the way business operates globally, offering substantial advantages to both buyers and sellers, because it can cope with a rapidly changing environment. Many industries have further motives for embracing the Web, as it offers huge savings on their marketing and distribution costs, which in certain cases, for example the airlines, can make up about a quarter of their total operating expenses. The Internet has made a big difference to aviation, with portable computers becoming essential in the process of booking and buying air travel. Simplifying booking and cutting out the cumbersome process of issuing card tickets can be very attractive to customers. Since 2000, an increasing number of airlines, such as Northwest and Swissair, have been offering online facilities for seat selection and check-in, as well as for booking and paying for flights.

e-Commerce will also allow businesses to learn more about their Web customers, so they can package offers tailored to their individual needs. This is what in marketing terms is called 'customer of one' and it applies to airlines, just as it does to cars or computers. Continuing with the same example, there are distinguishing characteristics between the different levels of airline Web sites. The most basic are 'brochure sites' which offer simple static information, not much different from the printed brochures found in the bricks-and-mortar travel agents. At the next level are the constantly updated versions of the 'brochure sites'.

The third level contains sites that obtain information from the customer as he logs on and builds a profile of his travel needs and preferences. It can answer requests for information, take bookings and issue e-mail confirmation of bookings. This sort of e-Commerce transaction is now quite common, especially for the no-frills, low-cost airlines. The next generation Web site will recognize and greet the customer by his or her name when s/he logs on and will know that s/he is a valuable customer. It will be able to analyse his travel history and suggest alternative itineraries that might suit him better.

Niche Marketing

No-frills, low-fare carriers such as EasyJet and Ryanair have been using this low-cost, high service strategy to carve out successful niches. The emergence of these new companies has increased the level of competition in the industry, putting established carriers under increasing threat of loss of business on their traditional routes and ultimately bankruptcy. One notable example is Swissair, and even British Airways has felt the pinch with the threat of its shares losing their blue-chip status. Other examples of industries that have made good use of the trend towards personalization through the Internet are the perfume and fashion industries. Custom fragrance marketers have been established, usually family-run businesses where the Internet has radically changed the direction of this niche market. In 2001 a number of new entrants have included Procter and Gamble with Reflect.com, Ashford.com, RomanceHer.com, Eleuria.com and Creativescent.com. The Internet is about to turn this niche market into a major profit-making category of prestige fragrance and force the major perfume companies to create custom divisions. Nevertheless these new ways of doing business are at risk for being untested and vulnerable to sudden market downturns or fashion changes.

Small and medium-size enterprises are the main beneficiaries of the low-cost marketing possibilities offered by the Internet, which can turn them from small niche players into global ones. A fundamental change is happening in the world of Asian marketing that could prove a bonanza for struggling companies. The Internet is providing low-cost ways for small to medium-size businesses to get their advertising message across, focusing on specific audiences. Asia has been experiencing a phenomenal growth in Internet advertising, whose potential demand has been recognized by US Internet advertising agencies.

DoubleClick Asia, a joint venture between New York-based Double Click and Hong Kong Web portal builder Asiacontent.com, has been able to track Internet users' movements by collecting 'cookies' or files embedded in users' Web browsers that log the pages they visit and for how long. This information allows marketing solution providers such as DotMedia China or Next Media to help their customers, which are local companies, to target their own local audience in a far more efficient way by posting relevant ads on their Web sites. Another interesting SME example is Charles Tyrwhitt, a UK manufacturer of mainly shirts, but also ties and other accessories, to the exclusive ABC1 men market.

The company has adopted a 'clicks and mortar' strategy, which hopefully will turn this British niche player into a global one. It will also reduce its brochure and marketing costs. The company's strong customer service culture is being translated on to the Net, where this is so important. The firm's success lies in its ability to carry more than 3,000 lines of stock at any one time, with each shirt being offered in up to forty-eight combinations of size, cuff and sleeve. The company is able to maximize sales by targeting groups of people more effectively than could ever be done through mail order.

The key to the success of niche e-businesses is first and foremost brand awareness. Second, expanding the customer base geographically is leading to the need for a greater product range to meet strong local preferences in style and fashion. The Internet has proved to be the perfect messenger for niche interests, serving individual tastes and diverse geographical demands. In certain industries, such as national media, which were previously dedicated to mass markets, the Internet is offering for the first time the possibility of meeting specialist demands. As successful online newspapers in the United States reach less than 25 per cent of their local Net users, some have tried to add an interest-based niche to their regional focus. For example, the *San Jose Mercury* is concentrating its online energies to SiliconValley.com, a specialist site for technology news. The objective is to have a network of loyal users by meeting specialist demand with detailed information. In the United Kingdom the commercial site Fish4, which is backed by local newspaper publishers, owned by the Guardian Media Group, is claiming to have reached the necessary critical mass of information to make a niche product. BBC News online is another example where the battle between general and niche is being fought. The way it uses its huge breadth of content, both broad-brush and localized, demonstrates the diversity of its users and their demands. In just one day 98,450 different stories were read, amounting to a staggering 20 per cent of all the stories the site has ever produced.

Understanding the Global Environment

For the e-Commerce organization shaping the direction of its global expansion it is vitally important to understand the external environment as a means of identification of opportunities and threats. An analysis of the variety of factors and environmental influences is necessary in order to allow a balance of internal capabilities and resources with the opportunities offered externally that ultimately would affect business planning and implementation within the organization. The elements of the external environment connected with the organization can be divided into four distinct groupings, known by the acronym STEP.

STRATEGIES FOR THE FUTURE

These opportunities presented by e-business preclude the option of waiting for the technologies to mature and the implications to become discernible and lucid. The rising popularity of the Internet, increasingly demanding customers and unrelenting expectations for expedited services, continuing cost constraints, and emerging opportunities for new revenues will compel colleges and universities to adopt an e-business strategy.

Institutions with a carefully constructed plan that considers institution-wide implications will substantially benefit from this transition. Others will be left to struggle and fret over why, where, how, and when to move into e-business, placing them at a competitive disadvantage for students, research grants, and contributions, in addition to hampering efforts to increase the effectiveness and efficiency of administrative processes.To navigate the stages of an e-business strategy successfully, institutions must do more than just enable on-line transactions over the Web. Assessing your institution's readiness or developing a strategic plan for e-business must include an examination of a multitude of capabilities, not just an evaluation of the campus Web site. The multifaceted challenges that must be confronted to succeed in e-business span the entire institution, necessitating close coordination and dependencies among disparate organizational entities. This is the true challenge of doing e-business.At Pricewater house Coopers, we have identified eight areas in which preparedness is vital to exploit the opportunities presented by e-business:

- E-business strategy
- Organization and capabilities
- Delivery and operations
- Processes
- Systems and technology
- Performance management
- Security
- Tax and legal

In each of the eight areas, you will need to assess your institution's preparedness, identify gaps, and develop plans to optimize your institution's readiness and improve its ability to provide Internet-enabled services. Assessment of these categories can serve as an initial gauge of your institution's e-business readiness. In essence, such a diagnosis determines where your institution is deficient in its preparedness. Armed with this information, your institution will be sufficiently well informed to develop a strategic plan for e-business and a corresponding implementation plan, significantly improving the likelihood of success in the increasingly complex and competitive world of e-business.

LESSONS LEARNED

In developing this strategic plan for e-business, your institution should leverage its own experience and that of others in the higher education industry. Other industries such as financial services and retail companies (for example, e-Trade, Dell, Schwab, and Amazon. com) offer insights on the development and deployment of successful e-business strategies.Based on our experiences, we have identified five key lessons learned that higher education institutions should incorporate into their strategic planning process:

- Link e-business objectives to critical business issues. Your rationale for e-business should be aligned with your institutional mission, strategies, and priorities. Simply put, "e-business" will become all business. If your institution's strategic objectives are to raise academic quality, reduce costs, increase student quality, or improve student service, e-business initiatives should be undertaken in support of those institution-wide strategic objectives.
- Focus on e-business as a business-driven project. E-business is more than a technology initiative; its impact will be pervasive and should be viewed as a mission-critical undertaking. Brand issues are paramount. Accordingly, the project sponsorship for an e-business

project should emanate from the president, provost, or executive vice president's office to ensure that sufficient importance and institution-wide perspective are embedded in this endeavor.

- Acknowledge that culture and change are more complicated than the technology. Once you have determined your e-business objectives (aligned as appropriate with your institution's strategic objectives) and designed the undertaking as a business-driven project, developing an effective change management plan is the next critical activity. Instituting the technology—the infrastructure, applications, or interfaces— is relatively straightforward, although resource intensive. Processes, policies, and organization will likely undergo a transformation. To do so effectively requires a formal change management plan replete with frequent communication of key messages to a variety of constituents.
- Do not treat e-business as just a way to communicate with customers; it will change the way you operate. If you view e-business as simply an interface, you will miss transformation opportunities. E-business is more than just enabling on-line transactions. It will lead to the substitution of network-based technologies and processes for physical locations, manual processes, or other expediting functions that necessitate human attention or increase costs but do not add actual value. These technologies transform an institution by altering customer service models, enabling personalization of services, providing services at any time, and establishing new relationships with suppliers and other key constituents.
- Ensure that business units take ownership, but make sure that central leadership, coordination, and development are also priorities. In colleges and universities, it is likely that the admissions office has initiated discussion with on-line admissions application vendors, the registrar has spoken with Campus Pipeline or a similar vendor, the directors of purchasing and accounts payable are intrigued by Commerce One's solution, and the advancement office is considering Harris On-line. Although initiative at the business unit level is necessary, unmanaged activities will ultimately distract institutional focus and resources. These individual process-specific decisions must be made only after carefully considering institution-wide objectives and priorities.

4

E-Business Technology in the Workplace

INTERNET AND WORLD WIDE WEB TECHNOLOGIES

The microcomputer or Personal Computer (PC) forms the basis of e-Commerce. The Internet would not have the wide reach that it has into peoples' homes in the absence of the PC. Most office PCs are linked to a computer network and PCs at home are connected to the Internet via modems or dedicated data transfer cables.

LOCAL AREA NETWORKS AND WIDE AREA NETWORKS

PCs on local area networks (LANs) and wide area networks (WANs) are connected to the Internet. LANs and WANs are digital computer networks that connect PCs to enable sharing of information between separate computers. LANs are limited to a geographical area such as an office, whereas WANs connect computers over a wider geographical area. The computers on a LAN or WAN share information in the form of addressed packets of data.

The capacity of a single computer is increased by connecting it to a LAN or WAN, as it can share computer Programmes and information. A computer that is linked to a network can download and use computer Programmes and share storage and printing facilities, and take advantage of network capabilities for sending and receiving data and information.

CLIENT-SERVER ARCHITECTURE

A computer on a LAN or WAN that provides resources like application Programmes or printer connections is known as a 'server'. A server provides other computers known as 'clients' on the LAN or WAN with software and other resources. This set-up is called client-server computing architecture. A server that is linked to the Internet is called a 'host computer'.

A server computer is capable of running server software, which needs to be compatible with the network operating system. The client and server are independent and perform specialized tasks to process information and run computer applications. If you use Microsoft Word on your computer, the client, it is probable that a server will have provided the Microsoft Word software for you to use. The client-server architecture is the basis of the Internet too.

THE INTERNET AND PROTOCOLS

The Internet is the sum total connection of LANs, WANs and stand-alone computers around the world. The term 'Internet' is short for 'inter-networking' or an interconnected set of networks. It is the global network of computers, whether the computer is on a LAN in an office, or a WAN in an industry extranet, or an independent computer in a private home. An Internet-connected computer is known as an Internet host computer. The Internet is also known as the 'Net', the 'Information superhighway' or 'Cyberspace'.

The set of rules for moving information over the Internet is called a 'protocol'. The transmission control protocol (TCP) is used for sending large amounts of information between host computers on the Internet. Vinton Cerf wrote the basic ideas for TCP on the back of an envelope over lunch, and in 1983 the core protocols of the Internet transmission control protocol/Internet protocol (TCP/IP) became the standard protocol for transmitting information over the Internet.

INTRANET

An intranet consists of networked internal connection of computers owned by an organization and makes use of Web technology. An intranet may be mounted on a LAN or a WAN. An intranet makes use of Internet technology such as TCP/IP, HTML, Java and HTTP to make it interoperable and to provide it with Web capability. The basic elements of an intranet are a computer network, a computer designated as a server containing server software and the Internet protocols TCP/IP.

An intranet offers several benefits to an organization: improved sharing and communication of information, open standards and cross-platform collaboration. For example, a car manufacturing company may connect its information systems on purchasing with its accounting information systems to form an intranet for sharing and processing information between two departments in the company.

An intranet is a company's own internal information transfer system that offers: e-mail, communication among different computers, connection to remote offices, a Web browser interface and special-interest news groups. For e-Commerce, an intranet is used to provide a corporate image and unified 'experience' for a customer that combines product information, ordering and customer care.

EXTRANET

An extranet is used for business-to-business (B2B) e-Commerce. It is the networked connection of computers of two or more companies. It is a private communication system to support trade and is used for communication and transactions between business partners, suppliers or special customers. For example, a car manufacturing company may connect its computers with its various suppliers of components for the cars it makes. Another example is the airline industry's OneWorld network, which enables customers to transfer seamlessly between airlines to reach their destinations.

DESIGN PRINCIPLES

Intranets and extranets share the same design principles formulated for the Internet. The Internet design principles are:

Interoperability. There are varying operating systems that control computer functions on the many different computers on the Internet. Normally a given operating system cannot communicate with a different one. A standard to enable varying operating systems to communicate with each other was introduced by the US Department of Defence, which originally financed the Internet. Interoperability means that independent implementations of Internet protocols can work seamlessly.

Consequently, operating system developers such as Microsoft or Apple incorporate software into their operating systems that enables them to operate with other computers over the Internet. Internet-compatible systems use the TCP/IP common protocol for communication. Interoperability for e-Commerce means that companies and customers do not have to purchase and upgrade software from the same vendors. Their computers will be able to communicate over the Internet because of the standard protocols.

Layering. The Internet can be regarded as a series of layers of software. The structure of the Internet is layered. It is a five-layer system consisting of: interconnect level (National Access Points, NAPs), national backbone providers, regional Internet providers, local Internet service providers, and the business and consumer market.The bottom layers of software, interconnect and network, are concerned with operating the computer hardware. The higher layers, business and consumer market, come closer to the needs of the person using the Internet.

The most relevant layer is the layer that processes the information required by the Internet user; this is called the 'application' layer. These different hardware and application layers need to communicate with each other and they do so by using well defined interfaces. The Internet layering standard has resulted in increased reliability of Internet software and it is invisible to the Internet user.

Simplicity. The layering has resulted in simplicity of software design. Each layer is concerned only with its own functionality, making its design simpler. For example, the layer concerned with physical devices like mouse operations are hidden from the higher layers that process information. This kind of simplicity has contributed to increased software reliability too.

Uniform naming and addressing. Each Internet host computer has an Internet Protocol (IP) address that uniquely identifies it on the Internet from the millions of other computers also on the Internet. The IP address is expressed in a uniform format or 'dotted quad'. An example is: '17.10.2.3'. As the dotted quad is not meaningful to humans the domain name system (DNS) is used to provide a symbolic name for the dotted quad. An example is: 'sol.brunel.ac.uk'. The DNS is capable of translating the symbolic name into the required IP address to enable Internet operations.

End-to-end protocols. The Internet does not process information. It enables the transfer of 'packets' of information between computers. This is called end-to-end protocol. The Internet enables the transfer of information or 'content' of the packet. The transmitting or receiving computers, known as the 'end' system, do the actual processing of information.

The combined use of the Internet, intranets and extranets by companies has resulted in the term 'virtual organization' or 'networked organization'. The virtual organization is to be contrasted with the physical organization; the latter is restricted by geographical, physical space. Companies can combine computer-networking technology with information technology (IT) and information systems (IS) to develop a network of computers that can capture, process and share information and knowledge in virtual or cyberspace, where time and space are defined differently from physical time and space. Amazon.com may be classed as a virtual organization. Virtual organizations tend to be flatter because access to information and knowledge is potentially open to all employees who have access to a PC.

THE WORLD WIDE WEB

The World Wide Web, also known as the 'Web' or 'WWW', consists of pages of information depicted as text, graphics, sound, or video clips. A Web page may contain Java applets - Java Programmes that are downloaded from the server and run on the local computer.

The Web consists of over a million Web servers, and an untold number of Web browsers. What distinguishes the Web from other computer media is its ability to link Web pages dynamically; this is known as hypertext links or simply links.

The Web combines computer network technology with hypertext to provide a 'global information system'. One Web page can be linked to another by a hypertext link and the user merely has to click on the link to display related information.

A link appears as highlighted on the Web page. It is this hypertext linking capability of the Web that makes it a powerful source of information. The Web is a client-server architecture system, and a Web user can access the Web servers with a Web browser such as Netscape or Microsoft Explorer.

HYPERTEXT

A document on the Web is composed using hypertext technology. Hypertext is an electronic document system that can be read non-sequentially and interactively.

The reader does not have to read it like a book, she/he can click on hyperlinks of related information. The Apollo space programme to record its documentation used a hypertext system. e-Commerce Web sites are built using hypertext documents, and other hypermedia.

HYPERTEXT TRANSFER PROTOCOL

The Web differs from the Internet by the protocol it uses to transfer information between computers. The Web uses the hypertext transfer protocol (HTTP) to connect and transfer hypertext documents stored on Web servers, also known as Web sites. All the computers on the Internet that use the HTTP protocol compose the Web.

THE WEB BROWSER

A Web browser is a graphical interface for searching, accessing and viewing hypertext and multimedia files on the Web. The first browser, called Mosaic, was invented by the US company Netscape Communications, founded in 1994 by Marc Andreessen. He set himself the problem of transferring sound and pictures over the Web. His solution was the first graphical Web browser.It allowed basic functions such as retrieving and displaying hypertext files. The growth of the Internet and the Web is largely because of the invention of the graphical browser which makes it easier for people to search and view information.

Two popular browsers are Netscape Communicator and Internet Explorer. They are more sophisticated than the original Mosaic browser and enable e-mail messaging, HTML authoring, and extensions such as scripting, plug-in and multimedia.

INFORMATION SEARCH ON THE WEB

In the e-retail literature, much is made of the *similarities* between the new electronic ways to sell goods to consumers and the traditional ways (bricks). One can talk about e-stores, e-shop fronts, e-shoppers, e-malls and so on. We highlight some of the *differences* between clicks and bricks.

These differences arise from the totally different technologies which are used in a clicks store compared with a bricks store, and the totally different approach used by e-shoppers to find goods and services, to compare prices and to generally browse around. The essential concept is *search* - the process by which e-shoppers find information about products and services.

BACKGROUND TO SEARCHING THE INTERNET AND THE WEB

The Internet is a worldwide network of servers and machines, originally set up (as the ARPAnet) to facilitate information exchange between US government contractors and university researchers . From the earliest days of the Internet, a major activity has been *searching* for information. As the Internet grew, a variety of tools were set up to help users perform searching to find the required information. Nowadays, the focus of activity is the World Wide Web, which uses Internet technology with an improved user interface, making huge amounts of information available to the end-user, often a home computer user. Much of this information is about products and services for mass distribution provided by e-retailers. The interface employed by most users is a graphical Web browser, typically Microsoft Internet Explorer or Netscape Navigator.

In practice much of the information is textual in nature, with graphical layout (such as the use of lists) to provide structure and additional graphics to provide other information and 'decoration'. Although much has been made of the idea of e-malls, where a group of e-shops congregate together like a conventional shopping mall, the typical user experience involves focusing on a specific Web site often linked to one company's offerings.

SURVEYS ON WHAT PEOPLE DO AND WHERE PEOPLE 'GO' ON THE WEB

A computer scientist would say that what e-shoppers actually do is to use a Web browser to examine data from the Web rendered into graphical images. A typical user would say something rather different - the experience is that you explore a virtual world and that at any moment you are at one 'place' in that world.

From then you might explore the place more deeply or move on to other places which are linked. Many surveys have been done to help us understand why people use the Web. There are four primary motives for Internet use: researching (in the most general sense), shopping, socializing and generalized surfing (for enjoyment).

Shehan (2002) carried out a cluster analysis of types of Internet sessions, finding that 'I need to find some information' was a significantly stronger motivation than all others. Visiting news sites, using search engines, searching for product information and using online databases together accounted for 34 per cent of users' online time. Searching for product information alone accounted for 7 per cent of online time, compared with only 1.7 per cent spent e-shopping.

Eighty-five per cent of all Internet traffic comes from 13 major search engines. Information search is important for consumers and it is important for e-retailers too: in a US study, the use of the Internet to search for information was the strongest predictor of e-shopping intention. In addition, information search improved shoppers' attitudes towards e-retailing a nd helped overcome the perceived barriers to e-shopping. Similarly, Fink and Laupase (2000) carried out an experiment with 30 Australian and 30 Malaysian participants who evaluated selected websites. They found evidence of a relationship between products and services and news stories. The authors argued that the impact of products and services displayed could be maximized through the presence of news stories providing information about recent developments.

We referred briefly to our study investigating shoppers' motivations in e-shopping. The respondents were a sample of 150 undergraduatestudents. Enjoyment was one of the main motivations and 'involvement' was one of the most important enjoyment dimensions. In line with previous work drawing attention to 'variety seeking', the most popular sites were Amazon, CD WOW and eBay, *i.e.* 'hedonic' e-retailers .Amazon and eBay are the UK's top two sites in terms of audience numbers.

It is particularly strong on involvement, with visitors spending on average 1 hour and 11 minutes on the site, one of the longest of UK e-retailers. Visitors return to the site frequently to check on items they are buying or selling. There is also a feedback feature on sellers that helps to build trust, and eBay is one of few UK e-retailers to achieve over one billion page views per month. Such sites enthusiastically embrace the 'involvement' aspect of enjoyment with features such as chat rooms, bulletin boards, customer written stories and product reviews, suggestion boxes and personalization of the Web site offers. In short, many of the features that make these sites involving, enjoyable and successful are based on satisfying shoppers' needs for information in one form or another. Some e-retailers use surfers' needs for information as a successful method of directing traffic to their sites. For example, outdoor equipment supplier L L Bean (www.llbean.com) provides information on national parks, and chemist/ drugstore Boots specializes in nutrition and health information.

SEARCHING AND FINDING ON THE WEB

Shoppers, then, spend a lot of time *searching*, and e-retailers are, of course, most interested in what they *find* ('Seek, and ye shall find!'). They would like shoppers to find information on their products and services at their virtual store, and to find (and execute) ordering and payment processes. They thus need to understand what technologies the shoppers use, and how they use these technologies, in order to improve the chances of sales and services on the Web. Thus, e-retailers who can help satisfy surfers' wants for information have a head start in selling to those customers.

THE AVERAGE WEB SESSION

Let us consider what average users do in an average Web session:

- The users sit down and start their Web browser, often set up so that the initial screen (the home page) points to some major Web site, and it displays a list of links to other sites and services. For example, the home page might be set to the Yahoo! main page (www.yahoo.com). Possibly they might decide to *focus* immediately on some site they know about and type in the Web address (URL) or use 'favourites' or 'bookmarks' to access that site.

- Otherwise, they look through the home page visually and *evaluate* the list, and make some decision based on what they are interested in.
- They might then decide to access a *search engine*, for example Google, (www.google.com) and, by entering suitable search phrases and hitting the Search button, instruct the engine to produce a list of relevant web pages with a brief summary of their contents. Having got that list, it is then scanned and evaluated.
- They might decide to examine a *directory system* related to their search goals, and scan through that and evaluate items.
- The process of scanning through lists for relevant items and/or using search engines is repeated until the relevant items are found. If nothing suitable is found, the search is refocused or *abandoned* at any point, or the search goals may be refocused from information retrieved, deliberately or not (some advertisement might pop up). The users might even go directly to some site, even if it does not come up on a directory or search-engine list, if they know the Web address (URL).

Let us now examine these in more detail.

They are:

- Focus
- Directories
- Search engines.

FOCUS

Suppose you want to purchase some hair conditioner. If you go down to the local town centre and locate a major shopping mall or high street area, you have expectations as to what you might find there and the ways you can quickly locate items of interest. For example, you would expect to be able to find a chain pharmacy store in a few minutes - in the United Kingdom, a branch of Boots or Superdrug. Having found such a store, you would expect to locate quickly a section with hair products and, equally quickly, a range of shampoos and conditioners. What you might also do is use some sort of directory (possibly the Yellow Pages) to locate stores of interest. Compared with the bricks experience, an e-shopper on the Web operates in a rather different way. On the Web, a user starts up a Web browser with some initial page, perhaps that of their Internet service provider. They then start searching for the item required, following appropriate links. Almost certainly they will use some sort of Web search engine. Obviously, we need to design web pages so that they are usable and attractive to the user. Nielsen (2000) has written extensively on Web site usability, and has pointed out a number of important considerations.

A prime component of making sites usable is clarity and focus. If the user finds the site difficult to use, and the design messy and unfocused, they will abandon the site and turn to searching elsewhere. Neilsen suggests some standards to create user consistency, good design and relevance, leading to a unified user experience across the site.

DIRECTORIES

People like lists, from the Seven Wonders of the Ancient World to the Top 20 pop songs. Directories are lists compiled around some specific topic, such as the telephone directory and trade directories. In the early days of the Web, people (editors) compiled lists of the most popular sites. As the number of sites grew, the lists became rather long. To improve accessibility, they were split into categories and sub-categories. Well known Web directories include Yahoo! and MSN.

Let us consider Yahoo! in a little detail. Yahoo! is compiled by human editors who also create a short description that is shown alongside the link to the Web address. The editors categorize the topics logically, in a way a search engine does not. For example, a category listed on the Yahoo! main page might be *Shopping*.

This might lead to *Electronics*, which might lead to *Cell Phones*. This might point to a list of cell phone items e-shoppers might be interested in. This hierarchical arrangement ensures that shoppers can fairly quickly get to items in which they are interested.

Improvements in search engines mean that directories are losing some value, but they are still useful for locating groups of relevant websites on a similar topic. It should be noted that directories of this nature can be very wide in scope, or they could be more focused, in the nature of a trade directory. To ensure contact with potential customers, e-retailers might consider something much more focused.

One point: note that Yahoo!, for example, is rather more than just a directory. It includes a search engine (formerly, the Google engine), and a range of services such as mail and instant messaging.

Such a service, which acts as a 'port' to many other Web and Internet services, is known as a *portal*. Portal owners hope that users will use their portal as their home page and point of departure, hence making them targets for selective advertising and other delights.

This does make portal sites attractive (if expensive) places to place web banners and other advertising material. The big portals are hard at work implementing a 'Search, Find and Obtain' model across information, shopping and entertainment channels. The effectiveness can be demonstrated by usage figures: MSN and Yahoo! are the most popular websites worldwide, each with 83 million users .

SEARCH ENGINES

Search engines on the Internet have been around some time. The first ones actually did a 'live' search of remote file systems holding documents (FTP servers), looking for filenames which matched search terms. When the Web became popular, researchers built Web search engines to try out new software and hardware on the huge amounts of data that became available. Later on, these experimental systems were commercialized. Well-known commercial search engine systems are Google (www.google.com) and AltaVista (www.altavista.com.).

There are actually *two* sorts of search engine involved.First, Programmes called 'crawlers' gather information about websites. This is done by starting with a list of 'well-known sites' and from there searching the sites they reference. This is an automatic process. The HTML (HyperText Markup Language) code corresponding to each web page is scanned for links to other sites.

In the HTML, such a link will appear like this: If this link is followed, the corresponding web page will also have links, and these too are followed. This process is continued, until millions of web pages are accessed. Each page is analysed for content. What this means is all the information in the page HTML - the title, the text of the body of the page and any additional information tagged on to the page (metainformation) - is extracted and examined for relevance. All this information is then put into a database (also called a catalogue or index). This process is repeated at regular intervals, possibly every two weeks.The database is indexed on content, and is made available to the e-shopper via a Web interface. Given some *search term*, such as 'shampoo', the database is searched for matching terms and the corresponding page URLs are retrieved, together with the page titles and summaries of the page contents.

This information is then formatted into a web page which is returned to the e-shopper. So the user inputs the word 'shampoo' and obtains a page of references to websites involving that term.

A few technical points:

- Following of links from any one page is only done to a certain 'depth', which means that it is important to put significant information on the Home Page or just a little 'below'.
- *Web crawlers* see a web page split into 'frames' as a number of pages,

and therefore explore these less deeply than pages without frames. Frames are best avoided if you want Web crawlers to extract as much information as possible from your pages.

- Web crawlers are not clever enough to deal with databases (for example, catalogues) which might be accessed from your pages. Really significant information should be able to be accessed as plain HTML pages, rather than by using some catalogue systems. Catalogues are really meant for human users.

Note that the process of database construction is automatic, but guided by concepts such as *well-known sites* and *relevance*. It is also possible to notify a search-engine system of a site for inclusion, which again guides the crawler. Websites that meet the criteria are added to the index whether they have been submitted for inclusion or not.

Popular Search Engines

Google (www.google.com) is the world's most popular search site, accounting for 60 per cent of all searches . Google compiles its catalogue of over four billion web pages very week or so. Despite being faster, larger and more efficient than competitors, even Google indexes only a fraction of the total web pages available.

However, the coverage is very wide. Although most e-shoppers use search engines, the typical user is usually not willing to spend much time formulating search terms, and often gets rather frustrated if the information they require is not returned. They might abandon the search, or perhaps try another search engine.

Many systems offer Boolean searching, which means that search terms and phrases can be linked, for example. Digital camera AND Canon AND inexpensive. Some systems also offer the option of fine-tuning the results by allowing the user to input terms used to rank (put in some order of precedence) the returned results.

The average e-shopper is not usually willing to learn how to set up these more sophisticated queries. They want a reasonable set of results with as little work formulating the query as possible. Otherwise, they tend to give up and try some other method.

They might use *metacrawlers*, which bring together results from various search engines and directories. Coverage is wide but operation can be cumbersome, with little fine-tuning possible, so these are not that popular.

The most useful systems as far as many e-shoppers are concerned are systems that allow natural language, for example a query such as: Where I can buy inexpensive Canon digital cameras? Systems such as

AskJeeeves (www.ask.com) specialize in such natural language queries. Observation by the authors shows that users often pose their questions in natural language whatever the system! They do this because no one has ever told them that they cannot, and because reasonable results are often returned, since many search engine systems filter *noise words* (such as 'the', 'and' and 'but') and use the remaining words as search terms and for ranking the results. Systems such as Google also make suggestions in an attempt to correct spelling results.

Growth in Search Engine Activity

Most of the growth in e-shopping is being driven by search engines like Google and other sites like the online marketplace eBay. Improved search quality, pioneered by Google, has made search engines an easy and efficient way for people to find things online - and for advertisers to find customers. At the same time, eBay, a haven for small businesses, has become the fastest-growing major shopping site, and much of Amazon's growth has come from serving as an intermediary for independent retailers.

Another example is that of Visa, which noted that online sales, including travel, have increased considerably, much more than sales using Visa cards with traditional retailers. A firm that compiles Internet research, online sales are rising by nearly 30 per cent per year, and soon 100 million people a year are expected to make online purchases.

A Price water house coopers survey indicates that not only are search capabilities and product information important to online shoppers when selecting an online shopping site, but they can help e-retailers turn shoppers into buyers and make the online shopping experience more like the on-land one. Search functions are the most popular online shopping feature. The majority of online shoppers - 77 per cent - have used a search function while shopping online and most of these users are satisfied enough with search functions to use them on a regular basis.

In addition to being the most popular features, survey results indicate that search capabilities and product information are most important to online shoppers when selecting an online shopping site. Search functionality and product information are ranked as the most important online shopping features by 43 per cent and 40 per cent of online shoppers, respectively.

INTERNET SEARCH ENGINES

The Internet is unarguably the most voluminous information store in the world. Finding information on the Internet requires complex computer algorithms. These algorithms form the backbone of Internet search engines designed to help people find the information they want. Organizations need search engines to find information about customers or business competitors or partners. Search engines are computer Programmes that locate specific Web pages, files or multimedia items stored on the Internet. Search engines such as Google or Autonomy use different algorithms or techniques to search for Web pages.

UNIFORM RESOURCE LOCATOR

The uniform resource locator (URL) is the address of a particular Web site on the Internet. It consists of domain names and a pathway that locates a particular host computer that is connected to the Internet. An example URL is www.yahoo.com or www.dell.com. A URL consists of the protocol that is to be used to make the Internet connection (the WWW in the examples), the name of the host computer ('Yahoo' or 'Dell') and the domain (.com). In the case of commercial companies, the name of the host computer connected to the Internet is usually the registered name of the company.

HYPERTEXT MARK-UP LANGUAGE

Hypertext mark-up language (HTML) is used to author information on a Web page. HTML documents are text files that are interpreted by a Web browser. The browser reads the HTML file and interprets the HTML instructions. The browser has to do this interpretation each time a hypertext file is loaded. A Web page can be divided into 'frames' or sub-pages.

Each frame is used to display separate but relevant information designed by the Web author. Multimedia can be facilitated by extensions to HTML or by 'plug-ins' or add-on Programmes that make the Web client more versatile to deal with additional media types. An example of extension is Secure HTTP that enables sophisticated encryption and decryption algorithms for sensitive e-Commerce data like payments for transactions.

It takes time to learn to write HTML code. Authoring tools are available for automatically converting documents in Microsoft Word to HTML files, ready to load on to a Web server. Hot Dog Pro, Adobe PageMill and Microsoft FrontPage are examples. A Web site consists of one or more Web pages linked together by hyperlinks. The contents of a Web site are known as 'content'. HTML is not capable of processing or interacting with Internet users. To process data captured through a Web form JavaScript is required.

MULTIMEDIA

Multimedia is a tool capable of providing the transfer of sound and images like pictures over the Internet. Multimedia applications require lots of memory and bandwidth - the physical capacity of data cables to carry and transfer data. For example, one minute of music requires 5 MB of data. The transfer of sound and images in real time requires special software which is added to TCP/IP and HTTP protocols. On the client end, a player is required to interpret the data and render it into sound or images. Multimedia Internet Mail Extensions or MIME is an Internet standard for multimedia Internet e-mail. MIME enables e-mail to be cast as types consisting of HTML, text, images or video. Example MIME types are: image/jpeg, video/ mpeg or application/pdf.

JAVA, APPLETS, JAVASCRIPT AND INTERACTIVITY

The Internet is popular because it is interactive. Interactivity means that the Internet user (or client) can actively request information from and provide information to the server. Such interactivity is important for e-Commerce applications. CGI script and JavaScript provide interactivity on the Internet.Java is a programming language originally intended for programming consumer electronic devices like microwave ovens, dishwashers or electronic clocks. As there are many manufacturers of these products, Java's developer, Sun Microsystems, designed Java to be ubiquitous, meaning that it should be operable on any manufacturer's device.

Virtual Java machines that are independent of PC operating systems interpret Java, a feature that makes it ideal for Internet programming. Java Programmes created for the Internet are called applets. Java applets are embedded in HTML documents.

An applet is a Java programme that is executed on the client machine. It is loaded by the Web browser and restricted to prevent security breaches. The applet is executed on a Java virtual machine in the browser.

JavaScript, originally called LiveScript, was developed independently of Java by Netscape to provide interactivity. It is used to process data captured via forms on the Internet and to create interactive Web sites, and both the server and the client side use it. JavaScript is embedded in HTML and is interpreted by a browser.Web pages that contain JavaScript can be transferred around the Internet, because JavaScript is platform-independent or interpreted. ActiveX is a competitor of JavaScript. Scripts can be used in e-Commerce to validate service or product order form entries.

COMMON GATEWAY INTERFACE

CGI Programmes are text files that consist of line or programming code similar to JavaScript; such Programmes are called CGI script. Pear is an example of CGI programming. CGI is used to create interactive Web sites that pass information from a Web browser to a server using a form, very useful for organizational needs. A form is a document that is created to interact with a user, take data from the user and send it to the server for processing, usually via a database.

CAMPUS E-BUSINESS

The unprecedented flow of information across networks and between organizations, coupled with the power of computers to extract, compile, organize, and republish information, has made e-business possible. These same capabilities are also raising significant concerns and issues related to the appropriate use of institutional information and the protection of information originating or residing in college and university information systems. The developmental phase facing colleges and universities today on the road to enabling e-business as one of integration. Our progress in adopting e-business in higher education will be enabled or constrained by institutions' abilities to develop, implement, enforce, and automate complex rules that authorize these consumers to partake of university services—for example:

- What rights will distant learners have regarding access to licensed university information resources?
- How can colleges and universities protect usage logs that record student and faculty library consumption activity for materials licensed from third parties?

The privacy, access, ownership, and security issues posed by e-business are extraordinarily complex and represent as much a set of cultural, behavioral, and policy issues as technical ones.

Colleges and universities have long—and correctly—been described as self-governing anarchies or adhocracies. Higher education's hallowed and well-established traditions of self-governance and shared governance are responsible for our remarkable history of achievement, service, and innovation. These traditions also make integration hard. In many ways, achieving the necessary level of technical integration to enable e-business is the least complex aspect of preparing the institution for e-business.

Many campus chief information officers (CIOs) understand what it means to reorient systems from their current functional office views to the end-user views (student, parent, alumni, inter-enterprise) that e-business will demand. In most cases, the technical tools to achieve this kind of integration exist. In short, technical integration is a significant issue that can be addressed by vision, talent, and money. The thornier integration challenges are cultural and relate to role definitions, authority and power, and values. These issues will define the boundaries of an institution's approach to, and its likelihood of success in, implementing e-business.

FUNDAMENTALS OF BUSINESS COMMUNICATION

Fundamentals of Business Communication distills the basic concepts and information from Ober' s "Contemporary Business Communication and places greater emphasis on grammar and mechanics. This brief text combines the traditional textbook format with a workbook and allows students to immediately test, apply, and reinforce the basics of business communication. Each chapter opens with an interview profiling managers from multinational companies (such as 3M), small entrepreneurial companies (such as village), and nonprofit organizations (such as The Wilderness Society). These discussions with industry insiders set the stage for key topics covered in the chapter. Language Arts topics appear in every third chapter to introduce or review basic grammar and mechanics. Ongoing examples provide a consistent thread of instruction, illustrate business communication in context, and reinforce the importance of audience analysis. After each major topic, "Checkpoints allow students to immediately review and test their understanding of the material just covered. Progressively increasing in degree of difficulty, these features ask students to recall, define, apply, and then critically analyse what they have learned. Activities and end-of-chapter exercises that follow the "3Ps model guide students through the assessment of a "problem or a typical business scenario involving effective communication, the process of determining how to respond to the situation, and the final "product—such as an e-mail or memo—created in response. Seven "Portfolio Projects allow students to demonstrate their communication skills to prospective employers. Students prepare: a routine informational message; claim; bad-news message; persuasive request; situational business report; videotape of an oral business presentation; and a resume, cover letter, and videotape of a practice interview.

THE IMPORTANCE OF COMMUNICATION

When he first started taking projects on RAC, he passed through a typical period of lurking; poking around and looking at all the details for various projects. He was even reading the comments from coders to buyers and vice versa, in their online resumes. It seems to me that there was a word that was present in most of the comments: "Excellent Communication", "Good Communication", "Communication is superb.

It is clear that many people were evaluating someone by his/her communication skills. Being a hardcore coder for many years I always believed that he must be judged by the final outcome of the project. In RAC, he discovered that this is partially true. A great implementation of a project will make the buyer accept the project 100% but if the communication is pour during the development of the project, neither the buyer nor the coder would like to cooperate again. Good communication will ensure repeating work between the same buyer and coder.

He strongly believe that the secret of successful projects is "Communication" If the buyer and the coder can communicate well, the project is only a matter of time to finish. Communication doesn't only mean that both parties have to speak the same language. It means more than that. It has to do with the wealth of information that is exchanged between them. Communication must be fluent, clear and enriched with meaningful information.

Many projects have failed to be completed and went to arbitration because the buyer and coder failed to communicate efficiently. Here is an example from my own personal experience. During the development of a project, the buyer was constantly sending me short, cryptic e-mails. I always had to reply back and clarify even minor details. Chatting with him online wasn't proved useful either. He didn't really know what he wanted. Sometimes, when he replied to my long e-mails it was hard to read his replies because he didn't even use paragraphs to separate my text from his.

When he finished the project, I got a 10 and a nice comment but only I, knew how hard it was to complete it. It was a nightmare. Most of my time on the project was spent trying to communicate with him. He estimated that I spent double the time that it was worth for this project. Do you think that this was an extreme example. Think again. It is very possible to happen to you if you fail to communicate. Buyers must clearly specify their needs before they post a project. You don't have to be a system analyst in order to do this efficiently. Write as many details as you can and give examples. Coders are not magicians. They can't guess what you want. During the development, constantly comment on the work. Always check the various steps and make sure that you are moving into the correct direction. Praise the coder if he finishes a nice tricky part of the project. Most coders are take pride in their work. Reward them if they take the extra mile for you.

Coders must have patience. Buyers aren't always experts in technical terms. Don't use technical lingoes to show off. It is better to explain things in simple words, one step at a time. In the long run this is going to save you time. If the buyer has a strong technical background about the project then you can use the appropriate terminology. During the development, keep a constant communication flow. Be sensitive about the buyers needs. Don't keep him in the dark about what you are doing. It is always a good idea to send daily short reports even for the smaller projects. This will assure that you are on the right track.

A successful project completion depends on many factors. "Communication" is the most important one. You can't go wrong if you make a lot of effort to communicate the best you can.

FORMS OF COMMUNICATION

Effective communicators have many tools at their disposal when they want to get across a message. Whether writing or speaking, they know how to put together the words that will convey their meaning. They reinforce their words with gestures and actions. They look you in the eye, listen to what you have to say, and think about your feelings and needs. At the same time, they study your reactions, picking up the nuances of your response by watching your face and body, listening to your tone of voice, and evaluating your words. They absorb information just as efficiently as they transmit it, relying on both non-verbal and verbal cues.

NON-VERBAL COMMUNICATION

The most basic form of communication is non-verbal. Anthropologists theorize that long before human beings used words to talk things over, our ancestors communicated with one another by using their bodies. They gritted their teeth to show anger; they smiled and touched one another to indicate affection. Although we have come a long way since those primitive times, we still use non-verbal cues to express superiority, dependence, dislike, respect, love, and other feelings.

Non-verbal communication differs from verbal communication in fundamental ways. For one thing, it is less structured, which makes it more difficult to study. A person cannot pick up a book on non-verbal language and master the vocabulary of gestures, expressions, and inflections that are common in our culture. We don't really know how people learn non-verbal behaviour. No one teaches a baby to cry or smile, yet these forms of self-expression are almost universal. Other types of non-verbal communication, such as the meaning of colors and certain gestures, vary from culture to culture.

Non-verbal communication also differs from verbal communication in terms of intent and spontaneity. We generally plan our words. When we say "please open the door," we have a conscious purpose. We think about the message, if only for a moment. But when we communicate non-verbally, we sometimes do so unconsciously. We don't mean to raise an eyebrow or blush. Those actions come naturally. Without our consent, our emotions are written all over our faces.

Functions of Non-Verbal Communication

Although non-verbal communication can stand alone, it frequently works with speech. Our words carry part of the message, and non-verbal signals carry the rest. Together, the two modes of expression make a powerful team, augmenting, reinforcing, and clarifying each other.

Experts in non-verbal communication suggest that it have six specific functions:

- To provide information, either consciously or unconsciously
- To regulate the flow of conversation
- To express emotion
- To qualify, complement, contradict, or expand verbal messages
- To control or influence others
- To facilitate specific tasks, such as teaching a person to swing a golf club.

Non-verbal communication plays a role in business too. For one thing, it helps establish credibility and leadership potential. If you can learn to manage the impression you create with your body language, facial characteristics, voice, and appearance, you can do a great deal to communicate that you are competent, trustworthy, and dynamic. For example, Wal-Mart founder Sam Walton has developed a homespun style that puts people at ease, thereby helping them to be more receptive, perhaps even more open.

Furthermore, if you can learn to read other people's non-verbal messages, you will be able to interpret their underlying attitudes and intentions more accurately. When dealing with co-workers, customers, and clients, watch carefully for small signs that reveal how the conversation is going. If you aren't having the effect you want, check your words; then, if your words are all right, try to be aware of the non-verbal meanings you are transmitting. At the same time, stay tuned to the non-verbal signals that the other person is sending.

VERBAL COMMUNICATION

Although you can express many things non-verbally, there are limits to what you can communicate without the help of language. If you want to discuss past events, ideas, or abstractions, you need words—symbols that stand for thoughts — arranged in meaningful patterns.

In the English language, we have a 750,000, although most of us recognize only about 20,000 of them. To create a thought with these words, we arrange them according to the rules of grammar, putting the various parts of speech in the proper sequence We then transmit the message in spoken or written form, hoping that someone will hear or read what we have to say. It shows how much time business people devote to the various types of verbal communication. They use speaking and writing to send messages; they use listening and reading to receive them.

PROCESS OF COMMUNICATION

Communication is the process of sharing thoughts, ideas, and emotions with others, and having those thoughts, ideas, and emotions understood. You need a sender, a message, and a receiver for communication to take place. Here are some other things that help communication to be effective:

Attention: The sender needs to pay attention to what he/she is trying to communicate, and choose the best words and body language to communicate with; the receiver needs to pay attention to what is being communicated by listening and watching.

Attitude: Both sender and receiver need to have a positive (and respectful) attitude. They should want to communicate, and be willing to work to see that communication can take place. Using negative or blaming words shows a poor attitude - using "I" messages and trying to understand the other's point shows a good attitude

Feedback: both sender and receiver can give feedback to each other, either by using words or by body language. This helps to show whether the communication is being understood correctly or not.

BARRIERS TO COMMUNICATION

There are many things that can hinder or prevent good communication. Here are some of the most common barriers:

Distraction: It is hard to understand if you are distracted by something else. When you are trying to communicate, make sure there is no competition for your attention like exciting things going on nearby or other people talking (cellphones, IMs, chat rooms, e-mail, etc.)

Blocks: Sometimes it's hard to communicate simply because you cannot send or receive the message. Loud noises can block communication, and so can things like lost phone signals and computers not being able to interface.

Poor Skills: Some people have not learned how to effectively listen, and do not understand what you are trying to communicate.

Attitude : Communication can also be affected by a poor attitude towards the other person, towards the subject, or just because the sender or receiver is having a bad day. Fear and mistrust can impede communication, as can boredom or lack of interest in the subject. For best communication, try to keep the emotions out of the way until you understand what is being communicated.

Poor Understanding: Sometimes the sender uses words that the receiver does not understand, or refers to cultural experiences that the receiver has not grown up with, so that communication is less effective. Try to use simple words if you are communicating something complicated, and make sure that both of you understand the context or cultural references.

Lack of Feedback : If the receiver does not give feedback, the sender does not know if the communication is effective or not; also, if the sender is not paying attention to the feedback, the communication will not be effective.

The best way to insure good communication is for both the sender and the receiver to use "I" messages - instead of saying "You hurt my feelings," or "That's stupid," you let the other person know how you feel by saying things like "I feel hurt when ___ happens," or "I feel angry when I hear someone say _____." Pay attention to how your voice sounds when you speak, and try to avoid sounding angry or condescending to the other person.

Avoid making hateful statements, insulting others, and complaining - instead, try to make helpful statements that can change the situation from negative to positive.

Dealing with Communication Barriers

No matter how good and effective a communicator one maybe, yet the fact is that one does face certain barriers, from time to time, which forces them to work on becoming even more effective in their skills to communicate. Given here are the communication barriers that occur while listening, speaking and in the case of non-verbal communications...

Listening Barriers

Interrupting the speaker

Not maintaining eye contact with the speaker

Rushing the speaker to complete what he/she has to say

Making the speaker feel as though he/she is wasting the listener's time

Being distracted by something that is not part of the on going communication

Getting ahead of the speaker and completing his/her thoughts

Ignoring the speaker's requests

Topping the speaker's story with one's own set of examples

Forgetting what is being discussed

Asking too many questions, for they sake of probing

Barriers While Speaking

Unclear messages

Lack of consistency in the communication process

Incomplete sentences

Not understanding the receiver

Not seeking clarifications while communicating

The other barriers include:

An individual's subjective viewpoint towards issues/people, which leads to assumptions.An emotional block, which can lead to an attitude of indifference, suspicion or hostility towards the subject.

An emotional block or bias that is based on a third party's view point, or on what you have read/heard.Words can have different meanings to different people, thus blocking communication.

Use of negative words Well before the current world financial crisis struck, organizations have sought inventive ways to engage in face-to-face meetings without the need to travel. Companies have turned to services such as Adobe Acrobat Connect Pro, Cisco WebEx, Citrix Got Meeting, and Microsoft Live Meeting as a means for workers in multiple locations to share presentations and otherwise collaborate. No question, these tools greatly reduce costly, productivity-sapping travel, with the added benefit of lowering a company's carbon footprint. Yet scratchy audio quality, out-of-sync slides, and tiny, Webcam-quality video often diminish these solutions' usefulness.

Prediction: Google Announces Twitter Acquisition

Similarly, more traditional videoconferencing systems (which have been around for decades) suffer from low utilization rates — partially because of complicated, unreliable technology. The door has now opened for telepresence solutions: a conferencing environment that seeks to mimic the in-person experience as much as possible. Several technologies make telepresence possible. High-definition video cameras and large, flat-panel monitors clearly display participants in life size. Optimized networks — making use of QoS and even application-aware protocol acceleration — help eliminate audio and video delay over long-distance and high-latency WANs. As such, participants can make eye contact with colleagues and immediately pick up on all-important visual cues — such as how someone reacts to an offer. Moreover, operating the systems can be as simple as using a television remote control or telephone.

Something for Everyone

In general, telepresence systems fall into three configurations. First, there are formal group setups, purpose-built rooms that accommodate four to eight participants.

Here you'll find warm wall coverings, soft lighting, three or four wall-mounted monitors, and a conventional conference room seating arrangement. In use, it's as if remote participants are sitting across the table from you. Second, you'll find small-to-midrange setups, which comprise a single monitor and one camera, suited for handling one to four users.

This option works well in executive offices, and some systems are mobile enough to be ferried among regular conference rooms. These less-costly systems work over existing networks, yet the picture and audio quality surpass that of early-generation videoconferencing solutions. None come with amenities such as plush suites, but they closely match expensive systems' picture quality and usability.

Finally, there are classroom-style rooms that can hold 30 participants or more. These facilities, which are used by corporate and educational institutions alike, usually have multiple monitors or video projectors.

The Cost of Collaboration

Even with falling hardware costs, a telepresence system doesn't come cheap. A group system at a single site that can accommodate 18 to 36 users can go for $350,000. One reason for the expense is that you typically don't install telepresence systems in any old room. An immersive face-to-face environment requires special lighting, acoustics, and furniture, which all factor into the price. And that doesn't count in-house (or contracted) network and support costs. But before you despair, take a serious look at how much money you're spending on employee and executive travel among your various offices: airline tickets, food, accommodations, and the like. Factor in how much productivity is lost during travel, as well as how much time that travel can add to moving forward with a project or deal. In the end, you may find fast payback on your investment. For instance, Cisco representatives say that their customers often recover a telepresence investment in six to nine months, according to independent audits.

Notably, there are ways to reduce telepresence costs, including equipment leases and renting time at conferencing facilities. If price is still a barrier, you could consider one of the lower-end, high-performance systems, which run for less than 10,000. Moreover, video chat applications are improving, too, though it's a real stretch to put them in the same category as fully developed videoconferencing solutions. Still, for little (or no) cost they let several people connect with very usable audio and visual quality.

5

Organizational and Management Change in the E-Business Era

The commercialization of the Internet has given rise to a range of new business concepts, and the popular imagination has been captured by the rise and fall of Internet start-ups - the dotcoms. This was particularly the case where the companies involved demonstrated new business models and offered customers novel value propositions.

The great 'e-Pioneers' are certainly worthy of attention and analysis. All businesses can learn much from their birth pangs and their experiences of the early days of the Internet era. But for most companies, online operations are not matters of innovation from scratch, but of organizational change and adaptation - even corporate transformation. As Kalakota and Robinson note. 'In the e-business world, companies must anticipate the need for transformation and be ready to re-examine their organisations to the core' (1999:8).

Quite apart from the dotcom saga, the Internet continues to have an enormous impact on established organizations. It is affecting how they operate and how they do business; it provides new opportunities for businesses of all sizes and has created a new sales channel. The ever-increasing scope of e-business change. Furthermore, even such radical restructuring cannot be regarded as just a one-off activity. As Butler *et al.* (1999) state, the network technologies that support this are built on silicon - *i.e. sand* - and 'as the sand shifts so does an e-business'. In other words, companies have to be prepared to reorganize and restructure themselves continuously. For this reason, understanding how to manage change effectively becomes essential.

As Stroud notes, 'The benefits that the Internet is expected to deliver will not be realised unless a company adapts its organisational structure and methods to meet the radical new ways of working that this new technology makes possible'. It is worth noting, however, that some companies have embraced the need for change perhaps *too* enthusiastically. One manager of a software company remarked, 'We start to get worried if change is not taking place every week even; the question is, will we get left behind?

We must change something. But often it's change for change's sake' (private conversation).At the other end of the scale, some companies remain reluctant to grapple with the opportunities offered by the Internet. In a piece of research conducted by Jupiter Communications in 2000, only 24 per cent of the US CEOs surveyed actually viewed their Web initiatives as an integrated part of their core business.The US experience, according to Cohan, is that companies generally fall into two broad camps with their e-Initiatives: being 'self-reinventing' in order to maintain market leadership, or else 'change-avoiding' by persevering with existing ways of doing business. As the Jupiter study implies, the self-reinventors are still in the minority, but these companies, according to Cohan, have the following characteristics:

- They believe it is better to attack their existing business models than allow competitors to do so.
- They are led by CEOs who are very concerned about keeping competitors from gaining access to their customers.
- Their CEOs have a financial incentive to reinvent the company in order to sustain rapid profit growth.
- Their CEOs are personally open to learning more about e-Commerce if that is what is necessary to maintain the strategic initiative in the industry.

Similarly, Siegel recommends that in developing e-Business strategies, self-reinventors spend time sharpening the 'big questions'. These include:

- Which business areas are we open to exploring, and which are we going to avoid?
- Which parts of our business are going online fastest?
- What changes do we expect from competitors?
- Which start-ups are going to put us out of business?
- Which of our competitors would make good partners?

These questions suggest a radical or transformational view of e-Business-related change, rather than an incremental one. This has major implications so far as the process of change management is concerned, as well as the likely successes and difficulties it will involve.

BARRIERS TO CHANGE

It is worth reporting here the recent findings of Rosabeth Moss Kanter, who undertook a survey of 785 companies to investigate the barriers to e-Business change.

The results are listed below in overall descending order of importance from 1 (most important) to 17 (least important).Bear in mind that companies more than 20 years old face fewer marketplace and technology barriers than younger ones do, but they face many more internal barriers - from decision-making uncertainty to divisional rivalries.

- The unit does not have staff with adequate technical or Web-specific skills.
- Customers and key markets do not want to change their behaviour.
- There are more important projects that require existing resources and time.
- Technology and tools are inadequate, unavailable or unreliable.
- It is hard to find the right partners to work with.
- Suppliers are not co-operative or not ready for e-Business.
- Employees are not comfortable with change.
- Leaders are not sure where to begin: they do not understand how to make the right choices.
- Top executives do not personally use computers and are not personally familiar with the Internet.
- Rivalries or conflicts between internal divisions get in the way.
- It is hard to find the capital for new investment.
- Managers fear a loss of status or privileged positions.
- Employees fear loss of jobs, or unions and employee groups fear loss of membership.
- Government rules and regulations get in the way.
- The company is successful as it is: leaders see no need for change.
- The company had a bad previous experience with new technology.
- It is a waste of time or money: it is not relevant to the business.

It is evident that there are a number of difficulties in implementing the intellectual, cultural and structural shifts necessary to succeed in a much more interactive business environment that requires a diverse range of skills.

Drobik notes that 'organisations need to wake up to the complications of being an e-business', but he claims that one of the biggest mistakes organisations make when implementing an e-business strategy is that they 'completely redesign the business in order to become an e-business'.In other words, organisations cannot simply 'switch' to e-business. He explains that success depends on 'mix management' - a mix in which traditional and e-business models coexist, which supports the central theme of this book.

ORGANIZATIONAL OBJECTIVES AND THE BUSINESS MODELS

In selecting the business model suited to a retail operation, the retailer will initially assess their marketing and sales objectives for the three principal retail channels: bricks and mortar, direct retailers and virtual retailers. Note that objectives are *samples* and not an exhaustive list.

Scoring the Retailer's objectives for Customers

The potential for a retail channel to meet the individual objectives for customers is assessed on a scale of 1 to 5. A retail channel with little potential to meet an objective scores 1 increasing to 5 for a retail channel with a high potential to meet the customer objectives.

The structure of each retail channel and the method of accessing the channel's target audience provide advantages for communicating certain information and appealing to certain human senses. For communicating information that appeals to the customers' senses of sight, sound, touch, taste and smell, there is currently no better medium than the face-to-face interaction possible in a physical retail store. This conclusion is reinforced by the 20/25 score for the bricks and mortar retailers. Restricted to audio and static visual images, direct retailers cannot provide moving images of new products or a tactile experience for a customer and this resulted in a score of 16/25. Encouragingly, research into direct retailing shows that such customers often retain the retailer's marketing correspondence to be reread in the future. Such correspondence may include details (*e.g.* retailer achievements) often overlooked while browsing in a retail store or un-clicked on the retailer's Web site.

Though computer software and hardware facilities for the Web are improving to encompass audio, video and tactile reproductions of the real world, the experience is still not a replacement for the communication facilities and immediate feedback of the store environment. As an advantage over the direct retailers, the virtual retailer's ability to include moving video and online search facilities enables improved demonstration ability for merchandise offered, giving the virtual retailer a score of 18/25.

Globalization created by the Internet means that many retail names formerly restricted to domestic markets have become internationally recognized brands. While some retailers have attempted to establish a physical bricks and mortar presence in overseas markets, the logistical costs and unique requirements of the overseas locations has for some retailers resulted in major losses and eventual withdrawal from the overseas market.

Direct retailers have utilized the well-established international postal and courier systems for decades. With little more than a sales orientation, many direct retailers have accepted orders from overseas customers, packaged the orders and passed the distribution responsibility to transport groups such as DHL (www.dhl.com) or FedEx (www.fedex.com). The transport groups arrange pickup of the packaged merchandise, export documents, customs clearances, final delivery and, in some cases, payment clearances. For a small direct retailer, such international sales provide new market revenues without a major investment in logistics infrastructure, *i.e.* a specialized international shipping group. A drawback for the direct retailer is not being known by potential customers in other parts of the country and overseas. Many of us have turned to the phonebook to look for a supplier, but what if you don't have every phonebook in the world? The answer is turn to the World Wide Web and use of search engines. The Internet has given every person with access to the Web an access to every virtual retailer, as testified by the meteoric growth of Amazon (www.amazon.com) from being the seller of books to a few avid readers to becoming one of the largest book and video retailers in the world, and all this exclusively online. Worldwide access to the Web is now so entrenched that successfully established direct retailers such as Lands End (www.landsend.com) established sophisticated order-taking websites and integrate sites into the retailer's marketing and distribution plans as an added retail channel.

Scoring the Retailer's Objectives for Staff

The potential for a retail channel to meet the retailer's objectives for staff is assessed on a scale of 1 to 5. A retail channel with little potential scores 1, increasing to 5 for a retail channel with a high potential to meet the individual staff objectives. The same score of 15/15 for staff objectives? It is because that, no matter what retail channels a marketer uses, staff must be prepared to provide the finest service possible within the constraints and advantages of that channel. Consider negative perception of a prospect should they ask a question concerning the exchange policy of the retailer's staff (face-to-face, by mail or through a Web site) only to receive the reply 'I don't know' and without the follow up 'but I will find out and get back to you by (x period)'. Quality support systems are also essential in all retail channels because it is the retailer's personnel who receive the ire of annoyed prospects when an electronic system (*e.g.* Web site or ordering facility) fails.

Scoring the Retailer's Objectives for Shareholders

The potential for a retail channel to meet the retailer's objectives for shareholders is assessed on a scale of 1 to 5. A retail channel with little potential scores 1 increasing to 5 for a retail channel with a high potential to meet the individual shareholder objectives. The immediacy of response and round-the-clock access of the Internet places the virtual retailer in an enviable position for providing shareholders with detailed information as demonstrated by the 15/15. Unlike the brief summaries of financial and business information conventionally available in an annual report, Web-based documents may incorporate interactive graphics and video to display information for more impact upon the shareholders. Not all shareholders will be retail customers and therefore exposed to the marketing communications provided by both bricks and mortar and direct retailers. To inform their shareholders these retailers traditionally use printed media and call-centre responses to shareholder enquiries, therefore giving both retail channels a score of 9/15. Though effective, such methods have high labour costs and are slower to update when compared with information storage and retrieval from Web-based retailing.

Scoring the Retailer's Ofor Suppliers, Partners and Dealers

The potential for a retail channel to meet the retailer's objectives for suppliers, partners and dealers is assessed on a scale of 1 to 5. A retail channel with little potential scores 1, increasing to 5 for a retail channel with a high potential to meet the individual supplier, partner and dealer objectives. Using the series of objectives and totalling the scores for each retail channel, the maximum potential score is 15.Synchronizing data records between the retailer and their suppliers, partners and dealers is essential to avoid such errors as:

- Missed or duplication of orders;
- Misdirected correspondence to personnel or addresses that have changed;
- Non-compliance with legislation (*e.g.* government reporting schedules);
- Missed targets (*e.g.* end of month summaries or sale dates).

Direct retailers have honed their record systems to finalize sales and associated records in the absence of physical customers to score a total of 10/15. When disputes with customers and suppliers do occur, it may take time for the direct retailers to consult and correlate the electronic and manual record systems. Bricks and mortar retailers also pay a great deal of attention to the daily summarizing of financial exchanges. Though important, third-party contact records (*e.g.* contact names at suppliers or shipping agents) may not be updated as regularly nor carry the same level of priority customer interactions and this lessens the overall score to 9/15. By the nature of their operational environment, virtual retailers depend upon efficient real-time data exchanges through the Internet network, which itself depends upon detailed and automated record-keeping of transmitted information. Such an improved information exchange with the relevant parties gave the virtual retailer a higher score of 13/15, assuming e-retailers and their third-party partners regularly update and utilize the pertinent data over the Internet.

Scoring the Retailer's Objectives for the Community

The potential for a retail channel to meet the stated retailer's objectives for the community is assessed on a scale of 1 to 5. A retail channel with little potential scores 1, increasing to 5 for a retail channel with a high potential to meet the individual community objectives. An integral component of modern marketing plans is keeping the community informed about the direction and intentions of the retailer. For each retail channel, there are alternative communications media to carry messages to the relevant community. The current communications media available to the bricks and mortar and direct retailers include print (*e.g.* newspapers) and broadcasting (*e.g.* television). Though extensive, such media may not reach every community person who has a stake in bricks and mortar and direct retailer channels and this restricts the total scores to 8/15 and 9/15 respectively. In communications to the community, the virtual retailers have an interactive advantage over the other two retail channels. The e-retailer's Web site may incorporate a series of messages to support their objectives for the community in a more convincing manner. Helping to communicate these messages through the Web site and achieving a score of 15/15, the retailer may include any of these online facilities:

- Hyperlinks to relevant websites
- Live footage (webcams streaming video)
- Storage of printable documents (*e.g. Adobe Acrobat* format)
- Interactive games
- E-mail exchanges.

As shown, each of the retail channels - bricks and mortar, direct and virtual - have varying degrees of suitability to meet organizational objectives. By summing the scores for each objective and each channel, the retailer will identify the retail channel with the greatest opportunity for marketing plan success. To reiterate, the objectives for the five retail participant groups are *samples* and *not* an exhaustive list for all retailers; the unique environments facing the retailers may require them to add or remove objectives.

Taking the results for each set of sample objectives, the results are 59/85 for direct retailers, 61/85 for bricks and mortar retailers and 76/85 for virtual retailers, placing the virtual retailer in the most effective position to meet the sample of objectives for the five retail participant groups. This does not restrict the retailer to a single channel.

The growing consumer acceptance of electronic shopping is allowing traditional retailers to expand into multiple retailing channels. To do this and provide the greater likelihood of meeting the retailer's multifaceted objectives, the channels chosen should be in order of their scores, which for this set of objectives is virtual retailing, followed by bricks and mortar retailing and finally direct retailing. Concentrating on the virtual retailer, the next stage is to gauge how suitable merchandise is for this particular retail channel.

E-RETAILING INTO AN ORGANIZATION

During the early commercialization of the Internet, when it became clear it would provide a new channel for the sale of products and services, there was common speculation that traditional retail was dead. Investors flocked towards dot.com stocks on the premise that a new economy was emerging where established organizations, with their inherent structural rigidity and reluctance to embrace change, could not compete with more nimble dot.com start-ups, founded on embracing e-commerce.

However, this 'either/or', 'bricks vs. clicks' paradigm was short-lived. Although there are many reports of dot.com successes that became spectacular failures, as well as examples of dot.com survivors and outright dot.com successes such as eBay, the evolving stars have been hybrids and, most often, established retailers who have successfully integrated e-commerce.

The integration of B2C e-commerce, namely e-retail, into established businesses, and begins by examining the reasons for traditional retailers to incorporate e-retail into their business model, considering some recent examples. It then goes on to review some frameworks that have been proposed to encompass strategies for integrating online and offline activities, and ends with consideration of the operational implications of such activities for the retailer.

WHY TRADITIONAL RETAILERS ADOPT E-RETAIL

The number of customers shopping online has increased markedly each year since the beginning of e-commerce in the mid-1990s. In the UK during November 2003, for example, online shopping was up 44 per cent on the previous year (ZDNet, 2003). This alone might be a reason for a traditional retailer to look at e-retail, but the influences on such decisions have varied with time and understanding of e-commerce.

Out of Fashion: Commerciality

Before the dot.com downturn in the spring of 2000, the word 'Internet' keyed into what seemed pervasive optimism for a new century. It meant youth, new possibilities and an opportunity to break with traditional business and create new rules. From the media and daily articles on achieved or projected *Initial Public Offering (IPO)* success, even game shows such as *The e-millionaire show*, which went out during peak viewing, to the restructuring of government and creation of new departments, such as the Office of the e-Envoy and a complement of online resources, the Internet could not be ignored. In the absence of a better reason, fashion alone was sufficient to drive most traditional businesses to consider moving into e-commerce, even if the boardroom rationale was to protect shareholder value.However, the shakeout of 2000 left fashion with the debris of countless failed start-ups. In its place came valuable lessons across e-commerce, and evidence for incumbent retailers that factors such as having an established brand provide significant advantages in e-retail and play a part in customer loyalty and increased profit.

Advantages of Being Established

Analysis of dot.com failures and comparison with traditional retailers in the same industry, for example eToys (www.etoys.com), which folded in 2000 and was subsequently bought by an established toy retailer, vs. Toys R Us (www.toysrus.com), which successfully opened an e-retail channel through collaboration with Amazon (www.amazon.com), has revealed several advantages for the established retailer. Newcomers have to attract customers, and much of their cash-burn and early debt is usually caused by brand-building and promotion. Established businesses, however, have an existing customer base and can build on brand values that are already in place. They also have existing marketing budgets usually able to furnish new online activity, and are experienced in the market they serve, unlike many start-ups. Further advantages, such as having an existing value network including suppliers, buying, fulfilment and the teams to support these functions, have been shown to be generous compensation for being late to market.

Benefits of e-retail

There are many strategic options for the adoption of e-retail and the level of involvement a business can choose in online activity, but clearly, e-retail, at the very least, represents an alternative or additional channel for traditional retailers. While opening new physical retail outlets can expand the geographical reach of a business and add convenience for consumers, retailing

online not only carries these benefits, but also offers further returns that are more specific to online trading. The Internet has global reach and provides the opportunity to trade internationally. Of course, this is not necessarily an advantage for a number of reasons, such as having to deal with multiple languages, currencies and even cultures, and managing far-flung logistics including returns, but, with foreign competition able to enjoy the potential of international trade online, businesses do need to consider their competitive position should they ignore e-retail.

Other broad benefits include the ability to trade 24/7 and operate with lower overheads in terms of staff and space, while more particular advantages include the ability to increase the number of customer 'touch points' and build more personalized customer experiences, products and relationships.

However, these e-retail advantages should not imply that an online presence is a recipe in itself for success; that kind of thinking was tried and failed with the dot.com boom and bust. Instead, if there is a recipe for successful integration, it is found in variants of established business practices, such as an understanding of the strengths and weaknesses of the business, for example in relation to technology awareness, which is a good indicator of e-commerce success. Most importantly, the adoption of e-retail relies on the competent formulation of an integration strategy.

STRATEGIES FOR INTEGRATION

Online shopping in the UK continues to grow and is expected to comprise over 5 per cent of the retail market by 2005. Such predictions can be somewhat self-fulfilling and help fuel enthusiasm for continued research and development, providing a constantly changing environment for any integration strategy. It is necessary to keep abreast of these developments as they all impinge on strategic decisions.

Overview of Current Developments

While the common e-retail interface remains the Web browser running on a personal computer, many companies have investigated alternative methods of interfacing with the customer. *T-commerce*, that is e-commerce over TV or instigated by TV commercials, is an important e-retail alternative, not least because 97 per cent of UK homes have one or more televisions, and take-up of interactive TV continues to rise. During Christmas 2003, 'Freeview' (the name for the free-to-air part of digital terrestrial television in the UK) was among the top ten queries on Internet search engines. In comparison, penetration of Internet via PC has been predicted to level off at 53 per cent by 2004. Dominos Pizza had early success in T-commerce using satellite, cable and the Web to achieve

98 per cent brand recognition in multi-channel homes, and other retailers, including Dixons and WHSmith have followed. The medium has also been particularly popular with the finance industry and has attracted several banks and building societies.

Other developments that strengthen opportunities for e-retail exist in advances in mobile phone technology. Recent developments include 3G, with data transfer speeds up to 2Mbps that can support video-level *interactivity*, and the growing deployment of *Wi-Fi* networks couples with widespread prediction that Wi-Fi is a key growth area that will fundamentally change Internet access. For example, there is an effort under way to turn Paris into one big Wi-Fi *hotspot*, by positioning access points above and below ground at all of the city's 372 metro stations, interconnected by fibre-optic cable.

The pilot phase of the project began in mid-2003, when Cisco announced that it was partnering with RATP (Régie Autonome des Transports Parisiens - the Paris public transport authority) in a proof of concept above ground at a dozen locations along the Bus 38 route. If the full project gains approval, Paris will have one of the largest Wi-Fi networks in the world.

The UK has its own significant developments, including building an advanced retail communications network at Birmingham's new Bullring shopping centre. As part of a dynamic retail environment, incorporating an intelligent buildings system and a multi-Gigabit cabling infrastructure, the 130 new shops are supplemented in the mall by 27 touch screen interactive kiosks, 25 plasma screens and 155 thin client terminals linked to one of the largest Wi-Fi networks in Europe. Among the large traditional retailers, Argos (www.argos.co.uk), a UK catalogue company with streamlined ordering and collection at high street stores, has been prominent in developing alternative ordering and reservation methods as well as full online retail.

The company has had success with in-store kiosks that provide fast track ordering and credit card payment, and was among the first to trial a text messaging 'text and take home' system for product reservation. Using the system, customers can text the catalogue number of an item to check its availability at a particular store, and then, in response to the text that confirms the item's price and stock position, can place a reservation on the product. The system reduces queuing and is part of the company's continuous innovation in ideas to increase customer convenience.

Murray Hennessy, MD of John Lewis Direct, believes that in e-retail, 'It's getting easier to be smarter' (IMRG, 2002). Software platforms for e-retail are now available off-the-shelf, and people in the industry are now more experienced.

However, no matter how accessible the technology of e-retail systems becomes, or how successful the big players have already been, companies that want to adopt e-retail need to understand what it offers and pursue an integration strategy that is appropriate to their business.

Strategic Options

A company's strategy towards e-retailing will be influenced by a number of factors, including its market sector and prospects for online and offline retail, in-house technical knowledge and experience of outsourcing, re-engineering and development projects, as well as its overall vision, desire and ability to operate in a very fast-changing and possibly unfamiliar commercial environment.In order to recognize the additional complexity that e-commerce is likely to introduce, it is useful to consider the digital and physical dimensions of a business in relation to the type of product, process and delivery agent involved, as shown in Figure 3.1.

This model, developed by Choi *et al.*, maintains currency, being used in recent works such as Chen (2001) and Turban *et al.* (2002), and conveys the prospect of choices and issues for a business contemplating e-commerce from a background of traditional commerce.

For a traditional retailer, the first questions regard how readily its products and services lend themselves to e-retailing, and then the degree to which the business can exploit electronic processes. One method for approaching these questions is described by the ES test and involves consideration of product attributes in terms of the five human senses and looking at consumer type and the familiarity of the consumer in purchasing the product..

Once a retailer has evaluated the potential of its products or services for e-retailing, it must then decide its position for e-retail adoption, and determine a course of action. De Kare-Silver (2001) lists ten options that can be arranged on a scale from 'no e-retail operations' to 'e-retail only', in order of increasing e-shopping responsiveness, paralleled with increasing commitment to e-retailing as shown in Figure 3.2.

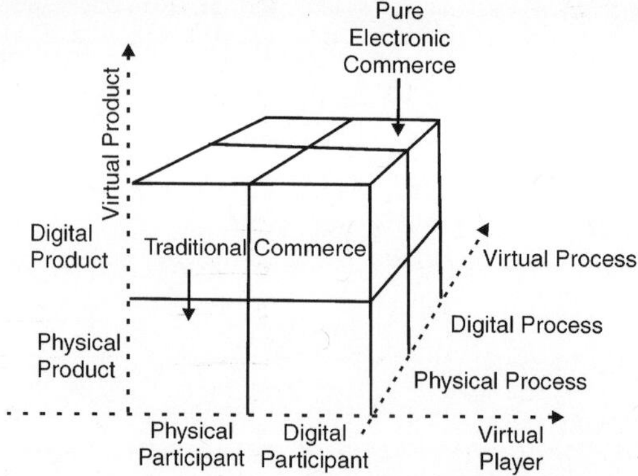

Fig. e-Commerce Digitization No e-retail Operations

This is the defensive option, based on revitalizing the 'experience' and social aspects of shopping based in towns and shopping centres. However, consumers now expect every organization to have at least an information Web site and an e-mail address.

Information only

Reluctance to tackle the disadvantages of e-retailing leads some well-known high street retailers (for example, Monsoon - www.monsoon.co.uk) to use the Internet purely as a marketing communication channel rather than for online sales.

Export

This approach is aimed at protecting the business of the high street stores while widening the potential customer base with e-channels. De Kare-Silver cites the example of bookseller Blackwells (www.bookshop.blackwell.co.uk), which has 82 outlets in university towns and campuses across the UK, but whose listing of one million specialist and academic titles is now available worldwide on the Web.

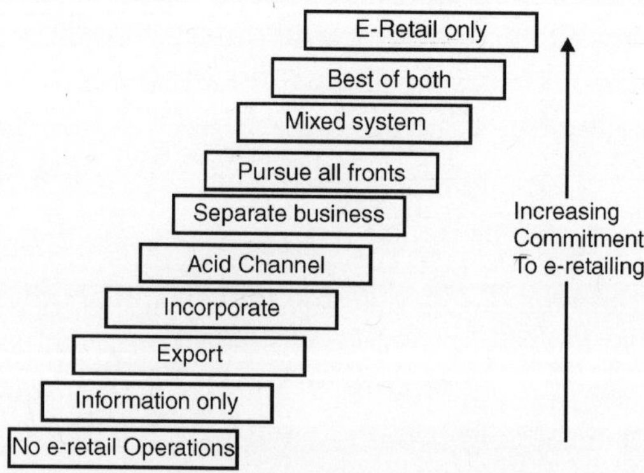

Fig. Strategic Options for Retailers

Incorporate into existing business

This option seeks to protect the existing stores by using an 'order and collect' system. The thinking is that, by coming to the store to collect the order, the shopper is more likely to think of extra purchases, or to pick up impulse buys. Safeway (www.safeway.co.uk) and Sainsburys (www. sainsburys .co.uk) tried this system but did not gain the popularity of market leader Tesco (Safeway withdrew from e-retail completely before being taken over by Morrisons, and Sainsburys introduced home delivery, initially based on warehouse picking centres rather than stores).

Add Another Channel

With this approach, retailers such as Next (market leader in online clothing sales, according to retail researcher Verdict) use e-retailing as an extra route to reach more of their target customers. Retailers in this category may be represented on an e-mall, saving much of the setting-up cost of a dedicated e-retailing operation.

Set up a Separate Business

The idea of the separate business is to offer competitive e-shopping benefits without alienating the existing customers for the high street operation, who probably pay higher prices. The separately branded direct operation has been popular for financial services - for example, Abbey National's e-bank 'Cahoot' (www.cahoot.co.uk).

Pursue All Fronts

An example of this is the National Westminster Bank multi-channel system, based on making every possible channel open to the customer: high street branches, direct mail, ATMs, phone, interactive TV and Internet (www.natwest.co.uk).

Mixed System

This approach recognizes that strong brands are essential to successful e-retailing. Brand strength is showcased in flagship stores in major cities - for example, Virgin Megastore (www.virginmega.com).

Best of Both Worlds

Is it possible to retain all the high street operations while at the same time being state-of-the-art in e-retailing? This is probably only practicable for a clear market leader in a sector, and represents a high-investment strategy, making it more difficult for competitors to catch up - the Tesco approach.

e-Retail Only

Few retailers are brave enough to close all high street outlets and operate only virtual shops. Pre-dot.com crash, though, a number of e-retail-only operations were developed, the best known and most successful being Amazon (www.amazon.com). However, even Amazon sees benefits in some 'real' presence, given its joint venture with Toys R Us (www.toysrus.co.uk). Only those operations high in e-shopping potential, such as travel, and with big budgets to build the brand (*e.g.* Lastminute.com - www.lastminute.com), are likely to be leaders with Internet-only operations.

MINI CASE STUDY 3.1: NETSHOP.CO.UK

Netshop Ltd is a privately owned company specializing in the online retail of computer networking products to end consumers. Evolving out of Homestead Electronics Ltd, a mail order electronics company founded in 1983, Netshop now forms part of a multi-business e-retail portfolio with offerings in diverse market segments.

The technology and mail order origins of the company, along with an established customer base and in-house knowledge of the networking market, assisted a smooth transition from mail order retail to e-retail, since much of the order processing and fulfilment infrastructure was already in place and the company possessed the necessary skills to develop its own transactional Web site and start small alongside its traditional business. Once its e-commerce systems were proven, they provided a platform for further online activities. The company's background as a family business, coupled with its attention to success factors in the e-retail marketplace, helped it foster an appreciation of customer expectations, and the requirement to be competent at more than just the technical process behind the shopping experience.

Many new customers arrive at the Netshop Web site from results at search engines such as Google (www.google.co.uk), and not all of them are seasoned e-consumers. Netshop recognizes this, and works to establish trust by giving prominent space to the company's physical address, the history of the company and telephone numbers so that customers are not forced to pursue an online transaction if they do not want to. Instead, prospective customers can phone and place an order, and even arrange to collect it, obviating the need to make credit card transactions online or by phone, or disclose address details. As the company says on its Web site, 'Talk to a real person at Netshop. We are not just another anonymous On-Line company!' This customer-oriented approach is augmented by several features that add value, such as extensive product information, news articles on new products and aspects of networking, FAQs and support pages, manufacturers' links, and free driver downloads, providing a multi-channel presence for a company that has chosen to move most of its operation online.

LOYALTY-BASED INTEGRATION STRATEGIES

The emphasis on focusing on people rather than products, coupled with the requirement for a business to align its strategy with its ability to operate in an e-retail environment, raises the question of how to formulate strategy for e-retail integration that takes these key requisites into account.

Recent research by Cuthbertson and Bridson (2003) proposes a framework to tackle this question and how the Internet changes the traditional store-based model of marketing, by setting it in the context of customer loyalty, which has long been acknowledged as an important factor in a firm's competitive position. Successful relationship marketing is underpinned by the ability to both acquire and retain customers over the long term, and the need to customise the relationship to the individual has been shown to be a critical factor.

Modelling the Online Retail Experience

Cuthbertson and Bridson suggest that the loyalty marketing strategy is dependent on the fundamental structure of the retailer-customer relationship, and put forward a categorization of retailer-customer relationships in an Online Retail Relationship Matrix as shown in Figure 3.3.This matrix uses the two principal components of the retailer-customer relationship - the retailer-led channel proposition to the customer and the customer-led channel access to the retailer - and divides these based on the focus of each party.The retailer may configure its offer as pureplay (online) or multi-channel, while the customer can choose to access the retailer directly or through a marketplace.

Examples of marketplaces include those that are online, such as DealTime/Shopping.com (www.dealtime.co.uk, now relaunched as part of www.shopping.com), or an interactive TV channel.The usefulness of the classification is that each category carries a higher likelihood of success for particular types of retailer, depending on the retailer's product/service. By mapping its type onto the matrix, a business can determine whether success is likely in a given configuration, with implications for the loyalty strategy that is most likely to succeed.The categories comprise:

- The digital retailer-customer relationship
- The ubiquitous retailer-customer relationship
- The focal retailer-customer relationship

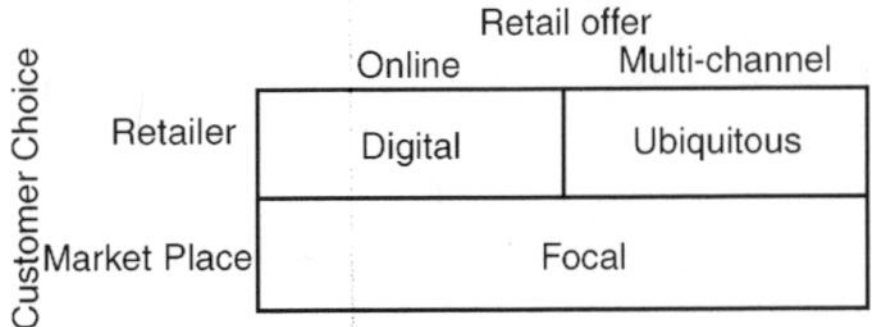

Fig. The Online Retail Relationship Matrix

THE DIGITAL RETAILER-CUSTOMER RELATIONSHIP

The digital retailer-customer relationship appears to be most applicable where: The service element at the point of transaction is low and the product can be distributed digitally. This could relate to the retail of software, and financial or travel services. For example, airlines that retail tickets direct are likely to be successful by adopting a digital retailer-customer relationship.

THE UBIQUITOUS RETAILER-CUSTOMER RELATIONSHIP

The ubiquitous retailer-customer relationship appears to be most applicable where: The retailer is selling a wide range of goods to customers where the frequency of purchase is relatively high, or selling expensive, technical products where the frequency of purchase is relatively low but a high degree of consideration is given to the purchase decision.A grocery retailer such as Tesco, or a car retailer such as Ford, are examples of where a ubiquitous retailer-customer relationship is likely to be most successful.

THE FOCAL RETAILER-CUSTOMER RELATIONSHIP

The focal retailer-customer relationship appears to be most applicable where: The retailer is a third party to the product/service vendor, and is providing customers with digital access to a range of goods, based on convenience. This applies to third party convenience retailers such as Shopping.com (www.shopping.com) or to those offering customers specialist access to goods, such as eBay (www.ebay.co.uk) or online communities.

Loyalty strategies for retailers with a focal retailer-customer relationship depend on closely understanding customer requirements and providing a selection of retail opportunities to easily convert to purchases, with a mechanism for the third party to benefit from the transaction.

USING LOYALTY MARKETING STRATEGIES

Cuthbertson and Bridson (2003) expand their model to identify the relevant loyalty strategy by proposing a matrix called the Purchaser-Purveyor Loyalty Matrix, shown in Figure 3.4, with five distinct choices: pure, pull, push, purchase and purge, each appropriate for different retailers, dependent on their particular marketing mix and competitive position. The definition of each loyalty strategy is as follows:

- A *pure* loyalty strategy is based on the existing or pure relationship between the retailer and its customers, and focuses on the retailer's product and service offer.
- A *push* loyalty strategy aims to push customers towards the retailer, and focuses on the retail location and channel.
- A *pull* loyalty strategy uses retailer promotion to pull the customer to the retailer or particular products.
- A *purchase* loyalty strategy concentrates on increasing the number and value of purchase transactions, irrespective of which particular retailer benefits.

- A *purge* loyalty strategy is used where a retailer attempts to purge all unnecessary cost and aims at providing all customers with the lowest price possible.

In general, it is observed that successful digital retailers follow a purge loyalty strategy, ubiquitous retailers follow a push and pull loyalty strategy, and focal retailers pursue a purchase strategy. These findings help put forward the appropriate loyalty strategy for any business attempting to integrate e-retail and, when used within the complete retailer-customer relationship model, go some way towards dealing with the complexity suggested by the e-commerce digitization view, and finding the appropriate choice among the ten strategic integration options.

Purveyor: Retailer offer	Purchaser: Customer perceived choice — Signal Retailer	Many Retailers
Focused offer	Pure	Push
Extended offer	Puff	Purchase
Price-led offer	Purge	

Fig. The Purchaser-Purveyor Loyalty Matrix

IMPLEMENTATION: CHANGE MANAGEMENT AND RESOURCE IMPLICATIONS

Even for businesses that develop the right e-retailing strategy with the appropriate mix of e-retail and traditional retail, and mindful of the organization's skill base, it is necessary to recognize that moving from theory to practice will have an impact across the organization, affecting resources and business processes. A fundamental re-evaluation of company strategy may lead to a radical overhaul of existing ways of doing business, with company structure and culture becoming much more customer-focused. Moving organizations towards such ways of working will have widespread consequences.

Resistance at all company levels may need to be overcome, with a corresponding need to build commitment and consensus around e-retailing strategies. However, in doing this, as noted earlier, companies must also deal with a paradox. As the dot.com crash showed, there are many strengths in bricks and mortar companies, particularly their customer base and brand profile, and organizational capabilities in areas such as supply chain management. Evolving a new business model must therefore avoid throwing out the 'best of the old'. Only by recognizing and rising to these challenges and dilemmas, and devoting sufficient time, resources and expertise to them, will companies make a success of their e-retailing ventures. In other words, they have to be prepared to reorganize and restructure themselves continuously, and therefore understanding how to manage change effectively becomes essential. As Stroud (1998) notes:The benefits that the Internet is expected to deliver will not be realised unless a company adapts its organisational structure and methods to meet the radical new ways of working that this new technology makes possible.

What is surprising is the reluctance of many companies to do this. In a piece of research conducted by Jupiter Communications (2001), only 24 per cent of US CEOs regarded their Web initiatives as an integrated part of their core business. The US experience is that companies generally fall into two broad camps with their e-initiatives: being 'self-reinventing' in order to maintain market leadership, or 'change avoiding' by persevering with existing ways of doing business. The Jupiter study suggests that self-reinventors are in the minority.

The central role played by technology in e-retailing will add a layer of technical complexity to what may already be a quite dynamic situation. However, the redesign of business processes and structures is far from a simple 'technical' matter, and involves significant social redesign. Such changes are likely to be politically controversial and therefore will always be open to disturbances and threats. The interests of a wide range of stakeholders may be threatened, there may be a high degree of uncertainty regarding what to do and how to do it, objectives may be less clear than usual, and resource requirements will be less well known. In addition, it may be more difficult to create shared perceptions of goals and build and maintain necessary commitment. So, in practical terms, management will need to become change agents, spending considerable time ensuring effective communication to encourage flexibility, address perceptions and generate involvement. To illustrate the problems that can ensue in such a situation, Badham *et al.* (1997) describe Merrill Lynch's move into online trading:

At the core of the change process was conflict at many levels within Merrill Lynch. There was conflict between the defenders of the brokers and their commissions and proponents of online investing. There was conflict between Merrill brokers who were concerned about losing customers to online brokers and Merrill brokers who were concerned about losing commissions. There was even conflict among Merrill executives between those who favoured setting up a separate online unit to compete with the brokers and those who favoured keeping the online unit under the same executive. There are of course technical challenges involved in moving from a physical or bricks and mortar organization to bricks and clicks. Here, a more 'virtual' form of organization may result, mixing traditional ways of working with electronic communications. One of the key problems for existing companies here is to integrate front and back end systems while mindful that their 'legacy infrastructure' might well still be essential to other aspects of the business. While start-up companies can leapfrog these problems, established ones face some difficult challenges. This was one of the reasons why it was originally speculated that Internet pureplays would become the dominant business model in the B2C e-commerce market place. This means that, when customers interact via the Web, placing orders and purchasing goods, the stock control and financial systems need to 'speak the same language' and carry out their part of the transactions. The problem is that many such back end systems are unlikely to be based on open Internet protocols and may even have been custom-built. Nonetheless, these systems are usually critical to a company's business, and include such details as bank account data and stock rotation information.

IT managers are loath to replace them with something new and untested. They may not even fully understand how their legacies work any longer. The people who built the systems may well have left the company, leaving present IT experts reluctant to tinker. Replacing such systems also takes time and requires particular IT skills and staff training - factors which may impede the developments that are critical to speedy innovation. There is one general criticism of the change management literature: that it tends to place considerable emphasis on strategies for overcoming different barriers to change, assuming that the 'traditional' companies in question have destructive, dogmatic cultures with bureaucratic tendencies. This insinuates that, at a basic level, such companies are almost by definition 'change-phobic'.

Many early writers made the rather enthusiastic presumption that Internet retailing was so revolutionary, traditional retailers would become obsolete. Traditional companies were criticized for being slow to engage and for adopting cautious 'toe in the water' strategies.

For example, Windham (2000) criticized traditional retailers for not finding 'the vision, commitment and guts to proceed', and interprets caution as 'e-denial'. In fact, it now seems that those companies that exercised a careful Web integration strategy have been the ones with the most durable strategies. They have in fact not resisted change, but instead embraced it in an incremental way by creating successful and sustainable online channels as part of holistic multi-channel strategies.

CASE STUDY 3.1: BOOTS (WWW.BOOTS.COM)

The case concerns the well-known bricks (and now also clicks) group, Boots the Chemist. Boots opened its first store in Nottingham in 1849, selling herbal remedies. Developing new products such as Ibuprofen (1969) and Nurofen (1983) has helped Boots become a leader in the pharmaceutical business. Boots is now in almost every high street, and is one of the largest pharmaceutical chains, selling medicines, toiletries, cosmetics, fragrances and photographic equipment. The launch of the Advantage loyalty card in 1997 helped Boots gain an insight into its customers and experience in data mining. The bricks stores, though, are approaching maturity in the retail life cycle and profits have been below expectations.

Boots has experimented with T-commerce, launching a 'Wellbeing' interactive digital TV channel in March 2001. However, due to the slow uptake, and the lack of consumer support, the service closed in December 2001. Boots still remains committed to the idea and intends to relaunch when the market is ready.

The Boots e-retailing site was launched in 2001. It is packed full of health and nutrition information content and is better stocked than most high street Boots, with 10,000 products available. Providing useful information can act strongly to drive e-shopping traffic. In its first year it turned over £4.3 million in sales. Customers can track their order progress online and there is currently no charge for deliveries (except for Saturday).

Returns can be posted back free. The site is renowned for customer satisfaction. According to a recent survey, 95 per cent of customers will shop at the site again. It is the only UK Web site authorized to sell Chanel and one of only two selling Esteé Lauder and Clinique. Boots has about one million e-shoppers, one of the largest customer bases of any UK e-retailer.

Promotion is largely via a targeted e-mail CRM/data mining system allowing personalization and offers relevant to individual consumers. Boots' experience with the loyalty card database is invaluable here. In addition, Boots uses 'link popularity engineering' to direct traffic to the site. The idea is to make the site a 'one stop shop' for health and well-being information. This makes the site popular with users and attracts links from other sites - characteristics that search engines use in determining rankings. The result is that if a surfer types 'well-being' into one of the major search engines (*e.g.* Google or Ask Jeeves) the first 'hits' will all be Boots - a mixture of sponsored and non-sponsored links.

The site was runner up for the 'E-business Web site of the Year' at the Computing magazine's Awards in 2001 and won the 'Best Website' award at the 2002 Santé Health and Beauty awards. *Sources*: Various, including Sunday Times (UK) Doors 'Webwatch' site test, Boots plc annual report and www.boots.com This case study was kindly contributed by Wayne Godfrey

CASE STUDY 3.2: TESCO (WWW.TESCO.COM)

Tesco is one of the UK's largest e-retailers and the world's biggest e-grocer, overturning the myth that shoppers will not buy fresh products because of the 'look and feel' factor. Indeed, the opposite is the case - of the top ten selling lines, seven are fresh, with skinless chicken breasts at number one.

Tesco has been active in telesales (at pilot locations) since 1995. The initial telesales pilot, at Ealing, West London, was developed from the home delivery service to less mobile consumers, subcontracted from the Local Authority. This low-tech operation was developed in 1996 into the pilot for e-retailing (rolled out nationally in 1999) - built on the proven delivery system and hand-picking from the shelves of the grocery stores. Tesco still uses this tried and reliable system for groceries in preference to a heavy investment in warehouse picking centres, although many non-food items such as books, CDs and DVD movies are now handled from a non-store facility. While Tesco's larger stores may carry only the top 50 CDs, Tesco.com claims to offer every CD currently available in the UK. Not only leading in grocery e-retailing, Tesco is rapidly gaining share in electricals, entertainment and clothing.

Despite the low-key approach, Tesco has invested £45 million in its e-retailing operation, including £15 million for the transaction system based on the ShoppingMagic proprietary system from Unipower. Customers can purchase any of the 40,000+ product lines for next-day delivery (for orders placed by 4.00 p.m.) for UK customers within delivery distance of a store (encompassing 97 per cent of the UK population). A limited product range is available for delivery worldwide. As an alternative to shoppers composing their shopping list online, Tesco sends them a monthly CD-ROM and information on special offers by mail.

Using the CD-ROM can speed up and simplify the ordering process, making it possible to save shopping lists and minimizing the effort in placing future orders. This is a significant 'convenience' benefit, since 80 per cent of grocery shopping is replenishment. Tesco follows the maxim 'make it easy for your customers to buy', accepting orders on the Web, CD-ROM, fax and telephone, and offering home delivery or collection and, of course, in-store shopping. WAP m-shopping was launched in 2001 followed by PDA in 2002. TV Internet had to close with the demise of ITV Digital, but at the time of writing is planned to return via BT Digital. In addition to groceries, consumers can buy books, music, clothes, PCs, and Internet and mobile phone services.

There are regular paper mailings and special offers, including non-food promotions such as 'The top 50 books 10 per cent cheaper than Amazon'. At £10 per customer, the cost of acquisition is low, compared to £50 to £100 for companies such as Amazon. Addressing the need for more social interaction, particularly for female shoppers, the Tesco site hosts the UK version of iVillage, providing information, chat rooms, travel, health and nutrition advice.

Tesco make use of the ready-digitized sales data for data mining and segmented offers. Targeted offers (for example via e-mail or SMS) are not perceived as spam by Tesco customers if they add value. HTML e-mails to customers achieve 10-30 per cent response rates. In one example, Tesco achieved a 28 per cent click-through to Unilever for a Dove promotion from 35,000 premium shampoo users. Tesco can use the lifestyle data from promotion responses to help plan other marketing initiatives. Running such promotions for manufacturers such as Unilever provides a valuable extra revenue stream for Tesco. In addition, there are affiliate deals with major portals based on cost-per-click or cost-per-sale.

Tesco's e-retailing joint ventures in Ireland, Korea (the country with the world's highest Internet penetration) and, particularly, the US allow the costs of development to be spread. New international markets can be entered at a fraction of the cost of starting from scratch.

Tesco has over one million registered customers, and an e-turnover of over £450 million. This success might well be attributed to Tesco's single-minded determination to provide customer satisfaction, using an easy-entry, cost-effective e-retailing system. Tesco's e-retailing operation has been in profit since 2001, with profit reaching almost £2 million by 2002. Despite the fast growth in e-retailing, e-shoppers spend over 25 per cent more than Tesco's bricks shoppers, which Tesco believes is not cannibalizing in-store sales. Indeed, bricks sales have continued to increase in real terms since the launch of the e-retailing operation.

Sources: Various, Fernie and McKinnon (2003) and www.tesco.com This case study was kindly contributed by Omar Chaudhry

E-SERVICE METRICS: A MANAGEMENT TOOL

Our research in the previous section revealed that interactivity was overwhelmingly important for achieving a perception of high e-service. This finding is even stronger when we add frequently asked questions (FAQs) to its role because this is a form of interactivity. In a sense the emphasis on interactivity is akin to the importance of personal service in the conventional literature. Interestingly, personal service was found to be the most important type of customer service in conventional retailing. Interactivity in the e-context includes two-way communication, the ability of the e-retailer to communicate to the user and the ability of the user to communicate with the e-retailer, responsiveness in answering questions (including the special case of FAQ) and personalization of the process.

Even without measurement, interactivity is clearly a good candidate as a capstone element in a powerful e-service programme. Similarly, we recommend that an e-retailer should audit its interactivity every year or so, along the lines suggested in the previous section (using, say, a critical incident analysis). If interactivity is found to be too low or not as high as desired, then steps can be undertaken to increase it, through, for example, increased customization or other means.

A second key finding of our research study is that interactivity needs to be supported by special offers, information, variety of items for sale and ease of use, as part of an integrated approach to e-service. An e-service audit of an e-retail site should incorporate all components of e-service.

A third key finding of our research is also very important for the practice of good e-service. We have shown that it is not sufficient to create and manage *positive e-service experiences*. Equally, the firm's e-commerce strategy needs to be able to handle *negative critical incidents*. The first point is that *even high-service sites* experience periodic problems in e-service. Show that high-service sites, while generally having a very high (72 per cent) positive incidence of interactivity, nonetheless had a 6 per cent (that is, non-zero) incidence of negative interactivity. The same pattern occurs in the areas of product variety and delivery. Firms need to take steps to continuously improve (that is, lower) the rate of negative incidents. Ideally, more interactivity may need to be built in if all other aspects of interactivity fail - this is the ultimate approach to service-failure recovery. Perhaps it is a toll-free phone service that is needed as a service in the last resort? A fourth key finding of our research that needs to be carefully considered by websites is that the solution for sites attempting to increase their e-service capability is not simply to *add* more information, an FAQ service or similar facility. Such actions are a necessary, though insufficient condition to becoming a high-service site. Take information, for example. Information incidents, both positive and negative, were important in determining membership of the e-retailer in a high-service or low-service category and the overall level of e-service of the site. Yet there was only a slight difference (and one that was *not* statistically significant) in the quantity of information across high-service and low-service sites. This suggests that the problem for some sites is not the *quantity* of information, but rather the *quality* and *relevance* of information. Thus the high rate (20 per cent) of negative incidents about information on the low-service sites may be due to overemphasis on the wrong information, that is, the wrong details, rather than the lack of information in general.

In summary, we suggest that e-retailers should regularly monitor or audit all of their e-service, at least as frequently as annually. The critical incident approach is a simple way of doing this and the method is robust because it captures both positive and negative incidents in e-service. Notwithstanding the merit of this approach, there are alternative ways of evaluating e-service and we turn to one of those in the next section.

E-RETAIL SERVICE QUALITY: AN ALTERNATIVE PERFORMANCE METRIC

Retail service quality entails the application of service quality as both a concept and measure to retailing. The landmark study in this respect is Dabholkar *et al*. (1996). One advantage of using a measure of (retail) service quality is that it represents a composite measure, pulling together a number of components of service, such as personal service, store design and problem-solving. So, instead of having to say that six or seven or whatever components of service are performing at the individual service level, we can combine our assessment into a composite service quality measure.More recently, researchers have extended their scope of retail service quality from conventional retailing to also include Internet or e-retailing. These studies include Zeithaml *et al.* (2000), Francis and White (2002a; 2002b), Janda *et al.* (2002) and Wolfinbarger and Gilly (2002). Each study uses slightly different dimensions (or items under each heading) of e-retail service quality, but generally the dimensions include:

- Web site design
- Security
- Ordering system
- Delivery system
- Communication.

The five dimensions of e-retail service quality provide an umbrella approach for e-retailers wishing to use an alternative measure of e-service performance. We offer no view as to whether this approach or the critical incident approach is better. Indeed, e-retailers could quite easily use both sets of metrics to evaluate their e-service, as they complement each other.At the time of going to press a major new article on e-retail quality has appeared, namely Wolfinbarger and Gilly (2003). This article seems to be the most comprehensive and methodical of all of the articles in this field and so we should highlight its findings. Four components of e-retail quality were identified, namely:

- Web site design (navigation, order processing, personalization);
- Fulfilment/reliability (receipt of correct goods, delivery on time);
- Privacy/security (security of credit card payments and privacy of shared information);
- Customer service (responsive to customer inquiries).

In terms of the predictive power of these four components, two of them (Web site design and fulfilment) were found to be the most important in contributing to overall quality, satisfaction and return purchases.

ADDITIONAL GUIDANCE ON PRACTICAL E-SERVICE PROVISION

A number of practical tools that could help the improved delivery of e-service for e-retailers. First, key concepts, such as interactivity and delivery, have been highlighted as having special importance. Second, the idea of e-service metrics is another practical tool ready for actual use by e-retailers. In addition to these ideas and tools, the reader might wish to consult a number of 'how to' books, including Sterne (1996), Cusack (1998) and Zemke and Connellan (2001).

We have analysed the total number of websites in the sample as well as sub-samples of *high-service* and *low-service* websites. We have also contrasted *positive* critical incidents from *negative* critical incidents. Perhaps an unexpected result, we found that the main e-service elements that drive positive e-service are *not* the same as the elements that cause negative critical incidents in e-service. Interactivity in particular, strongly supported by special offers and information about the product and firm, was the key component of positive e-service. In contrast, negative e-service experiences were most often associated with a lack of variety of items for sale and poor delivery arrangements.

We have suggested that interactivity could be the key capstone element for e-retailers trying to build a powerful e-service programme, with support from information, ease of use, variety and special offers. There is also a need to manage *service-failure recovery*, that is, the myriad of negative critical incidents. This may lead to the ultimate form of interactivity - namely an interactive service that handles the collective failure in all the other interactive mechanisms.

Two different taxonomies or classifications were used to explore the nature of e-services. We also argued that self-service is not a myth for e-services and should not be taken for granted. It needs to be properly designed to genuinely help the e-customer. Further, evaluating e-service performance is important for e-retailers, if they are to fully understand what attributes are needed by customers. Two different ways of measuring e-service performance were given, namely a critical incident approach and an e-retail service quality approach.

CASE STUDY : LEGAL SERVICES: BELL LEGAL GROUP (WWW.BELLLEGAL.COM.AU)

This is a legal services site of the Bell Legal Group on the Gold Coast, Australia, that offers a full range of legal services from corporate to individual issues. The site is typical of a service provider with a professional appearance and an abundance of information on the services that they provide. This site differs from many others due to the music and voice commentary on the home page.

The menu offers: our people, a group that lists employees' qualifications and experience with portrait photographs. It has the usual menu selection for contacts and queries with linked pages to a large range of predominantly Government websites related to legal matters ranging from privacy codes to taxation issues. The notion of providing an extra service through linkages to established sites is a fairly easy and cost-effective way of adding value to customers. Essentially it is a public service that is an option available to any e-commerce firm.

MOTORING ORGANIZATION: RAC (WWW.RAC.CO.UK)

This is a UK motoring organization that offers a range of services from breakdown to insurance coverage. The site is representative of a large organization that offers a multitude of services and requires careful navigation to locate particular information. This is made even more difficult with the amount of linked advertising and special deals scattered over the pages. If followed carefully the menu items on each page are self-explanatory and will lead to the desired location. The site is typical of similar motoring organizations worldwide that offer online services and information on their core and related products. While some of the site is intended to gain customers, there are some parts could be seen as public service, such as traffic conditions.The home page includes connection to localities, insurance for vehicles, property and holidays, motoring information for breakdown, technical reports and car care, holiday information, accommodation deals, vehicle hire, ship/airline bookings and tours. It also covers a range of finance options for loans and insurances as well as legal matters. The site is interesting enough, with standout colours, and is complemented with related photographs, coupled with an abundance of graphic deals.

MANAGEMENT OF DOMAIN NAMES

No serious commercial enterprise is without a domain name. Indeed the number of domain names that have been registered during the past five years could be graphically represented by an exponential curve. By 1995 approximately 100,000 domain names had been registered. At the beginning of 2000 this number had increased to 6 million. At the time of writing the number of domain names registered stood at more than 40 million.

Commonly there are no pre-conditions for registering a domain name and no restriction on the number of domain names that can be registered. In the case of start-ups or new ventures for existing businesses, it is important to register the chosen domain name as soon as possible, and certainly before any publicity about the business is released to the public.

There have been several cases in the past few years where a company has sent out a press release concerning a new business venture, including the proposed business name without having secured the domain name. The same day a member of the public who has seen the publicity surrounding the venture has registered the proposed business name as a domain name. Mediation with Nominet or dispute resolution with ICANN can produce a satisfactory resolution but will inevitably be expensive and time-consuming.

E-commerce businesses are advised to register all ccTLD variations of the domain name that relate to those countries where the client expects to do business as well as all gTLD's that are available. This prevents someone from registering the same SLD as the business, albeit with a different TLD.Businesses should also register all variations of the name, for example using hyphens where the SLD consists of more than one word or even common misspellings. This prevents anyone from taking unfair advantage of the goodwill in the business by engaging in the activity known as cybersquatting. An appropriate and sensible commercial strategy for domain name registrations, coupled with relevant trade mark registrations, can reduce the risks posed by cybersquatters. It should also be remembered that a domain name is not a property right as such. Rather, a domain name registration allows the registrant the exclusive use of that domain name for the period of registration. Registration periods are commonly either one or two years. It is vital that renewal is made otherwise use of the domain name will be lost.

Trade Marks and Branding

For the protection of a business or its product or service, the registration of a trade mark or service mark should be considered. An infringement action can then be brought against anyone using the same or similar mark in respect of a similar business in the jurisdiction of registration.

Where brand protection is not available by use of a registered trade mark (due to, for example, the business being unable to comply with the strict requirements of the registration process) some protection may be available from that branch of the law known as 'passing off'. This section considers the law of trade marks and passing off specifically in the context of protection of domain names.

Trade Marks

The fundamental difference between a trade mark and a domain name is that there can be several identical trade marks registered in different parts of the world, or even in the same jurisdiction, by different people. Each identical trade mark can relate to a different type of goods without any possibility of the trade mark use constituting an infringement.

By contrast there can only ever be one of each domain name, as such names are necessarily unique. Whilst use of an identical domain name to one registered by an e-business is therefore impossible, registration and use of a similar domain name by a third party is not unlikely. For example, although we may register the domain name, pwcarey.com, this does not stop someone else registering the domain name p-w-carey.com or pcarey.com.

In other words, the domain name registration system offers no protection against the registration of similar names. An action for trade mark infringement on the other hand can be brought against not only those persons who use an identical mark in relation to similar goods or services, but also against those who use a similar mark in relation to similar goods or services. E-businesses should therefore aim to support the protection of their brands by registering a trade mark for their domain names in each of their principal trading territories. Trade mark registrations can be undertaken by law firms or trade mark agents.

It is possible that use of a domain name by one person may constitute the infringement of a registered trade mark of another. The claimant must show, under s10 TMA 1994, that there has been use of an identical mark in relation to identical goods/services or use of a similar mark in relation to identical/similar goods/services where there is likelihood of confusion.

PASSING OFF

Where goodwill in a business is being used by another for their own benefit but that other is not using an identical or similar registered trade mark, the business may be able to bring an action for 'passing-off'. An action by one business against another or against an individual in the tort of passing off usually requires a misrepresentation in the course of trade, which leads to financial loss. An exception to the rule that to succeed in a passing off action the claimant must show that the defendant was using the same or similar mark in the course of trade was established in the context of domain names in the case of *BT and Others v. One in a Million Ltd* (1999) FSR.

In the case, brought by BT, Virgin, Sainsburys and others, the court held that the 'mere creation of an instrument of fraud' could amount to passing off. One in a Million Ltd was forced to give up its interest in certain domain names that it had registered such as sainsbury.com, virgin.com and bt.org. It had registered these domains in the hope of selling them to the relevant companies for a profit.

Some would argue that the companies should have had the foresight to resister these domain names themselves and should not expect the law to rescue them from their lack of commercial awareness. Nevertheless the court showed a willingness to adapt the common law to the changing commercial environment.

The laws of both trade mark infringement and passing off are difficult to prove and in any event litigation takes a good deal of time and money. For these reasons businesses that have found that others have registered domain names that they feel should in fact belong to themselves have chosen to engage in dispute resolution as an alternative to a court action.

CYBER SQUATTING AND DISPUTE RESOLUTION

Cyber squatting is the activity that involves the bad faith registration of trade marks as domain names. Where an e-business finds itself to be the victim of a cyber squatter there are a number of potential courses of action. In appropriate circumstances the cyber squatter can be sued in a court of law for infringement of a registered trade mark or in the tort of passing off. An alternative, and often cheaper and faster procedure is to enter into domain name dispute resolution.

Dispute resolution is a useful alternative to litigation for those cases where a claimant feels that they should be entitled to use a domain name that has been registered by someone else. Such a situation commonly arises under the existing procedure for domain name registrations, which is essentially a 'first-come-first-served'system. In most cases anyone can purchase the exclusive right to use a domain name, provided that no one has registered it beforehand. The *One in a Million Case* showed that it is possible to obtain a court order for the transfer of a domain name, but litigation is inevitably costly and time consuming. The Internet Corporation for Assigned Names and Numbers (ICANN) set up a dispute resolution system for the top-level generic domain names (.com,.net and.org) in December 1999.That system, known as the Uniform Dispute Resolution Policy (UDRP), has proved very popular and successful.

It is administered by four bodies (the best known of which is the World Intellectual Property Organisation) and frequently results in a domain name being transferred to the claimant. This section considers the dispute resolution procedures of ICANN and Nominet (which administers all.uk domain names).

ICANN DISPUTE RESOLUTION PROCEDURE

The important thing to bear in mind is that domain names are not property as such. The registrant's rights to use a domain name derives from the contract that it enters into with the registration authority. As far as gTLD's are concerned, the registration authority is ICANN (Internet Corporation for Assigned Names and Numbers). ICANN set up a Uniform Dispute Resolution Policy (UDRP), which became operational on 1 December 1999. The UDRP applies only to those domains administered by ICANN *i.e.* the three gTLD's.com,.net and.org. ICANN has subcontracted out the job of hearing and adjudicating on the disputes to four bodies (listed in Appendix five), the best known of which is the World Intellectual Property Organisation (WIPO). The UDRP relates only to an 'abusive registration'. This means that applicants will only be successful where they are able to show that:

- The disputed domain name is identical or confusingly similar to a trade mark or service mark in which the applicant has rights
- The registrant has no rights or legitimate interests in the domain name
- The domain name has been registered and is being used in bad faith.

Unfortunately the UDRP does not provide any guidance on how 'confusing similarity' is to be assessed. A 'legitimate interest' can be demonstrated by the registrant by showing some use or preparatory steps to use the domain name dating from prior to any notice by the applicant; evidence that the registrant is commonly known by the domain name or evidence that the registrant has engaged in a legitimate non-commercial use of the domain name.

'Bad faith', the most important element of the UDRP, can be shown where the registrant's main purpose in registering the domain name was to sell it to the applicant; where it was designed to prevent the applicant using its trade mark as a domain name or where there was an intention to attract users to the registrant's Web site by creating a likelihood of confusion with the applicant's mark. It should be noted that bad faith can be shown not only by a demand for money, but also by a request for services. In a case involving the domain name uwyoming.com the respondent wanted free tuition for his daughter at the

University of Wyoming, and in the gearmagazine.com case the respondent demanded the contract to build the complainant's Web site. In both cases the complainants were successful in getting the domain names transferred to themselves. If the applicant is successful at the arbitration hearing (which is by written submission, no live witnesses) then ICANN will immediately transfer the domain name to the applicant. By way of example, Julia Roberts was able to obtain reregistration of the domain name juliaroberts.com in her own name by using the UDRP.

By contrast Bruce Springsteen failed in a similar application for brucespringsteen.com, largely because the registrant was able to show legitimate use (for a Bruce Springsteen fan club Web site).

DISPUTE RESOLUTION FOR.UK DOMAIN NAMES

Nominet, the UK domain name registry, has announced its intention to radically update its dispute resolution procedure for applications by claimants against cybersquatters.

The principal criticism of the Nominet system to date has been that it does not allow transfers of the disputed domain name into the name of the claimant. Under the new system, to operate from Autumn 2001, Nominet will be able to remove the existing name from the register and replace it with that of the claimant.

The new system proposed by Nominet for all.uk domains is modelled on the UDRP but has some interesting differences.

At present the dispute resolution system available from Nominet, the second largest of the country code specific domain name registries, is a mediation service. It is free of charge and is undertaken by written submissions by the parties. Of the 1,200 mediations dealt with by Nominet since it began the service in 1997, approximately one third have been successfully resolved. Of the two thirds of claims that are not amicably resolved by the parties, the remaining alternative is litigation. Nominet will currently withdraw or suspend a domain name (but not transfer it) in the following circumstances:

- If the name is administered in a way that is likely to endanger the operation of the domain name system.
- If the basis on which the domain name was registered has changed.
- If Nominet finds that the name is being used in a manner likely to cause confusion to Internet users.
- Where Nominet UK has been informed that legal action has been commenced regarding use of the name.
- Where Nominet UK is of the opinion that one of the above is likely to occur.

The need for a new dispute resolution system arises out of increased public awareness in the activity known as 'cybersquatting' and the desire for a quick and effective procedure for the transfer of a.uk domain name which has been registered by a third party. There is also, according to Nominet, a perception that cybersquatting threatens the principles of a first-come-first-served registration system, and that self-regulation is preferable to an enforced solution.Under the proposals Nominet will continue to offer a mediation service for disputed domain names but the mediation will 'time-out' if it has been unsuccessful after ten working days.

The application will then be automatically referred to an independent expert who will be appointed in a 'cab-rank' fashion from a list held by Nominet (under the UDRP applicants can choose particular experts — there may be up to three experts deciding each case).

A fee — likely to be in the region of £500 to £1,000 — will be payable to Nominet for use of the service and all decisions of the experts will be published.In order to succeed in its application for domain name transfer, a claimant will be expected to show that the registration is 'abusive'.There is to be a two-stage test for abusive registrations. The claimant must show that:

- They have rights in respect of a name or mark which is identical or similar to a domain name.
- The registrant has and/or is using the domain name in bad faith.

This test is similar to that under the UDRP, except under the latter, the claimant must additionally show that the registrant has no rights or legitimate interest in the domain name. Under the UDRP where the mark of the claimant is not identical to the domain name, the claimant must show that it is 'confusingly similar', as opposed to merely 'similar', to the domain name. The central requirement for both the UDRP and the Nominet proposal is that the domain name be registered (or used) in bad faith. However, although the burden of proof under both schemes is on the claimant, the standard of proof is different. Under the Nominet proposal, the claimant will be expected to prove, *beyond a reasonable doubt*, the bad faith of the registrant.

Bad faith is commonly shown by a clear motive to siphon business goodwill away from the claimant or an attempt by the registrant to sell the domain name to the claimant at a grossly inflated price. It is unclear how the higher standard of proof will affect claims for the transfer of.uk domains.

FUTURE DEVELOPMENTS IN E-BUSINESS TECHNOLOGY

THE INTERNET

Just as the internal combustion engine (the motor car) and jet engine (aeroplane) have radically changed our lives, the Internet is beginning to do the same. In the short time of its existence the Internet has greatly affected business and society. The Internet's evolution and future development are set to continue. The TCP/IP protocol is evolving with the development of IPv6, the next generation of the Internet protocol. The improvements in IPv6 are scalability, security and support for real-time media quality. Companies such as Ciena Corporation are working on improving bandwidth. They have a product called Wave Division Multiplexing (WDM) that moves data at the speed of 100 billion bits per second (100,000,000,000 b.p.s.). This contrasts with the standard modem's 36,600 b.p.s.

THE WORLD WIDE WEB

The Web's HTTP protocol is evolving to encompass better performance and flexible interactions between clients and servers. Companies compete in complex and increasingly competitive markets. They do so by following, for example, competitive strategies of product differentiation or cost reduction. Similarly, *relationships* are becoming increasingly important in business models. Current developments in Web technology are best placed to enable companies to exploit their differences and build personal relationships with customers, suppliers or business partners. For example, the eXtensible Mark-up Language, the Semantic Web and other Internet developments are leading the way to providing tailoring capability in e-Business technology.

Extensible mark-up Language

The extensible mark-up language (XML) is gaining popularity over HTML with companies. XML offers companies the ability to define tags that uniquely describe their products, services or customer service culture. Companies can design XML tags to display price or product or service descriptions that cannot be done in HTML. In short, XML allows a company to tailor the feel and look of its Web site and order forms to its needs.

The Semantic Web

Semantic Web is the name given to developments in Web technology by the World Wide Web Consortium (W3C), headed by Tim Berners-Lee, who invented the Web. The Semantic Web enables communication of contextual data and information. Information makes sense to humans only when it is used in context. The Semantic Web enables such context to be captured in Web applications. The primary contribution of the Internet, the Web and associated technologies is to enable collaboration and sharing of information and knowledge among people. The types of collaboration are numerous, ranging from intra-organizational to inter-organizational and across the boundary of the organization with the customer. Future technology development will focus on this collaborative aspect of e-Commerce and will lead to radically different organizational structures and patterns of interaction among and between businesses and their customers.

6

Electronic Marketing Management

DISADVANTAGES AND ADVANTAGES OF E-SHOPPING FOR CONSUMERS

DISADVANTAGES

Consumers have been slow to embrace e-shopping. Back in 1996, the UK's largest e-consultancy, Cap Gemini, carried out an employee survey. The main disadvantages for shoppers, in ranked order were: 'Availability', 'Can't be in to receive delivery', 'Premium charged for delivery' and 'Can't see or feel the merchandise'. With years' more experience, many e-retailers still do not have satisfactory answers to these problems. Typical shopper comments have included: 'They left it in the garden and didn't tell me', 'It's a 24-hour shopping service but only a 6-hour delivery service' and 'Returning unwanted products is when it all goes low-tech' consumer surveys from Vincent *et al.*, 2000).

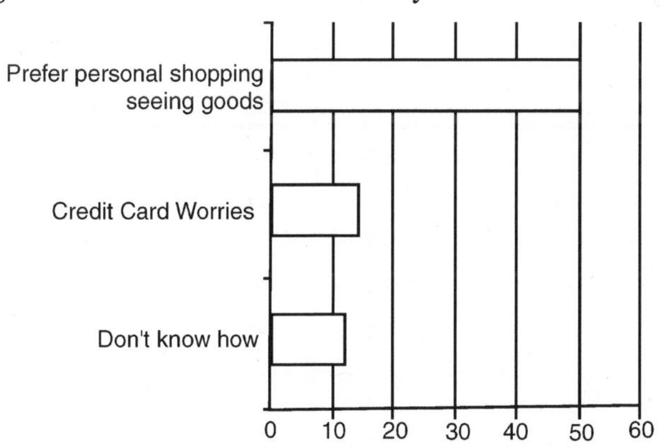

Fig. Why Internet-connected Consumers do not E-shop

Another survey reported, in ranked order, reasons why Internet-connected shoppers do not e-shop: 'Prefer personal shopping, seeing goods', 'Credit card worries' and 'Don't know how'. In 2001, Verdict confirmed security fears as the number one barrier to more consumers shopping online. Our own surveys (*e.g.* Dennis *et al.*, 2002a - discussed more fully in the following section) have indicated that sixth-form (year 12) pupils are avid e-shoppers using their parents' credit cards. This is an obvious security worry for parents, but also a nuisance for young people, restricting their e-shopping activities. Credit cards are only offered to those of 18 years of age and above, although alternative 'plastic cash' is available for children, with transactions authorized (in the example of the Solo card - www.solocard.co.uk) only up to what is in the bank account.

The disadvantage is that so far these cards are accepted by only a tiny fraction of (www.llbean.com) could claim to be the pioneer of mail order, selling goods to rural farmers since way back in the mid-1800s. Today the company has put their reputation for customer responsiveness, helpfulness, cheerfulness and reliability to use in becoming world leader in e-retailing outdoor equipment and clothing, with an efficient, award-winning site.

DISADVANTAGES OF E-SHOPPING FOR CONSUMERS

- Credit card and security worries
- Lack of personal and social interaction
- Can't see or feel the merchandise
- Don't know how
- Can't be in to receive delivery
- Premium charged for delivery
- Difficulties with returning goods for refund

ADVANTAGES

Counterbalancing the disadvantages and the slow responses of many UK e-retailers to addressing them, there is a number of advantages for shoppers. First, in ranked order from the Cap Gemini survey: 'Convenient/easy', 'Saves time' and 'Fits in with other activities'. Other commonly cited advantages, typified by responses to our own survey, include: 'Breadth and depth of products', 'Prices favourable' and 'Convenient' . According to Verdict, 'cost effectiveness' (rather than just low prices) is the key reason for shoppers to buy online, followed by convenience and ease of purchase.

ADVANTAGES OF E-SHOPPING FOR CONSUMERS

- Cost effective
- Convenient
- Easy
- Saves time
- Fits in with other activities
- Breadth and depth of products
- Easy search of many alternatives

- Personalization of presentation and merchandise
- Prices favourable

MOTIVES FOR E-SHOPPING

- Socializing
- Enjoyment
- Usefulness
- Ease of use
- Convenience
- Navigation
- Knowledge and ability to make a purchase
- Influence of friends and family

STUDY 1

We have already referred to this first study (initial results in Dennis *et al.*, 2002a) in the sections above. The method used was a questionnaire survey that compared shoppers' opinions of Internet shopping versus bricks shopping centres. The 308 respondents were sixth-form (year 12) and university undergraduate students - the shoppers of tomorrow. One of the main themes from the qualitative part of the study was a preference for shopping in shopping centres as more enjoyable and sociable. Shoppers who both e-shopped and shopped in shopping centres commented typically: 'Internet shopping is not a personal experience. You cannot try and see what you're buying.... Shopping [should] be very sociable.'Results from the questionnaire indicated that shoppers rated e-shopping higher than shopping centres for *favourable prices* and *convenience*. On the other hand, shopping centres were preferred for *positive image* and more emphatically for *customer service*. The results for the sixth-form (year 12) students, but the results for undergraduates were similar.

One striking figure is that 57 per cent of the sample were e-shoppers - compared with the UK average for all adults of around 15 percent. The average expenditure of the Internet shoppers on e-shopping was £22 per month, compared to £86 per month on conventional shopping. Thus, over half of the student sample shopped on the Internet, spending on average over 20 per cent of their non-food shopping by Internet.

SOCIAL MOTIVES FOR E-SHOPPING

- Social experiences outside the home
- Communications with others having a similar interest
- Peer group attraction
- Status and authority - raising the standing of the shopper in the eyes of friends and colleagues
- Virtual communities

STUDY 2

Our second study concerned motivations for e-shopping. Enjoyment, usefulness, ease of use, convenience, navigation, knowledge and ability to make a purchase, and the influence of friends and family were found to be important motivations.

Our results apply to students and are not representative of the average population. Indeed, these are people who within a few years are likely to be earning and spending significantly more than the national average. Bearing in mind this income effect and the high computer literacy of graduates, these are shoppers who will account for a disproportionately high percentage of discretionary income and comparison shopping.

Our results, and those of other researchers, show a consistent picture of the importance of the social and experiential aspects of e-shopping.

These motivators are being satisfied to good effect by the most successful e-retailers such as, for example, eBay - one of the most successful sites in terms of sales, time spent on the site and providing enjoyment.

ENJOYMENT AND E-SHOPPING

Enjoyment Motives for e-shopping

- Involvement
- Not boring
- Fun for its own sake

Enjoyment and social Features of e-retailing sites

- Chat rooms
- Bulletin boards
- Customer written stories
- Product reviews
- Suggestion boxes
- Personalization of offers

The most Popular 'Enjoyment' e-shopping sites (in Ranked order)

- Amazon (www.amazon.com)
- CD WOW (www.cd-wow.co.uk)
- eBay (auction, www.ebay.co.uk)
- Ticketmaster (show tickets, www.ticketmaster.co.uk)
- Ryanair (www.ryanair.co.uk)
- EasyJet (www.easyjet.co.uk)
- Opodo (air tickets, www.opodo.co.uk)

DIFFERENCES BETWEEN MALE AND FEMALE SHOPPING STYLES

Differences between male and female shopping styles may go back a long way. In hunter-gatherer societies, females tend to carry babies, are based around the camp and do the gathering. Males on the other hand are more likely to protect the group and do the hunting. Humans may have evolved in such a way that those best at their respective roles have been more likely to find a mate and to survive. For females, this meant excelling in gathering: finding the best food and other materials for the family. For males, it entailed being good hunters: fast, strong and decisive. Both sexes would look for those respective qualities in a potential mate, resulting in persistent traits. These differences in mate-seeking behaviour have survived into a wide cross-section of modern cultures (Buss, 1989). In Western consumer societies, gathering may have translated into comparison shopping, hunting into earning money to support the family.

Even in the US, where gender equality in the workplace is greater than most countries, differences in shopping styles can be clearly observed. The female style involves searching, comparing, weighing the advantages and disadvantages of alternatives, finding the best value and taking a pride in the shopping activity (Underhill, 1999). This pride is justified as on average women make a 10 per cent better cost saving than men do, making women the 'better shoppers' (Denison, 2003). Women see the activity of shopping as a satisfying experience in itself - *i.e.* a leisure activity. On the other hand, men see shopping as a mission and tend to go straight for what they want in a purposeful way (Underhill, 1999). For men, the focus is on 'the kill' - the actual moment of purchase when their heart rate quickens.

Evolutionary psychology has been founded on research demonstrating consistency of mating behaviour across widely different cultures. Accordingly, our own study has sought empirical evidence for an evolutionary basis to shopping sex differences by comparing shopping styles across cultures (reported in more detail in Dennis, 2004). Thirteen 'mini focus groups' wrote shopping scenarios about the national culture(s) that they were most familiar with. Fourteen cultural nationalities were represented: five judge participants represented the UK national culture, eight Continental European and 23 Asian, *i.e.* 36 judge participants in total. In general, there were some differences in shopping styles between the national cultures, but the differences between males and females were much more striking, reflecting the hunter and gatherer roles and providing support for the evolutionary hypothesis.

The stereotypes are not 100 per cent accurate but in the UK have been found to apply to 80 per cent of women and 70 per cent of men (Denison, 2003). The styles have been found to be equally valid for e-shopping (Lindquist and Kaufman-Scarborough, 2000). As with bricks shopping, the stereotype reverses when the product purchased is technical and expensive (Dholakia and Chiang, 2003).

COMMUNICATING WITH E-CONSUMER

It is one of the most quoted movie lines of all time and is very descriptive of how potential consumers have felt about venturing into e-retailing. 'Do ya' feel lucky?' or, more specifically in this context, 'do you have the courage to go online and shop after all that you have seen and heard about the dangers of e-retailing and do the benefits to you outweigh the fears?' The issue of risk as it pertains to online shopping, present the evolving profile of the e-customer, and consider both the advantages and disadvantages of an e-tailing experience.

THE PERCEIVED RISK OF E-SHOPPING

Shoppers often feel apprehension or risk when considering a purchase, especially from a new vendor. Perceived risk is a function of the uncertainty when making a purchase that may have unpleasant outcomes (Forsythe and Shi, 2003). Such risk is linked to both the type of merchandise being acquired and the channel or method of acquiring that merchandise. The reasons why non-store purchases fuel a shopper's perceived risk relate to the touch and accessibility issues, specifically:

- Not being able to touch merchandise before making a purchase.
- Barriers to returning merchandise.

WHAT DOES E-SHOPPING OFFER THE E-SHOPPER?

Shopper research by Tauber (1972, 1995) suggests the existence of personal and social consumer motives of shopping behaviour. Personal motives for shopping include role-playing, diversion, self-gratification, physical activity and sensory stimulation; social motives include meeting with others, peer group status and bargaining (Tauber, 1972, 1995; Midgley and Dowling, 1993).

For some individuals the shopping experience is enjoyable and treated as a leisure activity or for amusement (Westbrook and Black, 1985). Work by Reynolds (1974) and Berkowitz *et al.* (1979) established that, while non-store shoppers may enjoy shopping, they have a negative attitude towards the traditional store-based shopping environment because of such issues as overcrowding and a lack of parking. Later research includes work on catalogue shopping by Gehrt and Carter (1992) and cable television shopping by Eastlick and Liu (1997). Those authors found that the shopping enjoyment motivation is a positive influence for adoption of non-store shopping environments such as e-shopping through the Internet.

Whatever the shopping motivation of an individual, the result is not inevitable *shopping enjoyment* or purchase behaviour. For some individuals there is a feeling of apathy or reluctance towards shopping and this compels them to minimize the amount of time spent shopping. As part of a larger research project on multi-channel retailing, data was collected by the authors on the benefits expected from using the Web by customers of both business to consumer (B2C) and business to business (B2B) e-commerce. The variation in recipient profiles (personal versus business), the principal advantages sought from and given by the Web are principally the same. That is, the Web provides speedier ordering processes, faster usage, an effective search facility and up-to-date product-related information.

SYSTEMS MANAGEMENT

Senior managers must finally ensure that organizational processes are capable of implementing the e-commerce strategy. Information practices, human resources, performance measures, and customer management are all areas in which traditional systems may require adaptation to implement an e-commerce strategy.

- *Modernized Internal Processes: Using Information Effectively.* The cultural transformation described earlier may be enough to make e-commerce possible, but more must be done to maximize its benefits. Information practices must be adapted to promote transparency and availability.

  Changes must ensure that information flows freely throughout the company and is not hampered by artificial organizational boundaries or personal ambitions.
  - Modernized internal processes
  - Incentive-laden HR practices
  - Aligned performance measures
  - Improved customer management

In addition to information sharing, the decision-making processes of the company should be reconsidered. Cross-functional teams and remotely located teams should be assembled with greater frequency, with less emphasis on hierarchical reporting. Decision makers should also have greater self-governance and flexibility.

An important internal process is value chain management. Every company should identify ways to leverage the Internet in each part of the value chain, from procurement to distribution to delivery. In fact, failure to adopt e-commerce-specific cost savings will likely put a company at a serious competitive disadvantage. Strong supply chain management is often the basis for providing superior service. In the area of procurement, a company can reduce the cost of goods sold by obtaining products through the Internet. Distribution strategies must not only cut costs but also provide the fastest and most convenient customer service. Delivery strategies should maximize convenience and speed for customers, using both the Internet and the company's existing infrastructure to provide these benefits. The best supply-chain practices, however, depend on the type of offering.

- *Incentive-Laden HR Practices: Bringing Your People on Board.*

Compensation systems must be aligned with strategy and structure for the e-commerce venture to be a success. The CIO must be compensated as a member of the senior management team to signal the importance and respect shown for the IT function and the centrality and commitment to improved IT and e-commerce.

At lower organizational levels, compensation systems have additional consequences on alignment. By compensating e-commerce managers the same as managers in traditional commerce, the company sometimes fails to create the necessary incentives for e-commerce success. Though parallel compensation systems can often work, both market forces and the need for speed, creativity, flexibility, innovation, and extra diligence often requires additional incentives and rewards.

Differential compensation, often through stock options, can create an incentive to cannibalize from the company's traditional channels. Such practices can cause conflicts with traditional business units but are often necessary to optimize the use of each channel, especially during the formative years of the e-commerce initiative.

Typically, e-commerce compensation should be tied to the overall success of the venture rather than rewarding individual units or channels for performance. This is particularly relevant when the company is seeking full integration, because it helps ensure cooperation and seamlessness between departments.

The Internet also provides opportunities to improve the hiring process. Cisco is just one company that has found great benefits from hiring online, including lowered costs, faster filling of positions, and higher competence. Companies may also want to consider specialized HR practices for their IT departments.

- *Aligned Performance Measures: Planning for the Long-Term.* Strong measurement practices are among the cornerstones of all good systems. Performance measures for e-commerce must overcome the uncertainty and unique dynamics associated with the Internet, and they may be more frequently adjusted in response to real-time information. With these considerations, it is clear that no company should simply extend its existing performance measures to the e-commerce venture without extensive customization. Still, long-term cost differentials, balanced with a variety of financial, nonfinancial, and leading and lagging indicators, are particularly useful for successful e-commerce implementations.

Some skeptical companies have made unreasonable demands with respect to e-commerce performance. Because they misconceived e-commerce risks and rewards, they had unrealistic expectations of immediate growth and ROI that would not be demanded of any traditional long-term investment. Worse yet, they tied further investment to achievement of these goals, dooming e-commerce before it even could get off the ground. In most companies, new projects and ventures require short-term ROI, and revenue projections, many of which an e-commerce venture and its related projects may not meet. If the company decides to enter or expand e-commerce, it cannot hamstring the venture by insisting on such short-term requirements throughout.

E-commerce has also led many companies to create performance measures other than revenue, ROI, and traditional financial indicators. Some of the new, poorly designed performance measures have had a disastrous effect on strategy implementation.

For example, indiscriminate customer acquisition and attempting to maximize revenue through online advertising often have negative implications for long-term profitability. Single-purchase customers and advertising revenue independent of the company's value proposition are not sustainable strategies. Worse still are nonfinancial measures such as Web page hits and registered users, which may not even be tied to a short-term revenue stream.

In addition to measuring the performance of the business, e-commerce brings added importance to measuring the value and functionality of operations. Most e-commerce strategies will have a strong operational component, including cost savings from value chain management and cuts in labour costs for the online channel. Operational measures should be tracked by some dedicated resource and balanced between financial and nonfinancial assessments of operational performance.

Moreover, companies must create a value capture process to evaluate the success of IT projects associated with the e-commerce venture. Looking at nonfinancial performance measures, the value capture process can help convince skeptical employees of the importance of IT. Even with the value capture process, however, the full benefits of IT investment are often underestimated.

- *Improved Customer Management: Better Service and Better Data.* Companies must also reconsider the internal processes required to provide the high levels of customer service necessary in e-commerce. Online customers need access to some level of customer service at all times.

  There is a trade-off between service that entails a high level of human input and service that is automated and more cost-efficient. Finding the proper balance is a function of the company's offerings, its customer base, and customer feedback.

Customer data is a significant benefit in e-commerce, because of the vast amount that can be learned about customers during a Web site visit in contrast to an in-store visit. Many Web sites, however, have mistakenly focused only on counting hits and visits, while ignoring the more valuable information that can be gathered.

Tracking of customers' interaction with the Web site can be used to identify customers' price sensitivity and information preferences and to gauge satisfaction with the Web site design and accessibility. Gathering and using customer information is important to refine the value proposition and better allocate internal resources. Marketing strategies for the Web site can also be continually refined, using real-time information gathered from customers during their visits, a practice that Staples has used well.

Once a company has established an e-commerce strategy, organizational structure becomes a primary concern in the process of implementing that strategy. In many cases, e-commerce will not initially fit neatly into the existing organizational structure of a traditional company. E-commerce, even to the most technologically savvy company, represents a new channel for procurement, distribution, and sales. E-commerce ventures also put new demands on individuals and business units at every level of the company.

A dynamic model in which strong and supportive leadership and a well-formulated strategy provide the basis for transforming a company through e-commerce. To implement that strategy, structure and systems must be adapted for e-commerce.

Corporate strategy, structure, systems, resources and the external environment are all both inputs and constraints to the determination of e-commerce strategy, structure, and systems. Planning for an e-commerce venture should use the existing structure to determine what existing company strengths can be utilized or enhanced with e-commerce. Implicitly, even some companies that have been unsuccessful in e-commerce have grasped this fact.

But instead of treating existing structure as an input, companies have often treated it as an impediment to e-commerce, deciding to create an entirely new structure outside the organization. They believed that they could not create a new e-commerce structure inside the organization that could effectively implement the e-commerce strategy. They also did not believe they could integrate an e-commerce operation into the corporate strategy, structures, or systems. Sometimes e-commerce was split off as a separate company, sometimes it was separated as a separate functional or business unit, and in a few cases it was fully integrated.

These concerns have been at the core in the debate over structure in e-commerce. Through the late 1990s, companies feared the disruptive nature of e-commerce and were unwilling to make changes in existing company structures and systems. Many companies chose to separate e-commerce from the main company structure.

These separate-structure decisions included establishing separate business units far from company headquarters, creating separate management teams, outsourcing of the entire e-commerce platform, and selling large equity ownership of the e-commerce business to venture capitalists and other outside interests.

Many of these companies have belatedly realized the value of an integrated structure for e-commerce. High-profile failures may have served to convince uncommitted leaders, but the rationale for integration runs much deeper than an analysis of past outcomes. The application of fundamental business principles should also make the benefits of an integrated organizational structure abundantly clear.

Some previous discussions on e-commerce have divided the debate of e-commerce structure into a number of separate decision dimensions. Some have encouraged executives to consider integration or separation of equity, brand, management, and operations, while others focused on leveraging two dimensions, the financial and the operational. Although these dimensions are relevant in terms of developing an e-commerce structure, careful choices must be made.

Companies must rely on a well-developed and coordinated implementation of an e-commerce strategy, with aligned e-commerce structure and systems. It would have made little sense, for example, if Wells Fargo had integrated its management structure and operations and then followed in the footsteps of competitors, such as Bank One, by creating a new brand for e-com-merce. Likewise, Office Depot would likely have destroyed most of the benefits of its operational integration if it had sold equity in OfficeDepot.com to a venture capitalist.

In the final analysis, the most fundamental analysis is whether or not to integrate e-commerce, and this choice should direct all the subsequent financial, management, and operational decisions. The implementation of an e-commerce strategy can take different forms, and the structure and speed of implementation are part of the strategic choices. However, companies should make a commitment to long-term full integration. It is the path to that full corporate integration that is an issue. A lack of commitment to e-commerce integration can cause wavering dedication on the part of the company. While Bank of America is currently a leader in online banking, it faced early obstacles because it initially pursued an integrated e-commerce approach. It later moved on to a separate strategic business unit to foster creativity, and then had to switch back to an integrated approach.

Solutions are also described for problems faced when companies lack the internal capabily to fully implement the e-commerce strategies. Finally, the contexts in which external strategic alliances can be a desirable solution are presented.

THE ELECTRONIC INFORMATION ENVIRONMENT

The electronic information environment is an increasingly complex territory in which valuable resources can be found, but it is foreign to our usual senses. Many of the familiar problems and processes are found here but take a different form. What is our identity? What can we do here? How do we find resources? How do we traverse the environment with safety? How do we account for what we use? Do we share a common reference for time or place?The foundation of the electronic information environment is the complex of interconnected networks (including our campus networks) known as the global Internet. Accessible from desktops both within our campuses and via the Internet are an ever growing variety of databases, information servers, vendors doing business via e-commerce, computational servers, and a panoply of applications Programmes from e-mail to collaborative systems based on interactive virtual reality. E-commerce is developing rapidly in many forms and will enable reliable transaction of institutional business as well as new opportunities for individuals.

Our helpers in traveling the information environment are client software and Programmes that interact with other electronic entities by means of well-defined protocols. Just as in the analogue world, these protocols provide for successful interoperation among widely differing entities. The World Wide Web is an excellent example of this concept: the same set of complex text, graphics, audio, and video can be found and viewed on almost any modern computer regardless of what kind of computer might hold them. One significant advantage of this layered approach to complex systems is that individual pieces of the environment can be built or replaced without affecting the rest of the infrastructure. Another advantage is that end-user platforms can be tailored to different user communities and application needs. This layered approach must guide us in the development of essential information environment support services. Passports: The Authentication Service

The fundamental support service that will empower the network citizen is a universal, distributed, reliable, and robust digital credential system. Just as travelers must carry their passport when entering a different country, network citizens should carry a recognized credential when entering the electronic information environment. This credential, which can be validated by any service encountered, will ensure the authentic identity of the individual holding it.

Passports are recognized as authoritative around the world because the issuing authority is recognized by international treaty. So too should the network credential be recognized as authoritative so that network citizens can visit various sites and resources without having to resort to site-specific identification. Instead of an international treaty, there must be agreements among cooperating administrative domains to trust each other's credentials. Such agreements are based on understanding the methodology and management of the process for issuing the credentials.

The concept of a digital credential that refers to a single electronic identity is powerful because it can enable easy access to resources for the traveler.

The credential itself may not carry much information about the individual, much as the traditional passport carries not much more than a picture, an address, and a passport number. However, that passport number can be the key to determining additional attributes about the holder. In an analogous way, the digital credential should have an identifier (e-ID) that is unique to the credential holder and can be used as a key to discovering further identity information.

Relying on a single credential is fraught with the potential for abuse if it is mishandled. Since e-IDs will let travelers into many places, they must be issued only with strong assurance that individuals are who they claim to be. Once the e-ID is issued, the holder must recognize that it is an extension of his or her personal identity, protect it carefully, and never lend it to another person.

Even with reliable credentials, it will be desirable in many cases for an individual to have several e-IDs to be used for different purposes. All individuals and their organizations must consider the potential impact of a compromise of the security of any e-ID. For example, the manager of an administrative computing system might have an e-ID that carries with it special privileges. That e-ID should be used sparingly and only in conjunction with that system so that compromise of the more powerful e-ID would have consequences of a more limited scope and could be dealt with more readily. The system manager would use a less powerful e-ID when doing routine work, such as checking e-mail or writing reports.

An e-ID represents an assertion on the part of a registration authority that a known individual or entity is represented by that e-ID. If the registration authority is well designed and reliable, then services in cooperating administrative domains, or realms, can be comfortable accepting those externally registered e-IDs. Thus, in the general case, the e-ID must indicate not only the individual but also the registration authority that issued the e-ID. Ultimately this concept could be extended to commercial registration authorities so that, for example, high school students registered with a local electronic notary might be able to use their own credential's e-IDs in submitting electronic applications for admission to a college or university.

Once a campus has a robust digital credential issuance and authentication service in place with reliable operational support, all of the important campus server applications should be adapted to use this system. Parts of this process could take a long time since many applications are vendor supported and vendors are not yet responding to this broader vision. Until there is a well-established generalized authentication service, each server or application has little choice but to implement its own idiosyncratic method of authentication, and the network citizen must deal individually with each one encountered.

TICKETS AND PASSES: ATTRIBUTE AND ELIGIBILITY DATABASES

Eligibility, as distinct from authentication (which warrants the identity of a particular user), is an equally important support service in the electronic information environment. Eligibility helps define what network citizens may do or that to which they may gain access. It may be based on a person's e-ID or on any set of attributes associated with that e-ID, such as the person's affiliation with or within the institution, role, or current status. Often it is desirable to separate authentication service from eligibility and attribute functions, and it may be desirable to support them on different servers.

Eligibility does not necessarily imply authorization. The network citizen may be eligible to gain access to a resource, but at the time access is requested, the service might be oversubscribed or otherwise unavailable. For example, holding an airplane ticket may not result in authorization to board that flight. Authorization is a function of the service or application based on specific business rules. These rules might take into account a variety of factors in addition to the individual's identity, such as time of day, location of the individual, or the availability of resources.

In the historical model of mainframe computing, authentication (often referred to as access control) and authorization were often closely linked. Authorization usually was determined by loose association of attributes with the user account identifier (for example, "root" or "user, group, and other" in Unix systems) or by tables of authorized users. Since each system kept its own set of authorization data, management of these data in a consistent way across a large number of servers and client platforms was problematic, although a number of projects attempted to address aspects of this dilemma. Little thought was given to generalized information environment management mechanisms until the number of different systems and services began to grow dramatically.Today we need generalized and scalable network-based mechanisms not only for authentication but also for eligibility and attribute information. As an example of how this might be provided, suppose the network citizen requests access to a restricted database. The database server can simply query a specified attribute server, supplying the network citizen's e-ID, and receive information on the roles, affiliations, or other attributes defined for that individual. The database server then can apply a prescribed set of business rules to determine whether that particular network citizen is to be allowed access to the restricted data.

Suppose the network citizen's affiliation with the institution is "full professor and dean of the college." This might imply eligibility to view college budgetary data and approve spending plans and personnel actions, as well as to gain access to academic records and information. The same person might also be appointed to a multicampus task force on student diversity and because of that affiliation be eligible to retrieve sensitive student ethnicity and gender data. A database server that returned roles and affiliations for any given institutional e-ID would make management of this type of generalized eligibility much easier.

Such eligibility or affiliation data might be useful in transactions external to the institution as well. Appropriate individuals in any department could be given authority to submit electronic data interchange (EDI) purchase orders over the network, for example. A different set of individuals could have authority to approve payment of EDI-based invoices electronically. Workflow systems could identify individuals who need to be informed of such transactions for possible post-transaction audit.Whereas administration of an attribute service should be hierarchical and coordinated centrally, responsibility for actual eligibility data with respect to any given service should be distributed to conform with campus management structure. This is primarily an administrative rather than a technical issue. Suffice it to say that developing and managing a database service that combines all important attributes, roles, and affiliations and allows them to be managed by the office of record would provide important generality while maintaining the institution's established administrative structure.

WHO'S THERE? THE DEMOGRAPHICS DATABASE SERVICE

One particularly vexing problem is the maintenance of accurate personal data, such as home address, campus office address, or preferred e-mail address. Today there are far too many different databases wherein the same data are entered, usually by different individuals, from separate forms that must be filled out repetitively by the person who actually "owns" the information. For example, in many cases the same individual is both a student and an employee, which means that the same personal data often are maintained by entirely separate offices. Clearly it would be desirable to have a single comprehensive database of record that would hold information about all members of the campus community and in which personal data could be maintained by the relevant individual or appropriately designated staff.With strong authentication and a well-designed attribute service, it would be possible to build such a demographics database system. It might well be combined with a basic eligibility service so that a single database system supports both. Fields within a record would have associated rules for access or updating. All institutional applications that require use of personal data would use this comprehensive demographics database by either periodic downloading or indirect relational reference. In particular, on-line directory services for locating campus community members would use this authoritative database as their data source.

Campus network citizens could be responsible for maintaining all of their own personal data and also could check on the completeness or accuracy of other attribute data, such as payroll title or salary, status toward a degree, or the parameters of their employee benefits.

MAPS AND GUIDEBOOKS: DIRECTORY SERVICES

Information services and resources abound on campuses and beyond. The community of users changes and moves about, and the topology of the network changes periodically. How does a network citizen find anyone else or any particular service or information?

The Domain Name Service was the first widespread directory service in support of the information environment. Other common directories exist today, such as directories of people and searchable databases of information resources. Many more kinds of maps and guidebooks are needed to serve the new and complex information resources we are deploying. For example, the network citizen might want to find an on-line copy of Van Gogh's Child with Orange and the nearest colour printer that she or he is eligible to use and that is capable of high-resolution, large-format printing. New resource location services must support more complex data and search strategies.

A well-managed set of directory servers and search engines for information objects will help the network citizen discover resources and navigate easily throughout the electronic information environment.

SAFE PASSAGE: ENCRYPTION AND DIGITAL SIGNATURES

Authentication and access control alone are not sufficient to guarantee safe passage throughout the electronic information environment. Passwords can be guessed or stolen, data can be monitored in transit, and identities sometimes can be forged. The strongest defence against these challenges involves the use of modern encryption methods to ensure privacy of data transmission and create the digital equivalent of a pen-and-ink signature.

Our networks are truly open systems, which is one of their strengths as well as a source of many vulnerabilities. Any transmission might be intercepted, and any data received might be questionable. Attacking computers on the Internet has become a rampant obsession among certain curious and occasionally antisocial groups. Fortunately, modern encryption technology offers potential solutions for most of these concerns. Encryption of data while in transit can protect privacy as well as the confidentiality and integrity of data. The technology required to implement data encryption has become commonplace and should be considered for all administrative or other institutional business applications. Encryption alone may not guarantee authenticity, however. We need the equivalent of a seal or at least a recognized signature associated with the contents of the document.

A digital signature must be some set of data that cannot be forged and that binds the contents of a digital document to a specific individual, role, or other entity. It must be something that only the signing entity could have created and must be verifiable by anyone in the electronic information environment.

Standards now exist for creating this type of digital signature using public key cryptography (PKC). Clearly digital signatures of this sort would enable a wide variety of institutional business to be transacted over the network with at least as reliable verification and auditability as we have now with paper forms and manual signatures.A public key infrastructure (PKI) is critical to enabling the use of encryption and digital signatures. Fundamental to the PKI is a unique pair of very large prime numbers, generated for each credential holder, that are keys used for encryption and decryption of information. Software on the network citizen's workstation generates this pair of encryption keys and gives one of them (the "public" key) to the PKI certificate authority (CA). The other key (the "private" key) is closely guarded by the network citizen. The CA stores the public key in a directory along with the PKI certificate. Upon request, the CA or directory server provides any registered user's public key to any application that needs it.

In addition to support of the local community, a CA must have a way to find other trusted CAs on other campuses or anywhere else in the electronic information environment. This ability is part of an overall PKI and may be implemented in a number of different ways.The basis for trusting a traditional signature is either direct knowledge or the ability to look it up in an archive maintained by a trusted authority, such as a bank. In the digital world, trust must be established through Pre-established contracts based on mutual understanding of business practices, the basis for registering individuals with the CA, and the viability of the cooperating CAs.

The resulting so-called web of trust must be scalable to millions of users in thousands of locations. This can be achieved through a hierarchical model wherein a community-based CA registers subordinate CAs after verifying their viability. A consortium of college and university campuses, for example, could operate such a certificate authority and the associated services on behalf of its members. This CA in turn could register under national and international CAs to allow fully general and trustworthy access to verifiable public key directory servers anywhere in the world. A campus PKI with its root certificate authority also could register subordinate CAs for departments, the library, or special-purpose requirements.

Until and unless encryption mechanisms and support services are in use, no one should send anything of value or of a sensitive nature, such as a credit card number, over the data network.

SHARING LIMITED RESOURCES: LICENSE SERVERS

The network citizen is now equipped with the basic tools for verifying identity, invoking authority, and concluding transactions safely. These capabilities enable easy and appropriate access to a wide variety of resources within our electronic information environment. Unfortunately, not all of those resources are without significant cost to the institution.

A traditional library might hold five copies of a popular book or journal. Ideally this would be enough to meet the peak demand at any one time for this resource. It would not be economical to purchase one copy for every registered patron, yet we often provide software and other resources in this cost-inefficient way.It is quite possible for software or other digital resources to be purchased by subscription, much like printed documents today.

The cost of such a subscription would be based at least in part on the size of the simultaneous user community. For example, a physics department might purchase a subscription for twenty simultaneous "users" of a virtual physics laboratory software package. During laboratory classes, the students make use of the software on computers located in the facility. In the evening, when doing homework, up to twenty students could make use of the same "subscription" to run the software on their own personal computer.

One way to enable this type of sharing of expensive resources is a network-based license server (NLS). The NLS serves as a clearinghouse to ensure conformance with the terms of the institution's subscription. An early implementation of the NLS concept was available with the Apollo domain computers.

Macintosh and PC versions of license servers offer similar capabilities. Standardizing on an openly available NLS technology would enable publishers to develop products that could fit readily into our electronic information environment. A single NLS could moderate access to a wide variety of licensed resources, including databases and documents as well as software.

PAYING THE BILLS: AUTOMATED DEBIT THAND UNIFIED INVOICING

Much of the electronic information environment today is accessible without direct cost to the network citizen. However, as the real costs become significant, the campus may need to find efficient ways at least to account for the usage of expensive resources and possibly allocate some of the acquisition and support costs toward the end users. A building block that could help achieve this is an efficient network accounting server.

Ultimately every member of the campus community, as defined in the campus's demographics database and corresponding eligibility servers, could have one or more "virtual accounts."

Transactions for services would be posted to a designated network accounting server using encrypted data flows. A wide variety of network citizen services, from print-on-demand syllabi to lunches and storehouse items, could be accounted for in this way.

The network citizen should expect a single statement each month describing all services used and any costs incurred anywhere within the institution. This might include transactions with external partners as well. Eventually this monthly accounting could result in an automated debit against an external financial service, much like debit cards are used today.

WHAT TIME IS IT? THE NETWORK TIME SERVER

It may not seem obvious but many of the services we are developing need to have a common frame of reference for time. Billing information, for example, must show accurately the date and approximate time of the transaction. Network management information often needs time stamps to be accurate to within a few milliseconds. Electronic postmark or notary services must have an auditable date and time guaranteed to be within a known degree of accuracy. Thus, an important element in the set of enabling services within our information environment is the network time server.Technologies in support of network time services exist today and are deployed on most campuses.

However, not all of these are synchronized with each other or with a universal time standard, such as the National Institute of Standards and Technology broadcast standard time service.Even where synchronized network time servers exist, not all essential end systems can take advantage of them yet. Campus information technology managers must understand the importance of this element of distributed systems and take appropriate steps to ensure integration of this service.Our network citizens may wish to set their own "electronic watch" from this service as well. Most modern workstations can be configured with automatic utilities to accomplish this.

WHERE TO NOW?

The building blocks I have identified are all part of a larger set of standards that comprise an information technology architecture. The basic enabling services include the following features:

- A coordinated set of authentication servers
- An attribute and demographic database server on each campus that can include a wide variety of information, including affiliation and eligibility data
- Directory and resource location servers
- PKI servers that manage certificates and public encryption keys for individual users and make possible digital signature verification
- Electronic license servers in support of site-licensed software, library materials, and databases
- Billing transaction servers that can handle a large volume of small-value debit records extremely efficiently
- Time servers and digital notary servers that form the basis for reliable and verifiable on-line content and digital institutional archives

The building blocks might relate to each other and to the communications system and applications Programmes. Other building blocks might include software version control servers.

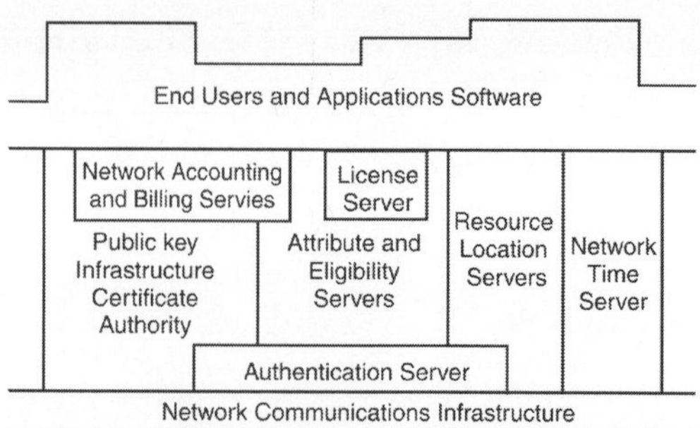

Fig. Information Environment Building Blocks with Common Interoperable Solutions for Basic Supporting Services

Campus users have access to the latest version of critical application Programmes, and alias servers to support consistent mapping between e-IDs and e-mail addresses or traditional identifiers such as employee number or student ID number. Current and potential technologies behind each of the building blocks described above are in different states of development and deployment.

With persistent vision and cooperative efforts, we can refine and deploy appropriate versions of all these enabling services over the next few years. If we do not start now, it may become very difficult to develop and retrofit a coordinated set of these services later. There is much to be done before network citizens are fully empowered. Information Policy to Support

CAMPUS E-BUSINESS

The unprecedented flow of information across networks and between organizations, coupled with the power of computers to extract, compile, organize, and republish information, has made e-business possible. These same capabilities are also raising significant concerns and issues related to the appropriate use of institutional information and the protection of information originating or residing in college and university information systems. The developmental phase facing colleges and universities today on the road to enabling e-business as one of integration. Our progress in adopting e-business in higher education will be enabled or constrained by institutions' abilities to develop, implement, enforce, and automate complex rules that authorize these consumers to partake of university services—for example:

- What rights will distant learners have regarding access to licensed university information resources?
- How can colleges and universities protect usage logs that record student and faculty library consumption activity for materials licensed from third parties?

The privacy, access, ownership, and security issues posed by e-business are extraordinarily complex and represent as much a set of cultural, behavioral, and policy issues as technical ones.Colleges and universities have long—and correctly—been described as self-governing anarchies or adhocracies. Higher education's hallowed and well-established traditions of self-governance and shared governance are responsible for our remarkable history of achievement, service, and innovation. These traditions also make integration hard. In many ways, achieving the necessary level of technical integration to enable e-business is the least complex aspect of preparing the institution for e-business.

Many campus chief information officers (CIOs) understand what it means to reorient systems from their current functional office views to the end-user views (student, parent, alumni, inter-enterprise) that e-business will demand. In most cases, the technical tools to achieve this kind of integration exist. In short, technical integration is a significant issue that can be addressed by vision, talent, and money. The thornier integration challenges are cultural and relate to role definitions, authority and power, and values. These issues will define the boundaries of an institution's approach to, and its likelihood of success in, implementing e-business.

COMMERCIAL INTELLIGENCE AND KNOWLEDGE MANAGEMENT IN MARKETING

Commercial intelligence and knowledge management are being addressed on varying levels of sophistication, often usually emanating from IT departments. Instead they need to be a key process in the definition, implementation and ongoing measurement of the commercial strategy.

Information gathering has emerged as a natural activity of the sales force, research and development, purchasing and marketing functions by nature of their regular external contacts. Until now this has been a disparate activity suffering from, on the one hand, the natural tendency to contain information within departmental boundaries or, on the other, exhibiting reluctance to share information within the business.

e-Commerce has imposed new, reduced time scales in direct marketing activity. Previously the direct marketer could anticipate when a mailing or phone call was effected and, within some degree of control, when a response would be generated. Access to the Web has reduced this element of control. A marketer can no longer engineer when a contact may wish to encounter his message, proposition or brand, or, indeed, come across it. As companies move seamlessly across borders, this process will become increasingly involved. A complex struggle will take place. Enlightened multinational corporations may gain advantage over leaner and fitter small and medium-size enterprises (SMEs) through the tactical use of information, whilst empowered SMEs may outsmart those larger competitors that remain with the traditional methods.

There is a need to establish valid methods of acquiring data from customers and visitors to e-Commerce Web sites and applying the resultant information and knowledge to drive variations in Web site content and appearance and to determine commercial propositions and further data acquisition. Customers and prospects presented with the same Web pages on each visit and being expected to reactively search for relevant products and offers will soon tire of e-Commerce and the marketer will lose the opportunity to develop a true relationship with the customer. Similarly, a visitor to a site presented with a vast array of qualification questions would be equally turned off. Tailoring the view of the site to the visitor will mean that qualification questions can be posed on an incremental basis, to populate the database using a hierarchy of importance to drive the questionnaire.

The development of the Web has coincided with the appearance of new, intuitive data analysis tools employing techniques that provide for the delivery of information and the definition and interpretation of patterns within that information, within time frames conducive to achieving the required dynamics.

CASE STUDY

The company had a large corporate account-based database on an IBM AS400 platform (addressing different transactional or customer service needs), plus a number of small department-owned databases run on PCs that included a Marketing database that was held externally and a system for managing events and conferences.*The problem*No links existed between the Marketing and Events databases or between the Events database and the AS400 systems. This meant that there were duplicate records but nowhere could the company achieve a total view of the contacts.

Nor were there any business intelligence (BI) tools; the Marketing Department was relying on pre-set reports. Each time a marketing campaign was planned, selections had to be made from each of the databases and discrete extracts run; these were then provided to the mailing house, which undertook a de-duplication process subject to predetermined selection hierarchies, to provide the final mailing file.The objective was to provide:

- A single, comprehensive view of a customer's dealings.
- Improvement in the quality of management information.
- A means to acquire and retain useful client information in a database.

The CRM issues demanded a central data repository. The recommendations were for the company to audit its data and pass it through a cleansing and enhancement process, prior to matching the duplicate records and merging data according to preset business rules.

The central AS400 system was augmented, with all additional data and each contact flagged by status (*e.g.* customer, prospect, enquirer, etc.). Regularly refreshed extracts were exported into a data mart (analysis universe), which was further augmented with qualifying data that the central system could not hold or for which development on the AS400 system was not economic and summarized or aggregated transactional histories. Business intelligence tools were introduced alongside the universe to facilitate querying, *ad hoc* analyses and campaign planning and management.

In this way the company was able to leverage the investment in the transactional system, could close down the satellite databases in the departments and introduce additional purpose-specific data without the need for costly redevelopment of the central system. For the first time the company would have a total customer view and could begin to maximize the opportunities from customer-centric CRM.

As the knowledge culture grows, so the interest in data throughout the enterprise also grows. The benefits of combining information from different departments, from different regions, even from different businesses, are being realized. Software tools such as intelligent agents search for meaningful additions to the knowledge base and data marts with business intelligence software facilitate the analysis of extensive data sets from disparate sources right on the desktops, within hours rather than months and without the mammoth budgets normally associated with corporate data warehouses.

This overall concept, taking the basic principles of data-driven marketing so successfully implemented in direct mail and telemarketing, aims to establish a process for creating the 'back back-end' of e-Commerce, its link to both internal and external marketing data and knowledge bases and the implementation of customer relationship management.The existence and growth of the Web and the increasing exponents of the medium have implications on both sides of the data-driven communications equation. On the one hand, the Web provides a novel, exciting and convenient medium for delivering a message to customers and prospective customers. On the other, it presents a channel for data collection that makes possible concepts that were only hypothetical in the past.

The beginning of the 1990s saw the introduction of data driving a variety of media beyond the traditional direct mail. For instance, computers were interfaced with telecommunications equipment to derive applications to assist in the management of customer relationships, enabling call centre agents to prepare themselves for calls, access customers' records and have repeat calls from a customer always channelled through to one agent. Or data being used to drive variations in customer magazines and newsletters, with such notable examples as Rover's internationally acclaimed *Catalyst* magazine bringing lifestyle versionalization and reader personalization to the realm of contract publishing.

However, in all these cases the systems that drove them relied upon pre-selection and qualification of the data. The industry even talked about unqualified contacts as being *suspects* rather than prospects. The sheer wealth of information available on the Web, the ability to identify and acquire it and the tools now available to manage it in all its varying formats and structures all mean that disparate data, wherever they may reside, could be made available to add qualification, enhancement or verification to a marketer's database. The natural corollary to that is a keener degree of customer profiling and targeting and a greater level of personalization of message, proposition and presentation.

Previously the data process was often presented as a funnel to depict a channel for information that is open to as much as possible at the top, but which needs a process of filtering and selection to be applied to that information so that the best is allowed to pass through into the business process. The down side was that controls had to be in place at the top to guard against overflow, which could mean the loss of both bad and good potential information.

The new information channel is less of a funnel and more of a wide conduit. It still allows as much as possible in at the top, but there is less need for those controls since the value of the data cannot be predetermined. Valid, but unstructured, data can be fed in from a multitude of sources, both internal and external, and their value determined once any links are identified. The information can then be attributed to the records on the database and parameters to drive the relationship established.

These new concepts also have implications for clustering and segmentation. Combinations of demographic and behavioural criteria have traditionally defined clusters. Once defined, these have been used to drive product development and marketing activity. Cluster sets change their content and their direction; individuals join and leave as new information is learned about them and as the importance of the business rules inherent in the data relationships is recognized. This means that the clusters are volatile and dynamic. Their dynamism must be tracked and the changes identified in order to keep the marketing strategy and communications schedule on track.

Marketers can find that markets for their products are dwindling, readership for their magazines is flagging and response to their once attractive offers reduced.This may not be because the product is any lower in quality or the price has leapt; it can be that the customer profile once associated with that product or marker has changed shape and has moved out of the target zone for that marketer. As considered above, has the customer turned thirty-one and so is no longer eligible for a Club 18-30 vacation? Has the child reached an age where his parents are no longer interested in nappies?

These changes and new viable targets must be recognized to effect and maintain product and communications strategies. Early warning of changes in customer profiles can be provided from constant data feeds with triggers identified to drive proposition, communication channel and delivery.

THE ROLE OF THE MARKETING DATABASE

A database may be defined as a comprehensive collection of interrelated data, which can be accurately manipulated or retrieved. A marketing database will typically contain details of customers and the transactional or behavioural histories associated with those customers and can benefit all the elements of the marketing mix, whether in broadcast or direct communications or in sales promotion or PR.

There is a role for the database in supporting advertising, market research, product development, sales force management and motivation and sales promotion. Hence the concept of Database Marketing should not be confused with Direct Marketing, nor should it be considered a medium in itself, competing with others in the marketing mix, but rather as a tool to improve performance, efficiency and effectiveness in marketing communications.

The marketing database helps develop a clear, *actionable* understanding of customers and develop a dialogue that ideally should always be relevant, timely and focused on qualified opportunities.

Database Marketing of the 1980s and 1990s strove for *one-to-one* relationships and its success has been commendable *within the context of the available techniques*. New concepts, tools and expertise will now help deliver an outcome that is closer to the vision. The increased awareness and availability of data within organizations has coincided with the appearance of new, intuitive data analysis tools. This combination allows the derivation of information and interpretation of trends within time frames conducive to achieving the required dynamics.

As companies seek to integrate their suppliers, their customers and their marketing partners in complex relationship structures, new quantities of data are becoming accessible for exchange and sharing and the value of the data as a corporate asset is increasing.

The existence and growth of the World Wide Web and the increasing exponents of the medium have implications on both sides of the data-driven communications equation. On the one hand, the Web provides a novel, exciting and convenient medium for delivering a message to customers and prospective customers. On the other, it presents a channel for data collection that makes possible concepts that were only hypothetical in the past.

WORKING WITH DATA

Data are things that are given, facts that when combined with other facts can constitute information. Jenkinson (1995) identified four types of explicit data, referred to as Primary Research, Secondary, Performance and External. Whilst these types remain valid, some broadening of the definitions is required to gain a better understanding of how they link and are complementary:

- *Basic data.* Rather than being just primary research data received directly from the customer, basic data may be viewed generically as the most fundamental elements, acquired usually as part of a standard business process. These will include a customer's name and address, e-mail address, definitions of the company's products or services, its URL, pricing, campaign definitions, branches and channels of distribution, sales force or dealer network.

- *Qualifying data.* Qualifying data are data from any source that in any way add description to the basic data. For example, a company may wish to collect the demographics of its customers (age, sex, income, occupation), their lifestyle information or geographical profiles.
- *Behavioural or transactional data.* These are data that record how customers have reacted, what they have bought or enquired about and all the transactional information a company may hold.
- *Externally sourced data.* External data cover everything that augments, qualifies or enhances the basic data that are acquired from outside the business and outside the relationship with customers or suppliers. For example, companies may rent or buy lists of prospects to add to their database or may acquire additional data to enhance their existing records such as correcting the postcode or adding qualifying data elements.

There is a fifth type of data. It is not explicit but is known as *tacit* data. These are data that are normally held in the minds of the people using the database. The data represent their understanding of their relationship with their customers or suppliers; they are the low-level view acquired through experience or local knowledge and are intuitive, intimate and topical. Their inclusion enables the explicit data to be put into context and interpreted and helps convert information into manageable knowledge, itself a combination of data and information-processing technology with human creativity and innovation.

SOURCES OF DATA

There are a variety of methods for acquiring data into the business. Some are a function of the business processes such as completing a sale or taking an enquiry. Others may be contrived tactics with the main objective of collecting a particular item of data for the database. Essentially, data can be acquired from six types of source:

- Leveraging current business processes,
- Tactical activity,
- Purchase lists,
- Marketing partners,
- Enhancement from external sources,
- Business information vendors.

Leveraging Current Business Processes

Business processes can be amended so that new information is acquired as part of regular activities; for example, adding questions to an application form, having a telesales agent ask additional questions or having a sales person qualify a prospect prior to making a sales call. Companies must satisfy themselves that they are acquiring all the data they can from the encounter with the customer or prospect (or even supplier). Most common data sources are:

- *Sales.* Does the company collect details for each sale? Is the basis of the customer database to be found in the accounts department?
- *Web site registrations.* Customer registrations are a reliable source of information so long as the precautions for data quality have been applied. Companies often take this opportunity to ask some additional questions to acquire qualifying information for the database.
- *Enquiries/help line.* When customers and prospects call in or complete an enquiry screen on the Web site there is an opportunity for the company to acquire additional information or qualify or verify data already held.
- *Complaints.* This may be the first occasion a company has to acquire even primary data about this customer - perhaps also take the opportunity to acquire some additional information. Record the complaint on the database; classify it and its outcome so that this can be used in later relationship management. A properly handled complaint can mean a more satisfied customer. Often a customer whose major complaint was handled well becomes a better customer than one who experienced a number of minor complaints.
- *Redemptions.* Sales promotion campaigns or consumer competitions can yield valuable data if one or two relevant questions are added to the entry form.
- *Marketing research and surveys.* Such surveys can provide high-level data that can be extrapolated across the database.
- *Accounts.* Ascertain spend levels, returns and credit control issues, all of which may be used as segmentation or selection criteria for marketing initiatives.
- *Third parties and marketing partners.* Companies may identify non-competitive marketers whose target markets are similar to their own; there may be opportunities for piggy-back activities or cross-marketing or joint venture initiatives.
- *Branches and channels.* Companies with front-line contact with their customer base will identify opportunities for data gathering.
- *Servicing.* Do customers have to come back to have their product serviced? This provides an opportunity both for data gathering and timelyverification.

Tactical Activity

Companies may launch specific tactical promotional campaigns, the object of which is to augment the database or acquire additional data. They could include:

- *Sales promotions, prize draws and competitions.* These all provide the opportunity to collect entrants' details. The techniques can be used tactically to gather primary information (*e.g.* prospecting or customer identification) or for data enhancement, by requiring entrants to proffer new information about themselves or their household.
- *PR events.* Those who attend company events, product launches, etc., demonstrate an affinity with the brand. Primary and qualifying data can be captured as qualification of entry or through sales promotion or prize draw techniques at the event.

The increasing use of the Internet for customer data acquisition has introduced a key benefit to database marketers. The wide acceptance of customers to use registration or query form screens obviates the cost of data capture and potentially increases the accuracy of input. With all other media the hard copy captured data have to be punched in, either by a company employee or more usually by a data entry bureau that may be on the other side of the world, and this can impose a considerable cost on the exercise.

Purchase or Rent lists

Companies can acquire lists from external sources to augment their database, expanding the volume of prospects or qualifying or updating existing records. Some will be available for purchase, others on a lease basis, allowing a pre-defined number of uses or unlimited use within a specified time period.

Most lists are available on a one-use rental basis. Leased and rented lists will be seeded with names of contacts to guard against illicit use of the data. Reputable list managers or brokers should be able to furnish this detail and will provide a data mandate confirming the origin and ownership of the data and any data protection implications. The British List Brokers' Association or the Institute of Direct Marketing can give advice on choosing a list supplier.

CASE STUDY: MISTAKEN IDENTITIES

An estate agent dealing in very expensive properties wished to acquire a list of householders in the smartest areas of England. It went to the trouble of selecting those neighbourhoods with the highest Council Tax bandings and translating them into the specific postcodes it felt defined the geographical areas it desired.

The agent then merely requested names and addresses in those areas from a list broker supplying data from the electoral roll. By requesting data purely by postcode, and with no other qualifying data, the selection it received comprised a list of people living in those areas which included chauffeurs, cooks and household staff. Given the type of householders in those areas, many were not on the electoral roll, since they were overseas nationals, or people for whom these properties were second or third homes.

Marketing Partners

Data can also be acquired through data swaps with other organizations with which there is an affinity. There are some industries that have formally created data pools used by members who may even be competing (*e.g.* charities). Formal marketing partnerships can also yield data from a number of contributors and partners will have predetermined access and use. All these must of course comply with data protection best practice and legislation.

Data Enhancement from External Sources

Additional qualification data can be sourced externally. Postcodes and postal address structuring can be applied either by specialist bureaux or by using software that has as its reference the postal address files of the countries in which the company is marketing. There are around 200 national postal administrations around the world providing this data.

This rapid addressing concept has been widely adopted by call centres that need to ensure swift and accurate address entry; entering the postcode drives the automatic population of most of the address. Web site registration is being made easier and more accurate by providing a similar function using the postal address files. The site visitor merely has to enter his postcode for the majority of the address to be populated in the appropriate fields.

It should be noted, however, that this process provides such results only in territories where the postcode can be linked to a discrete selection of addresses, as in the United Kingdom. The move towards the 5+4 format in the United States will help to some degree, but those countries using the standard European four- or five-digit code or clones of the US-originated 5-digit zip code can proceed only as far as confirmation of city. Some countries, for example the Republic of Ireland, have no postal codes at all.

Adding Qualifying Data

Companies that specialize in qualified databases can match a subject company's data to theirs and provide the missing information. Companies such as Claritas, Consumer Surveys, Consodata and Experian have established databases of millions of households in the United Kingdom and continental Europe. Each record is qualified by an extensive array of research factors that can provide demographic and lifestyle information for consumer databases, and social value grouping information can be acquired and added in, thereby adding both explicit and aspirational/ attitudinal (psychographic) elements for profiling.

Some data companies can also provide purchase intention for specific types of products or services.The psychographic aspect can be a major influence on segmentation. Psychographics is not, as some believe, synonymous with lifestyles. Two households may have identical demographics and be differentiated by their lifestyle preferences, but further differentiation may be achieved by understanding their aspirations and attitudes towards the product, the brand or their own profile.

CASE STUDY: ROVER

Rover, the motor manufacturer, needed to identify prospects for a new mid-range car. Having used demographic and lifestyle questionnaires across its new car owner database, it had a robust profile of the prospects it sought. Mailing lists were recommended that met this profile, and one particular list seemed especially apt. To be certain, a selection of names was tested by telephone research. Whilst the demographics and lifestyles were accurate, the psychographics were not. These people were so concerned with their personal image that they preferred to have a pre-owned, larger prestige car with perhaps a personalized licence plate on their driveway rather than a brand-new but smaller car. The list was a list of second-hand car snobs and not of any great use to Rover's new car sales task, and hence Rover's proposition would be irrelevant to a prospect on that list.For business-to-business, similarly, business demographic criteria (turnover, number of employees, type of premises, sector, etc.) can be added, as can the job titles of business contacts and the names of people in specific job functions. Arrangements can be put in place for changes of important elements, like key personnel, to be provided on a proactive basis so that the quality of the data can be readily maintained.

Business Information Vendors

Business information vendors can also provide information on sectors or performance within certain markets, specific company information, competitor activities and even information on weather, travel and currency fluctuations can be provided on a 'constant awareness' basis and can be integrated into the data strategy.

Adding Research Data

Research data can be both discrete and general. If research is discrete then it can be matched back to the subject, providing specific qualification criteria for those who respond. Information can then be extrapolated across other similar subjects to provide selection criteria, expanded profiles or segmentation.

Other Data Elements

Some data elements may be 'organically generated' within the database.

Such data are referred to as *derived* data and may be acquired as a result of analysis or applying specific calculations. A simple example may be the automatic calculation of customers' age from their date of birth or the creation of banded values such as age groups (twenty-one to thirty-five, fifty-plus, etc.) from discrete personal data. More complex algorithms can be applied to generate scores or propensity quotients that can be used as additional selection or segmentation criteria.

There is overhead attached to holding data in terms of storage, disk space and the implication on hardware and software. There is also a management overhead - the greater the amount of data held, the more management time will be required in data checking, handling data problems and administering the database. There is also a data protection implication: are you acquiring and holding data that really you have no use for and should not be collecting as it is irrelevant to your business?

DATA QUALITY

The value of the data in the database will relate directly to its quality and integrity. It is possible to achieve meaningful results without sophisticated modelling, so long as you have high-quality, robust and reliable data. The better the quality of the data, the more reliable the answers will be to queries run against the database.

Validation processes help with quality and integrity, making sure that the data being added to the database is valid. Business rules manage the validation process, and reference tables ensure conformity and adherence to standards and should be applied in all aspects of data acquisition and use. When designing a data capture device, like an entry form or application screen on a Web site, or when capturing data either using in-house data entry resources or an external data punching bureau, the brief should be the same, with all referring to the same set of rules.

The analytical or selectivity applications of the database rely on conformity; hence the table of references ensures that only values within the predetermined set may be entered into the database. For example, a Web site registration form may request details of how the customer first accessed the site. Normally termed the source code, or media code, this is an important piece of data, since not only does it provide feedback on marketing response but it also establishes a criterion on which customers could be selected for future contact.

If left to their own devices to complete a free text field, customers may enter, a free text string complete with typographical errors. Using a reference table of acceptable responses, conformity is assured and the quality of the data is maintained. Bear in mind also the data storage overhead: the free text string has to be held verbatim, whilst the selected value in a table need only be held as a code reference.

Key Issues to Manage

Data acquisition - are all marketing initiatives sharing the same data goals, are the needs of other departments being taken into consideration?

Decay

Data will decay over time. Business data tend to decay at a greater rate, since people move jobs, companies move premises or reorganize, acquire or are acquired by other companies or go out of business more often than individuals move house. Estimates suggest that 30 per cent of management and professional staff change positions annually.

Data Appraisal

In order to assess the quality of the data, an audit should be carried out. View the data on screen or in hard copy - most databases will allow the user to export data into a more familiar environment, like Microsoft Excel, where you can either view the data or print out the spreadsheets if more convenient, checking for key indicators regarding the reliability of the data.

BASIC OF INTERNAL MARKETING

The basic premise behind *internal marketing* is that a company's communications with its customers and other external stakeholders are unlikely to be effective unless employees within the firm are aware of (and prepared to buy into) the message that the firm is trying to put across. It is fashionable to refer to employees as 'internal customers'. If all employees are clear about the company's mission, objectives and strategy then there is a much better chance that customers will get the same message. Research has shown that firms where employees understand organizational goals had considerably higher returns on capital than those where employees felt excluded or uninformed. It has been estimated that more than 20 per cent of a firm's communications are actually with itself rather than with external stakeholders. Yet internal communications are rarely accorded the same degree of attention and resources as external communications. Sometimes very basic errors are made. For example, if the person responsible for mailing out corporate brochures is not told that a facility for customers to e-mail such requests to the firm has been implemented, incoming messages may well be ignored by that person in the mistaken assumption that someone else is dealing with them. It should now be evident that the principles of internal marketing mirror those of human resource management.

Organizational structure was once the way in which companies could control the flow of information within the firm. Clear hierarchies of responsibility meant that information flowed slowly up and down functional areas, but was often not made available to other parts of the organization, or could be excluded from certain individuals. Individuals' position in the management hierarchy could be ascertained by the degree of access they had to important information. Powerful fiefdoms could be established by individuals who controlled access to such information. With the development of internal company intranets, it is possible (in theory at least) for such information access barriers to be transcended. Real-time access to information can be available to any employee with Internet access, and the activities of diverse functional areas may become transparent to employees at all hierarchical levels. In practice, of course, decision makers can still choose to restrict access through passwords or firewalls. There are obvious benefits here to a marketer analysing market conditions or customer behaviour, but the sheer volume of information now available to organizations can create problems of its own.

For established firms looking to add online channels to their existing marketing activities, many of the marketing challenges are internal. Significant organizational change may be involved and effective communication within the firm of the need for change and the role of each employee in effecting it is essential to ensure staff commitment. Internal customers can be segmented into supporters, neutrals and opponents of change and communications with each group phrased appropriately. It is particularly vital to ensure 'buy-in' from key decision makers with the authority to enforce change, as well as from potential *champions* (sometimes referred to as 'rainmakers') who will drive the project forwards and communicate their enthusiasm to others.

Inappropriate cultural norms can militate against successful relationship building. Too often, customer care programmes are instigated as a 'quick fix', without making any changes in management behaviour, or attempts to evaluate the success of the programme. While press attention has focused on the achievements (and, more recently, the struggles) of Internet entrepreneurs, little mention has been made of the service workers who make up the bulk of the demand for labour in new technology industries. Many work in call centres that have been dubbed 'the new sweatshops'. In service-intensive organizations the power is in the hands of lower-level, front-line employees, upon whose handling of service encounters managers must depend for the achievement of organizational objectives.

As Piercy notes: 'Too many employees who deal directly with customers are damaging the product, service or corporate brand every time they open their mouths. ' For example, the technique of 'mystery shopping', where researchers anonymously check out the quality of service provided by staff, may well be feared and resented. Dissatisfied or demotivated staff can try to sabotage enforced 'smiling' policies or even wear their name badges upside down. One major UK DIY retailer implemented a customer care programme that required shop floor staff to be much more proactive in serving customers and suggesting suitable products. What management failed to note was the limited extent of employee commitment and willingness to accept the extra pressures associated with such responsibility. Instead of feeling empowered and motivated by the 'upgrading' of their jobs, many staff resented the interference and preferred the security and predictability of sitting at the till all day.Although 'clicks and mortar' organizations might be expected to struggle with integrating online relationship building, it is interesting that the 'dotcom' brigade does not seem to be immune to the problem. Leibovich, in an article appropriately entitled 'Service workers without a smile', provides an interesting account of employment conditions at Amazon, world-famous for its ground-breaking policies of online customer relationship building. Staff are pressured to work as quickly as possible in order to achieve customer satisfaction targets, particularly those who earn low wages packing books at the firm's distribution centres or answering e-mails from customers. The author notes: 'Customer service employees work in a patchwork of cubicles scattered over three downtown Seattle buildings.

The quarters have an old industrial feel, with gritty exteriors that belie the company's sleek online identity'.As mentioned earlier, the principles of internal marketing can also be extended to prospective employees with the notion of *employer branding*, in recognition that employees are a significant source of competitive advantage in a market place where products and services are easily copied. Employer branding involves treating staff and potential staff as internal customers. The aim is to acquire a reputation as a good firm to work for, thereby attracting and retaining the brightest and most dedicated employees, enabling the firm to stand out from its competitors. In an age where people expect to work for a number of firms (or indeed for themselves) during the course of their career, retaining key staff is becoming more and more difficult. Some firms are experimenting with paternity leave, flexible work arrangements and empowerment of staff or open communications through simplified management hierarchies in order to be seen as a 'good employer'. 'Forward-looking companies are working on the assumption that they have to do a continuous selling job on the employee'.

The relationship between internal marketing and relationship marketing. In what may be regarded as the ultimate integration of internal marketing and customer relationship marketing, Ulrich (1989) advises giving customers a major role in staff recruitment, promotion and development, appraisal and reward systems. While this policy may be too radical for many organizations, it can be seen from this discussion that a suitable internal climate is a necessary first step in the development of a customer orientation, rarely a simple task for an established organization. In much of the human resources literature, relationships between employees have received far less attention than relationships between employees and managers. Even discussions of team working often focus on what the team can deliver for the manager, the company or the customer. This is a pity. Employee-employee relationships are extremely important for organizations for many reasons, as they can:

- Help to create a positive and constructive company climate and culture.
- Provide an important source of allegiance to the company through commitment to colleagues.
- Create channels for knowledge exchange, particularly informal or tacit knowledge, vital for product and service delivery and quality.
- Provide a vital basis for internal marketing, particularly through building 'internal customers' and internal customer relations, for example, between departments. Although formal internal service-level agreements can help, it is often informal personal relations and agreements that get the job done more efficiently and effectively, and improve a company's service quality overall.

Perhaps one of the most over-hyped assertions made by organizations is the desire to have motivated staff committed to the company. In reality, there are numerous examples of organizations in which such statements are mere rhetoric not backed up by action. What are the sources of employee commitment? In practice, this can be achieved through a variety of means that have to be very carefully tailored to specific types of work and whether or not employees are working individually or within groups. Very broadly, we can think of the ways in which motivation - making employees more willing to undertake their work for the good of themselves and the company as a result of personal drive and commitment, making them identify more strongly with, and be more loyal to, their work, their work teams and the company - is generated as follows:

'Hard' Reward Strategies

These might include:

- Reward for performance above the standards or targets set, such as financial bonuses, or forms of remuneration over and above the basic wage, which can be offered on a regular basis (*e.g.* daily, monthly or yearly).
- One-off rewards such as all-expenses-paid holidays, meals, shopping vouchers, etc., for good performance. Such rewards are often used for staff performance that is well regarded by customers as a signal of what kind of care is valued by customers and, in turn, by the organization.
- Share options are an excellent way of getting employees literally to 'buy into' the company's business performance. It also helps to draw employees' attention to aspects of a company's performance that lie outside their immediate job (*e.g.* changes and opportunities in the competitive environment).

'Soft' Formal Reward Strategies

These might include deciding on and then publicizing 'Employee of the Month/ Year' winners, where the winners are made known to the organization in newsletters, posters or on the company intranet. A 'hard' reward may be given, but a primary objective is to publicize good performance and to share knowledge about how that good performance was achieved with both employees and, of course, customers.

'Soft' Informal Reward Strategies

- *Team meetings.* Time for reflection is difficult in a busy environment, but 'time out' not only to seek improvements but also to share success can provide positive and constructive feedback on individual and team performance.
- *Regular positive feedback.* How can employees know if they are doing a good job or not? The good colleague, supervisor or manager will not just wait until the annual appraisal but can provide such feedback as frequently as they wish. Informal feedback and praise for a job well done are a primary source of maintaining motivation among staff, often referred to as the *organizational climate*. A strong motivational climate is very important at any time, but can be vital at times of crisis and change, in order to maintain focus when things may become uncertain or difficult.

INVOLVEMENT AND PARTICIPATION

Again, it would be easy to be cynical about gaining employee commitment. It could be argued that commitment is often thought about as a one-way street where the employee is expected to commit heavily to the company but the company expects to put in the minimum of effort. Some of the rewards listed earlier can provide commitment, but more can also be done. The most effective mechanisms operate through involvement and participation processes. Blackburn and Cornelius (2001) have suggested that involvement and participation can add value to workplace organizations, certainly by generating employee commitment but also by encouraging workplace learning. So, for example, problem-solving meetings can help information exchange about actual and potential problems and their solutions. The key is really how 'participative' are participation processes?In unionized firms there may be joint consultation between management and unions on matters such as pay and conditions. In non-unionized firms, involvement and participation are often achieved through the following:

- *Team briefings* where managers brief employees on actual or possible changes, and feedback and suggestions are sought.
- *Problem-solving and quality circles* in which front-line issues are discussed and suggestions for improvement and change made.

- *Empowerment interventions* where employees are given the autonomy to make decisions about specific aspects of their work without having to consult with their supervisors or managers.

The company culture and organizational climate play a vital role in determining the willingness of both managers and employees to pursue these approaches. Further, the more exploitative the culture and demotivating the climate, the less likely such approaches will be taken seriously or succeed.

The Value-added of e-HRM

Perhaps one of the most exciting developments that all organizations can exploit is e-HRM. e-HRM concerns the use of electronic means for managing key aspects of HRM. Once again, a note of caution: the technology may be the means but it is not the end: the value of e-HRM is highly dependent upon a number of factors, including:

- The basic quality and relevance of the e-HRM systems in use.
- Whether employees, managers and HR professionals are adequately trained to use e-HRM systems.
- How effectively e-HRM is integrated with other more conventional systems of HRM, including strategic HRM.
- Identification of the most appropriate Internet and intranet systems that meet the organization's needs.

7

Internet Commerce and Marketing

RISING POPULARITY OF THE INTERNET

The Internet is fast approaching ubiquitous access, especially among college students, due to increasing computer ownership and commonplace Internet usage. Specifically, 55 percent of college students own a computer, and over 92 percent have access to one. Furthermore, many of these computer users are active Internet users. Among four-year college students, 85.4 percent use e-mail, and 86.6 percent use the Internet.

Current obstacles are expected to dissipate in the future. The biggest complaint today about the Internet-its slowness if connected through a modem-will eventually disappear as bandwidth, particularly to "the last mile, " becomes more abundant. The technologies that will make this possible will be cable modems, asynchronous transfer mode (ATM), xDSL, frame relay, low-earth-orbiting satellites, and an advanced Internet.

INCREASING DEMANDS AND EXPECTATIONS

Today's students are technologically savvy and proficient. They have grown up accustomed to automated teller machines, toll-free numbers, next-day delivery, and even the Internet. They are able to procure books, CDs, and even term papers (much to the chagrin of educators) over the World Wide Web and increasingly expect the same type of instant fulfillment of needs and wants. Queues on campus for course registration, feedback from advisers, financial aid decisions, degree audits, and other services-will be met with disdain and vocal dissatisfaction.

Similarly, due to services that they are able to receive from other Web-based companies, students—and staff and faculty—increasingly will expect services to be available on a 24x7 basis (twenty-four hours a day, seven days a week) and to be personalized based on their needs and interests. As in other industries, only the Web and associated e-business applications can provide this functionality for colleges and universities. For example, Amazon.com remembers book preferences and provides suggestions to customers. Can online course registration applications provide suggestions on course electives based on past preferences or other variables such as meeting time, professor, learning style and assignments, academic area, number of credits, background of fellow students, prerequisites, impact on degree completion, instructor and course rating by previous students, preparedness for other classes, or even cost of textbooks? Can a Web-based application recall a principal investigator's area of interest and provide customized information and services accordingly?

Colleges and universities increasingly will need to understand the functionality resident in best-in-class portals (gateways to the Web) and service providers from other industries to anticipate student, faculty, and staff expectations. Researching the current services and plans available only at other colleges and universities will be insufficient and shortsighted.

CONTINUING COST CONSTRAINTS

Even with favorable demographics and unique economic prosperity (and record tax receipts), cost pressures continue on the campuses of colleges and universities. In the early 1990s, colleges faced deficits that mandated across-the-board cutbacks. Today, across-theboard cutbacks have been replaced by the need for rapid, strategic reallocations. Resources are needed for enterprise systems implementations, expanded use of technology in the classroom, investments in technological infrastructure, capital improvements, and other mission-critical expenditures. Budget processes throughout the industry are being redesigned to unearth resources from underperforming Programmes or inefficient processes to enable reinvestment in higher-priority initiatives.

The search to do more with less will continue unfettered, so that colleges and universities can aggressively pursue strategic opportunities in the midst of increasing competition. To accomplish these objectives, institutions increasingly will look to e-business applications to reduce administrative costs, especially in business-tobusiness services, by reducing manual activities.

OPPORTUNITIES FOR NEW REVENUES

Universities increasingly have diversified revenue streams with research grants and contracts (with an increasing percentage from the corporate sector), fundraising receipts, advertising, and continuingeducation students. Each of these areas will require the utilization of e-business approaches to generate new—and even retain current— revenues. As has been documented, colleges and universities increasingly depend on continuing-education students, revenues, and "profits." However, distance education will become a required core competency for succeeding in continuing education.

Technology-based education—e-learning—is growing at a faster rate than classroom education, and leading to a dramatic shift. According to International

Data Corporation, technology-based information technology (IT) training is forecast to increase to 55 percent of U.S. training by 2002, up from 21 percent in 1998, thereby displacing classroom training as the method of choice for delivering IT-related education and training. Admittedly, the IT industry is an early adopter of electronic education and training. However, as colleges and universities seek to increase—or even just retain—continuing-education revenues, their success will depend on their ability to make the transition to and integrate technology-based approaches.

IMPLICATIONS

The business case for adopting an e-business strategy is compelling, and the urgency to do so will grow. We have identified four immediate implications as to how this expected change in delivery of services will affect colleges and universities in the short term:

- In all areas, multiple vendors with a broad array of products will cause increased confusion as institutions determine whether to build or buy and compete or collaborate.
- The Internet will affect process, organization, and policies.
- The Internet will raise a host of other new issues—tax, legal, security, and skills.
- Integrating information management will be a crucial challenge to enable institutions to leverage fully the benefits of doing business electronically.

PROCESS, ORGANIZATION, AND POLICIES

The promises of reengineering remain unrealized for many institutions. In many instances, large, expensive Programmes designed to institute change have been only partially implemented, often with less-than-expected results. As a result, it is likely that few fret the passing of the reengineering trend. Many institutions, however, have replaced these process improvement projects with still larger (and order-of-magnitude more expensive) enterprise systems implemen-tations. (These implementations are often referred to as ERP implementations, for their enterprise resource planning approach to integrating student, financial, and human resources systems.)

In this context, the influx of e-business projects or initiatives may be welcomed with less than open arms due partially to fatigue from these previous efforts. Conversely, others may be eager to embrace an e-business strategy as the vehicle to achieve organizational restructuring with more tangible and expeditious results.

The implementation of e-business applications, similar to reengineering and ERP projects, will require process redesign, organization restructuring and alignment, new job descriptions, and review and revision of policies.

Thus, they will be met with similar skepticism and resistance and necessitate institution-wide change management strategies to ensure success. The enabler may have changed—in this case, Internet-based applications—but these projects will require institutions to continue the difficult and often arduous restructuring efforts. Institutions that have realized significant progress from previous efforts will be able to leverage these initiatives and should experience a higher probability of success.

Academic policies too will require reexamination. Policies and processes related to articulation, faculty evaluation, faculty development, and assessment of student outcomes, among many others, will require review and revision by institutions that expect to succeed in the delivery of on-line courses, Programmes, and supporting services.

TAX, LEGAL, AND SECURITY ISSUES

Although there are similarities with previous institutional improvement efforts, new challenges exist as well. Implementing e-business applications will require institutions to examine tax, legal, and security issues. In the area of tax and legal issues, institutions will be forced to examine intellectual property issues, review Internet-based revenues for unrelated business income tax (UBIT), and document legal and audit trails. Security issues, while examined in ERP implementations, will be heightened in importance since vendors and other constituents will have expanded access to institutional data and systems requiring firewalls, authentication, encryption, confidentiality and integrity controls, and enhanced management of security breaches. These issues elevate risk management challenges to the top of the agenda of senior management at all colleges and universities.

GROWTH OF THE MOBILE INTERNET

The growth of the mobile Internet now exceeds that of the PC version. Mobile communications offer considerable potential to marketers because of their unrivalled combination of:

- Instant response;
- Personalized content (as each customer has a unique telephone number);
- Scope for geographical location tracking.

The potential for mobile networks is particularly high in developing countries that do not have an established wired telephone network and hence no established PC-based Internet services. In the Philippines, for example, SMS messaging has recently taken off rapidly, and mobile Internet services therefore offer huge marketing opportunities in these emerging markets.There has been a lot of hype recently about the potential of location-based technology in particular. However, current services are very basic, and it is important to remember that there is some way to go before they become sufficiently reliable and useful to have a broad appeal.For example, variations on the scenario whereby a customer is called on their phone and advised of a special breakfast offer just as they walk to work past a Starbucks outlet, have been heralded as the ultimate in personalized promotional campaigns.

There are a number of practical difficulties, though, such as customers' reluctance to be bombarded with intrusive advertising messages and the challenge of communicating effectively with the wide range of mobile devices and standards currently in use. The usefulness of wireless devices has recently been improved by new standards such as Jini and Bluetooth that connect wireless devices to other electronic products:

- Jini (www.jini.com) allows mobile phones, PCs and personal digital assistants (PDAs) to collaborate as part of an intelligent network, without the need for the correct device driver to be added to the operating system before a new device can be used.
- Bluetooth (www.bluetooth.com) is particularly useful for linking mobile devices because it does not require any wire connections. For example, it could allow a user on a mobile in a car to transfer data from an office PC directly to a home printer.

Keynote systems (www.keynote.com) recently launched a mobile performance measurement service to compare the services offered by all the major UK networks. It can measure delivery times, network comparisons, handset performance and geographic availability, thereby allowing content providers, networks or manufacturers to judge how successful their services have been. It also allows consumers to benchmark performance and make informed purchase decisions. In addition, for a detailed comparison of the characteristics of different mobile technologies. Mobile phones are now rapidly evolving and becoming 'pocket portals' that provide a range of personalized services including e-mail and text messaging with just one monthly bill. Before discussing some of the recent and pending innovations in this area, we shall review developments over the past two or three years.The first mobiles to offer Internet access, using Wireless Application Protocol (WAP), were introduced in 1999. The information displayed had to be especially formatted for a small screen area, and the limited functionality fell well short of the often extreme levels of industry hype.

The telecommunications industry broke one of the central rules of marketing, which states that promotional campaigns should 'under-promise' and 'over-deliver' rather than the other way round. Users found that navigating between pages on a mobile phone could be an extremely laborious process, for which they were paying by the minute for connection charges. During 2000, many early users abandoned mobile commerce after disappointing experiences.While mobile commerce is useful for 'distress' purchases such as parking, actually browsing the Web on a mobile phone is hardly a straightforward and stress-free experience. However, there have been successes to date, notably with mobile banking and gambling services.'Second-generation' mobile phones introduced early in 2001 offer faster connection speeds and are starting to carry advertising. High response rates are currently enjoyed by advertisers, and the most successful campaigns have been run by companies such as the *Sun* newspaper, which has used the mobile channel to advertise competitions being run in the paper itself.In other words, the *Sun* is using online advertising to drive its traditional core business - which is offline newspaper sales. Mobile advertising still represents a very small percentage of company promotional spend in comparison with more traditional media such as radio and television, but the figure is increasing. Business services via mobile channels are currently few and far between, but early experiments are under way with order placing, stock-checking availability and order tracking to facilitate supply chain integration.

The much-hyped but still awaited third generation of mobile communications (3G) is expected to deliver sound and images and be 'always on'. Auctions held in 2000 for the licences to operate 3G services netted the UK government over £20 billion, but since then the share prices of the 'successful' telecommunication firms that purchased them have been severely dented.

The technology competing with WAP is called Short Message Systems (SMS), and it is currently by far the more successful in terms of user numbers. SMS is a derivative of numeric paging technology, which has been in existence for many years, updated for two-way communication.

To illustrate the rapid growth of SMS, consider the following figures:

- In 1998, mobile phones had a 20 per cent market penetration in the UK and some *1 million* text messages were sent.

As with the growth of the PC-based Internet, it seems that communications with staff and customers are currently adding most value at this early stage, while the widespread acceptance of mobile transactions is still some way away. One must also bear in mind that not all these applications will be relevant to all companies all the time, and in most cases they will complement rather than replace existing channels.

The key skill for marketers is to focus on the particular aspects of mobile marketing that will add value to customers in their specific industry contexts. We will now examine each of these areas in turn, drawing upon a number of examples to illustrate this important point.

CONTENT PROVISION AND ADVERTISING

Mobile advertising is expected to grow exponentially following a slow start in the difficult economic conditions of 2000-1. The long-anticipated 3G technology will offer far more scope for creative advertising than the small black and white text-only screens that have dominated the market until recently. It seems to be commonly accepted that busy professional people do not want their important business interrupted by marketing messages on their mobile phones.However, we all at least tolerate advertisements while watching movies ... so firms that specialize in placing advertisements on mobile firms are at the moment focusing their advertisement placement on mobile entertainment services rather than on business ones. Placing adverts in mobile games that users are playing when they have time to spare is likely to be more acceptable than if a user is interrupted while trying to link up remotely to a company for business purposes.

In exchange for the entertainment value in the game, it is reasonable to expect that the customer will tolerate (and, companies of course will hope, respond to) the advertising message. For example, Stone reports that Mobliss, a US-based wireless marketing agency, worked with Tribune Media in turning its 'Jumble' brand (a scrambled-word game) into a multi-player wireless game.

It was also an effective advertising tool because the words used in the puzzles could be directly related to the advertiser's company or product. The advertisements can be displayed as either graphical images or text and themed to correlate with the creative campaign that the advertiser is running offline. In either case, with mobile Internet access, customers also have the ability to click a button and be connected directly to the advertiser's call centre.Mobliss has also launched a snow report system at www.mysnowreport.com where customers can go online and build in their preferences for particular resorts. Then a text message detailing snow conditions can be sent to the customer's phone.By forming partnerships with companies like the travel agency Moguls that are trying to reach the skier demographic (high income, high expenditure), a customer is able to check out the snow conditions at a resort, and then follow an advertiser's link that is offering a discounted package trip to that resort.

Then another link will connect the customer to the call centre to speak to a ski-travel agent. In these circumstances, the customer is more likely to perceive the advertisement as a benefit rather than as just a nuisance.

Targeting is very effective because if a user is enquiring about snow conditions, then almost by definition they are themselves a skier. In addition, the fact that the overwhelming majority of people currently using mobile Web services are males aged 20-39 with incomes over £30,000 is of course very appealing to advertisers.

Traditional magazines have been experiencing a fall in advertising revenues over the past couple of years due to the global economic slowdown. The ability to offer interactivity through SMS can make a publication more appealing to companies seeking to place advertisements, while at the same time winning new readers for the magazine itself.

So, for example, a company seeking to run a mobile advertising campaign to promote its brand could:

- First, rent a database of readers of a particular magazine that fit the demographic profile of their target group;
- Second, send text messages promoting a competition linked to the brand that is set out in the paper-based magazine.

Stone (2002) reports that a few companies have begun sending coupons as messages to wireless devices in order to unload 'perishable' services such concert seats or restaurant tables. He describes the example of PlanetHopper, a small company based in New York, which is focusing upon the entertainment industry.It has partnered General Cinemas, theatres and Shecky's guide to bars and clubs to provide the wireless coupons. By advertising in cinemas and in some 200 New York bars and restaurants, it drew some 20,000 users who opted in to get the promotional messages.

The key to success is 'opt in' messaging, as people's tolerance of spam messages falls. *The Economist* (2001) recommends that to avoid giving offence, mobile advertisements must:

- Be optional (meaning actively requested by users);
- Be personalized;
- Be moderate in volume;
- Be free to the recipient;
- Offer a means to unsubscribe.

The article goes on to report on a recent initiative by a mobile advertising company called the Mobile Trial, in which advertisements as text messages had an average response rate of 10-20 per cent. This is much higher than usual rates for direct mail (3 per cent) and Internet banner advertisements (less than 1 per cent).

DIRECT MAIL

Direct mail has become increasingly important as a means of audience contact. We discuss direct mail only briefly in this section, but will take a more detailed look, at how it can be used in a public communication campaign.

It is easy to obtain usage statistics on the mass media since there are only a relatively few outlets. Over the years industry watchers have gathered reliable and detailed information on how people use radio and television and even the eleven thousand magazines currently in publication. Direct mail statistics are more difficult to assemble. Every business, agency, and organization serves as its own outlet. While there may be hundreds or thousands of media channels, there are millions of direct mail channels, making it impossible to compile specific usage information. Direct mail usage is therefore based on assumptions and extrapolations, and even compilers of these statistics caution that there is a reasonable margin of error in the data. Nonetheless, the DMA has attempted to track the use of direct mail based in part on U.S. Postal Service reports. Over the years there has been a steady increase in the mailing technique. Between 1982 and 1985, there was a 40 percent increase in the total number of direct mail pieces. In 1985 the DMA reports there were more than 55 billion direct mailings within the United States and 16 million from the United States to overseas destinations.

From these figures it is evident that direct mail is becoming increasingly popular among U.S. companies and organizations. They are using direct mail to get their messages across to voters, consumers, and supporters. They are sending letters, brochures, fliers, coupons, and dozens of other forms to convince, cajole, inform, and stir people about issues of all sorts. Direct mail picks up where the mass media leave off. Direct mail provides targeted and personal contact with audiences. Computers, sophisticated mailing lists, and other technological advancements have made direct mail a convenient and affordable way to reach specific audience members. It enables communicators to shape their messages to meet individual needs.

An effective communication Programme must account for all essential elements of the communication process. Occasionally, a seat-of-the-pants campaign brings about the intended education or persuasion of an audience, but such examples are few and far between. The mass communication process has become far too complex in recent times to allow campaigns based on a hunch to have much success. With the expanded array of available media options, exposure patterns of audiences have become more complicated and difficult to pinpoint by intuition.

The vast array of messages competing for attention diminishes the probability that audiences will recognize any one of them and that, by even a smaller chance, the message will have an intended effect on individuals. One observer estimates the average American is exposed to some sixteen hundred commercial messages per day but notices only eighty of them. Only twelve of these messages, Parker says, elicit any response at all from the recipient. In order to be among the fortunate few to win the notice of an audience, communicators must draw from a variety of techniques to improve their chances in the competitive information marketplace.

The complexity of media exposure patterns and competition for audience attention present obstacles that some public communicators are willing to concede when they conduct a seat-of-the-pants campaign. Most acknowledge the inadequacy of such an approach, however, when faced with current message production and placement charges. Production and distribution of messages are expensive. Radio spots may cost several hundreds to several thousands of dollars to produce. A thirty-second radio spot aired during drive time in an average city may cost as much as four hundred dollars or more. Television spot production has run as high as several hundred thousand dollars for a thirty-second network-quality advertisement, although the average is a little under $100,000. Smaller television stations may charge several hundred to several thousand dollars to air a thirty-second spot during prime time, and for the same time slot, networks typically charge between $150,000 and $200,000. Of course, for special Programmes, network rates can be even more shocking.

THE SMCR MODEL

The Competition for Audiences

In a poorly planned public communication Programme, not only does the communicator stand to miss the audience entirely, either because of a poor selection of media or inadequate message preparation, but also, given the sizable charges for time and space, he or she may waste money in the process. Recognizing this waste compels business and political communicators to abandon seat-of-the-pants strategies. Over the years a good deal of practical experience, field research, and academic study have unfolded essential components of the communication process that serve to guide the business communicator in making intelligent decisions.

They assist the communicator in asking appropriate questions about the audience, media, issues at hand, and goals for the communication Programme. Informed strategies enable the communicator to see important links among these components and the interrelationships that serve to explain how the manipulation of one component affects other components.

A useful starting point for an examination of the communication process is with the Berlo model, which records four principal components inherent in nearly all communication scenarios: a Source, a Message, a Channel, and a Receiver (SMCR). Certainly this is communication in its most basic form. A source sends a message through some kind of channel to a receiver. Who says what, how, and to whom? Nearly every communication event, no matter how simple or complex, involves these four components.

This elementary model is fundamentally simple yet beguilingly complex. It is accurate yet, it is not complete. Basic communication students study this model to gain an understanding of communication. We will use it here as a paradigm for complex public communication strategies.

The Source

The source, which in a majority of cases will be the company, spokesperson, or political candidate, is that individual or group who is perceived by a receiver as the originator of the message. Who does the receiver think is the source of a message?

For instance, when Bill Cosby performs E. F. Hutton's television commercials, there is a strong likelihood that Bill Cosby is considered by most television viewers to be the source of the message—not the investment firm. A senatorial candidate may hire a speech writer during a campaign, but when the candidate delivers that speech, he or she will be perceived by the audience to be the source of that message, not the speech writer.

Perceptions of the receiver, then, are critical in discussions of the source. Despite those who may be behind the scenes of a public communication, it is essential to consider audience perceptions of who the source may be.

Audience notions about the source are no small matter in the public communication process. The image projected by that source, as a composite of physical appearance, voice, demeanor, and more, may be the most critical feature of the entire communication event. That image determines the message acceptance by and the impact on an audience. A source that comes across well to audience members will promote attention and enhance the persuasiveness of the message. A source that fails to appeal to the intended audience will yield poor results.

Perhaps because the importance of the source has long been known to public communicators, a good deal of research in past years has focused on the characteristics associated with an effective source.

Specifically, these studies have asked what makes a source believable to an audience and what enhances the capacity of that source to persuade an audience to accept the message. What is it that makes a source credible to an audience? Although we will provide an in-depth examination for the purposes of this introduction we will note that in most studies three component parts constitute source credibility: trustworthiness, expertise, and charisma. Trustworthiness deals with the inherent faith and confidence audience members place in the source. First, the source that does not have a stake in an issue and so stands to gain little from an audience's acceptance of a message will be viewed as more trustworthy. Additionally, if the source is known to audience members and has, over time, consistently provided good, honest, and accurate information, he or she will probably be perceived as trustworthy and the message viewed more positively. For years, CBS news anchor Walter Cronkite provided information that audiences perceived to be factual and believable, and so he was rated consistently as among the most trustworthy people in America.

Expertise is often measured by college degrees, years of experience in a field, awards, and citations for excellence. A source who can demonstrate expertise reveals his or her capacity to deal authoritatively with a topic. An aeronautical engineer will be perceived by audiences as having high expertise when discussing flight characteristics of a new aircraft. The president of a successful brokerage firm will be perceived as an expert on stock market matters. Note, however, that expertise is subject specific. Although the stockbroker may know Dow Jones, this investment expert is out of his or her element when discussing aeronautical designs. Audiences recognize these limitations and are quick to confine source expertise to subject areas. Finally, charisma, or dynamism as it is sometimes called, is the peculiar quality possessed by some people that grants them special influence over others. Although this trait is ascribed to the source, it is really a matter of personality, appearance, and demeanor recognized by the receiver as compelling features of that source. Some audience members may sense strong charismatic qualities in a source, while others are unable to detect such presence. A teenager, for instance, may be driven to near hysteria by the magnetism of a rock star. The teen's parents, however, may not recognize anything remotely attractive in the same musician. Charisma, then, like trustworthiness and to a lesser extent expertise, is a trait perceived to reside in a source.

Two features of source credibility emerge from this brief discussion. First, each of the component parts of credibility is imputed to the source by the receiver. It could be argued that the source may possess certain qualities of trustworthiness, expertise, and dynamism that can be measured on an absolute scale. For example, the source may have no evident stake in the issue at hand and may have consistently provided accurate information. Furthermore, this source may have college degrees to demonstrate expertise and may be an attractive person who can speak well and move audiences. Unless the intended receivers recognize and value these features, they are meaningless. In sum, we can consider the credibility of a source only as a function of the receiver's perceptions. Therefore, public communicators should plan their strategy not only to get out the message but to get out the message about the messenger as well.

The second observation about source credibility also involves the receivers: Audience members vary considerably over what constitutes a credible source. Different receivers ascribe different levels of credibility to a source because of different value structures, exposure levels, interests, and a host of other factors that make one audience member unlike another. There is no such thing as a generic, highly credible source that can be effective with all audiences.

There are only some sources that are perceived as highly credible by some receivers. In order to maximize the benefits from selecting a highly credible source, the public communicator must carefully match source characteristics with concerns of the intended audience. Often this means the communicator must give up one audience in Favour of another or develop a stratified campaign that presents different messages borne by different sources to different receiver groups. "One source fits all" may not work in any given campaign. We may need to reach young audiences with a sports figure, religious audiences with a member of the clergy, professional audiences with a respected authority in the field. To make such a determination, we must examine the group and the nature of the topic. These features of source credibility suggest a noteworthy dimension of complexity in the public communication process.

E-MANAGEMENT E-MAIL

Before proceeding to look at the law of e-commerce, it is useful to consider some particular aspects of e-business management. There is no doubt that, for the managers of any commercial enterprise, the Internet presents the most significant universal challenge that has yet been presented in the history of commerce.

It is tempting to think of the Internet as merely an electronic expression of what has gone before: e-mails replace typed letters, websites replace glossy brochures and electronic invoices replace their paper equivalents. But the Internet is not merely a more efficient replacement for existing systems.

Its significance lies in its ability to be not merely a communications device, but a market, an information system and a manufacturing tool. It allows managers to do not only what they have done before communicating with suppliers, advertising products and services, collecting customer data and obtaining payment more efficiently, cheaply and comprehensively, but also opens up significant new possibilities for the core operations of every business. Of course it is the potential to increase productivity and cut costs that is a most attractive feature of the Internet, and this must not be overlooked. Suppose, for example, you are a car manufacturer. Traditionally you have obtained orders for new cars from a network of showrooms that have in turn obtained orders from their customers.

Where outsourcing has been required, you have placed orders with your suppliers. Assembly takes place, the car is customised to the customer's requirements and is shipped to the dealer. With the Internet comes the possibility of the customer placing their order online.

They can choose their accessories and colour scheme and create a virtual image of how the car will look on-screen before proceeding with their order. Direct electronic communication of the order eradicates possible mis-communication in, and later arguments over, choice of specification. The delivery date can be electronically calculated and arrangements for payment can be finalised. The manufacturer's automated system will communicate electronically with suppliers so that the alloy wheels, or whatever has been selected, can be delivered precisely when needed for fitting to the vehicle. The finished product can be delivered via an intermediary dealer or direct to the customer.

E-MAIL

The spread of electronic communication brings transparency and openness to the management process. The ease with which an e-mail can be forwarded to hundreds or thousands of people changes the nature of communication — one must now assume that not just the recipient will read an e-mail that is sent to him.

It is no longer possible to hide behind mountains of paperwork or to 'lose' a letter to which it is currently not desirable to respond.It is common knowledge that the ability to send and forward e-mails causes two main concerns for employers. The first is that time will be wasted — some employees spend several hours each week in sending e-mails to friends. The second is that the employer will incur some liability as a result of the content of such e-mails. Both these concerns can be met by an 'e-mail policy', which should be clear and comprehensive.

It should set out the employer's attitude to e-mail and explain that employees'e-mails will be monitored (if this is desired) to ensure quality of service and appropriateness of communication. The presence of such a policy should have the effect of employees exercising some caution when sending and forwarding e-mails.

It should also mean that embarrassing incidents such as the Norton Rose 'blow job' e-mail debacle can be avoided. It should be noted that the monitoring of employee e-mails has data protection and privacy implications that are beyond the scope of this Report.A related issue is that of pornography. Pornographic images are popular with employees but cause great concern for employers.

Not only do they waste employee time, they cause offence and clog vital server space. They could also lead to liability for the employer. To avoid the sort of situation experienced by Orange when it dismissed 30 employees for downloading and distributing pornographic images, a clear statement should be made to employees of the employer's attitude to this activity.

To stem the flow closer to its source, the business should consider installing software capable of screening-out unwanted material.E-businesses should remember that an e-mail is a business document in the same way as is a letter or a fax. E-mails must therefore comply with the requirements of the Companies Act 1985, namely that the following information must appear:

- The full name of the company;
- The registered number of the company;
- The address of the registered office; and
- The country of registration of the company.

HUMAN RESOURCES

Given the current climate of short-term working practices and the need to have efficient and productive staff, e-businesses need to focus on staff attraction and retention. E-businesses, generally speaking, need fewer but better staff. This may require a review of working conditions, working practices, pay structures and benefits.

The e-business revolution has, significantly, created new jobs that did not exist in the offline economy — examples include Web site designers, knowledge management officers and e-business managers.Workers in e-business are increasingly flexible, many working from home or onthe-road. Rather than being feared, such practices should be embraced by businesses.Not only do they lead to a lowering of overheads (heat, light and a desk in the office are not required for mobile workers) but they can create greater satisfaction and loyalty amongst staff. Appropriate communication infrastructures should be employed so that staff are kept fully informed of events 'back at the office'and are able to communicate with other staff members, as well as customers and suppliers. Where sales teams spend much of their time out of the office, they too should be kept fully informed and accountable.

The lack of office presence of individual employees and the globalisation of businesses mean that the 'drink after work' and the 'training weekend' become increasingly difficult. Many businesses are developing corporate portals for their business to employee (B2E) communications.

Such portals can prove invaluable in providing information and training to employees. Larger companies can additionally use the portals as an online job market and to provide maps of buildings and photographs and locations of staff. Some companies motivate employees to log on to the portal on a daily basis by posting the share prices of the company or by displaying a list of employee birthdays for the relevant week. A section of the portal can be used for selling the company's products to the employees. The Internet can be used for recruiting staff. Potential job applicants can be given up-to-date information on vacancies, be taken on a virtual tour of the business and be invited to apply online. Communications between the HR department and job applicant can be undertaken by e-mail. The expense of using a recruitment agent can be saved.

CUSTOMERS

The Internet gives rise to the possibility of a wider marketplace. Customers may now be located anywhere on the planet but have equal access to the marketing material of the business. Systems should be set up to deal with this new global presence.

Better information on customers is available from the monitoring of their activities whilst visiting the Web site. Using cookies it is possible to 'personalise' the content of the site for each particular customer. Knowing that a customer lives in Oxford, for example, it is possible to display a banner advertisement for an Oxford-based pizza restaurant on your homepage.

Were a different customer to visit the homepage, the advertisement would be of a different kind. Location-specific and targeted advertising have data protection implications and detailed proposals should be submitted to a data protection lawyer before procedures are implemented.

As the technology grows, so do customers' expectations. Customers will expect to be kept informed of the process of their order and will want more information than would have previously been available. Electronic order tracking systems should be available to customers online to provide them with this information. DHL, for example, has a system which enables a customer to see the location of their package at each stage of its journey and to know the precise moment that it is 'signed-for' by the recipient.

E-MAIL MARKETING CAMPAIGN

- Acquire e-mail addresses (*e.g.* of people who have registered to receive information)
- Obtain permission to use the e-mail address for marketing. This is best done at the time of collection, *e.g.* registration or free samples may only be possible if the respondent checks the 'yes' box
- Select the addresses to target for the particular message
- Execute the campaign (possibly in conjunction with other communications channels)
- Respond to customer replies
- Correct and clean the e-mail list
- Track and measure the campaign performance.

SHORT MESSAGE SYSTEMS (SMSS) AND MULTIMEDIA MESSAGING SERVICES (MMSS)

While mobile phones and other mobile devices can be useful for 'distress' purchases such as paying a congestion charge (to drive into a city), the growth of m-commerce has been slow, even since the introduction of 3G. Nevertheless, even though it represents a small proportion of marketing budgets, advertising via *short message systems (SMSs)* and *multimedia messaging services (MMSs)* achieves high response rates.

Because of this, spending on mobile advertising has been predicted to rocket to £6 billion over the next year or two. Mobile advertising is growing in popularity not just because of the high response, but also because mobile Web users represent an attractive demographic, with the majority being males aged 20-39 with incomes over £30,000. They are well segmented as a target for games, gambling and travel services - currently the biggest mobile advertising categories.For example, in the US, the marketing agency Mobliss has launched Snow Report (www.mysnowreport.com). Customers who have registered their interests can receive text messages detailing snow conditions at winter sports resorts. Recipients of the message can follow a link for a travel package to the resort.

As with e-mail, the key to success is opt-in, with customers giving permission for these marketing activities when they register for the information service.

VIRAL MARKETING

Viral marketing is growing as more companies use it to promote and brand their products and services. For example, the low-budget horror movie *The Blair Witch Project* owed worldwide success to a vast volume of 'word of mouse' recommendations passed around Internet chat rooms. These campaigns are becoming more sophisticated with tracking of open, click-through and success rates.A potential problem with viral marketing campaigns is that the company is reliant on each individual in the chain to have permission to send such messages to each recipient. In many cases this is not done: viral marketing spreads much spam. The responsible marketer will be using tracking systems that can be used for follow-up of sample recipients to ensure that they do not object to such communications.As an example of *opt-out* viral marketing, consider the hypothetical way that this book could be promoted. Prospects may initially receive an information-only message, for example an invitation to a marketing conference, ending with something along the lines of: Please forward this message to anyone else who may be interested. In the future we may want to inform you of other services and products in which we think you may be interested. If you do not wish to receive such messages, please contact the sender to be removed from the list.

BANNERS, POP-UPS AND INTERSTITIALS

Online advertising expenditure on media such as banners and pop-ups is growing and has reached well over £150 million per year (£30 million more than cinema advertising, for example).

The interstitial a pop-up that interrupts browsing to show an ad - is a much more active form of advertising than banners. Some people using the Web for a specific purpose find these irritating, though. Online advertising company RealMedia (www.uk.realmedia.com) is using a less-intrusive system called adPointer. This generates an ad when the cursor has not moved for a specific time.Schemes that incentivize users to look at advertisements have been around for some years, but in the UK Bananalotto.com (www.bananalotto.com) has raised the stakes by offering the chance to win one million pounds as you click the banner ad. KPE, the media and entertainment consultancy, has developed around ten games for their clients. Managing Director Paul Zwillberg says:

* This section is summarized and adapted from Marketing Business e-business supplement So much of the Internet has been characterised by repurposing things that worked well in print or TV. 'Advergaming' is... a new combination that's made for the medium.... You take one of the most popular uses of interactive content and marry it with tried and tested advertising models like brand association, trial or data capture and you get something really wonderful.

CUSTOMER RELATIONSHIPS

The direct mail and e-mail activities described above are part of the management of customer relationships. Building on these basic communication tools, the most successful e-retailers such as Amazon (www.amazon.com) and Tesco (www.tesco.com) use various techniques of data mining, personalization and customization.

For example, Amazon customizes the web page, making offers for new books, music or movies that are likely to be of interest based on past purchase patterns.

Tesco likewise personalizes its communi-cations and special offers almost down to the level of the individual. These e-retailers are thus able to satisfy customers more specifically and therefore are better using the customer relationship and data mining tools.

WEB ATMOSPHERICS

Web atmospherics is too important and complex a topic for this single section, in greater depth. Briefly, atmospherics includes *visual* (*e.g.* text, design, colour management, video clips, 3-D), *aural* (*e.g.* music or sound effects) and *olfactory* (*e.g.* perfume and samples) stimuli. The Edmunds (www.edmunds. com) car sales site is a good example of the use of exciting downloads of video and sound effects to illustrate cars in action. With effects like this, there is a need to avoid long download times.

Perfume is available by e-retail, although most suppliers rely on description and well-known brands, rather than offering samples, for example Perfumania (www.mydesign erperfume.com): 'Contains citron, rose, jasmine and is accented with honeysuckle, vanilla and oakmoss making Allure by Chanel perfect for romantic use'.

Atmospherics, even when fairly low-tech, have much to offer in communications mix design.

LINK POPULARITY

Search engines use 'link popularity' in locating and ranking sites. Improving link popularity by persuading other sites to link to yours raises a site in search-engine rankings and is therefore a critical aspect of the communications mix.

CASE STUDY: EBAY.CO.UK

The eBay site was founded in the US in 1995, originally under the name Auctionweb. The UK site was launched in 1999, growing after a slow start to become the UK's top e-commerce site measured by monthly audience numbers, with 6.8 million people (compared with Amazon's 6.1 million and Tesco's 2.7 million). In the year to March 2003, eBay's audience increased by 160 per cent, compared to Amazon's 28 per cent. Internet growth overall was only 7 per cent.The figures are 'a significant sign of the potential of [the most profitable and successful Internet players] to sell to consumers', according to Nielsen/ NetRatings (www.nielsen-netratings.com), who supplied the figures. Cheap though most individual products may be, eBay still sells over £1 billion of them per year.If eBay were considered to be an e-retailer, this would make them number one in UK market share. While many dot.coms are mainly hype, eBay is profitable, making a quarter of a billion dollars on worldwide operations in 2001. It survived the dot.com crash relatively unscathed and the share price rose from US$18 in 1998 to US$110 by 2003.Visitors to eBay spend an average of 1 hour and 11 minutes per month on the site - one of the longest of any UK site.

Visitors return to the site to check the status of items they are bidding for or selling and ebay.co.uk is one of very few e-retailers to achieve over a billion pages views per month.Many UK users are earning a healthy living as 'power sellers', taking advantage of the worldwide market to offer everything from sports utility vehicles (SUVs) to comics, records and oddments like garden gnomes, T-shirts and kettles.

In the same way as the major bricks retailers are suffering increasing competition from charity shops and car-boot sales, so the established e-retailers face growing competition from online auctions.Most sellers are private individuals. For example, Pat Austin makes £30,000 per year selling an assortment of bric-a-brac that she finds in charity shops, car-boot sales and physical auctions.

She sells 1,000+ items per year and 99.9 per cent of her transactions have been positive. It is a full-time job, though, with correspondence and despatch taking up the mornings and sourcing goods the afternoons. Rosie English has a turnover of £100,000+ selling high-class women's fashion for prices of £100 to £1,000+.

She reads the fashion press to identify what editors recommend and what celebrities are wearing, then buys from sample and factory sales or direct from designers. However, eBay is not all one-person businesses, as the 'big boys' are seeing the opportunities and joining in with companies like Dell, Dixons and Sears using eBay to shift excess stock.It's a case of 'buyer beware', as auction sites do not take responsibility for deals that go wrong and offer only low insurance cover for losses. The way for buyers to identify the most reliable sellers is from feedback ratings - many regular sellers have hundreds of positive ratings.

E-COMMERCE CONTRACTS

Virtually all commercial transactions are undertaken in the setting of a legally binding contract. Indeed, without the presence of such a contract the parties would generally be unwilling to perform their obligations (such as the delivery of goods, the performance of a service or the payment of money) under the transaction.Contracts provide certainty as to the obligations of each party and, more importantly, a guarantee of the right to sue the non-performing party for breach.The law of contract dates back centuries, and has equal application to an ecommerce transaction as an offline contract. But the nature of an e-commerce transaction gives rise to some special problems that do not arise offline:

- Formation of the contract — for each party to have confidence that the performance of its obligations will have legal effect, it is of vital importance that the contract has actually been formed at the time of that performance. In the offline world the existence of a contract can be evidenced in many ways — such as a signature on a printed order form or a note of a conversation — that are not available in the online world.
- Incorporation of contractual terms — commercial transactions take place under a set of contractual rules. Usually these rules are set out in written form and will apply to the contract by virtue of being 'incorporated' within it. In the offline world terms are included in a contract by agreement. There is a considerable body of caselaw that describes how and why such terms will be incorporated. That caselaw may not, and indeed in some cases cannot, apply to online transactions.
- Non face-to-face transactions — e-commerce transactions, by their definition, take place electronically. The advantage of this is that the parties do not need to be in each other's presence at the time of formation of the contract. One disadvantage of this is that the law treats differently those contracts that are entered into between a business and a consumer 'at a distance' — the e-business must comply with a set of rules that do not generally apply to its offline competitors.

FORMATION OF A CONTRACT

It is generally well-known that a legally binding contract will arise where there is an offer to do something that is met by an unconditional acceptance of that offer. By way of example, where X offers to pay £250 for the delivery of a case of champagne to her home and Y agrees to perform that task for that sum of money, a contract is formed. To complicate matters, the law distinguishes an *offer* from an 'invitation to treat'.

An *invitation to treat* is something that might appear to be an offer, but in fact is not. An example is the display of goods in a shop window or on the shelf of a supermarket. It has long been decided that such displays are not offers and that therefore they cannot be 'accepted'.This is the rule that prevents a customer from being able to force a shopkeeper to sell goods to him at the displayed price, even where that price is clearly erroneous.

Whilst in the offline world it is easy to determine when a particular communication is an offer or an invitation to treat, such a distinction is unclear in a virtual transaction. Argos recently felt the effect of this when it mistakenly advertised televisions on its Web site with a price tag of £2.99 instead of £299.When several people placed orders for the televisions Argos realised its mistake and refused to supply the televisions at the price advertised. One 'purchaser' sued the company for failure to deliver on the contract that she said had been created. The case was settled before it reached trial so we do not know what the judge would have decided. Although we can speculate that, in English law at least, a Web site is probably an invitation to treat as opposed to an offer, it would be wise for e-businesses to make clear the status of pricing and other information on their sites.

INCORPORATION OF TERMS

Of central importance to the e-commerce transaction are the terms and conditions on which the contract is based and by which it is governed. An e-business will always wish to trade on those terms that are favourable to it. For example, the business may wish to state that it is not to be held liable for late delivery of goods, or that its total liability for defective goods is to be limited to a certain monetary figure.

In most cases this will be done by the insertion of terms and conditions on the Web site and by making some reference to them during the contracting process. By completing the transaction the customers will effectively be binding themselves to those terms and conditions. For the reasons mentioned above it is important for the terms and conditions of trade to form part of the contract.

Without them we must rely on the 'default position' provided by the law and this is rarely ideal for a seller. The difficulty with e-commerce transactions is incorporating the terms into the contract is rarely a straightforward matter.

There are various techniques, such as those listed below:

- Click-through with acceptance — here the customer is required to click on a button which says,'I accept' or similar. This is the best position for the e-commerce business because the acceptance by the customer is clear and traceable. However, there is a perception that customers may be 'put off' by the need for this formality.
- Click-through without acceptance — the customer is required to scroll through the conditions but there is no acceptance button. Here there will be, at the very least, implied acceptance by the customer if they continue with the transaction after having scrolled through the terms and conditions.
- Reference with link — here the customer is referred to terms and conditions of trade but not forced to scroll through them. However, there is a link that will take the customer to the terms should they wish to see them. This is not ideal but may amount to 'incorporation by reference' under English law — this has not yet been tested by the courts in the context of online transactions.

- Reference without link — there is a reference to terms and conditions of trade but they do not appear on the site. Again this is an attempt at incorporation by reference. It is the least satisfactory method and is unlikely to have the desired effect in an e-commerce transaction as there is no reason why the terms and conditions could not appear somewhere on the Web site.

The legal formalities for online trading are expected to grow. The European Union, for example, has recently proposed several new laws which will govern e-commerce in the future. With this in mind, businesses would be wise to adopt a policy of requiring those persons they contract with online to click an 'acceptance button' to demonstrate their assent to the terms and conditions displayed on the Web site.

UNFAIR TERMS

E-businesses must be aware that since 1999 certain terms in their contracts with consumers will be void, *i.e.* unenforceable and of no legal effect. The Unfair Terms in Consumer Contracts Regulations 1999 (S.I. 1999 No. 2083) apply, by definition, only to B2C contracts.For the purpose of the Regulations a 'consumer' is a person acting privately and not in the course of business. In contracts with such persons any unfair term is void. An 'unfair' term is one which,'contrary to the requirements of good faith, causes a significant imbalance in the consumer's rights under the contract, to the detriment of the consumer'.

Examples of terms that would be regarded as unfair under the Regulations include:

- Allowing the business to change the characteristics of goods or services offered without recourse to the consumer; and
- Allowing the business to terminate the contract without reasonable notice of such termination being given to the consumer.

THE DISTANCE SELLING REGULATIONS

A consumer who purchases goods or services from an e-commerce business is protected to a greater degree than a business purchaser is. It is important therefore, at an early stage, to determine whether the e-business will engage in B2B or B2C transactions.

In many cases of course the e-business will wish to trade with both businesses and individual customers. Where the e-business anticipates that part of its customer base will be individual consumers, the so-called 'Distance Selling Regulations' become relevant.

The Consumer Protection (Distance Selling) Regulations 2000 came into force on 31 October 2000.They apply to contracts between a business and a consumer that are not 'face-to-face' *e.g.* contracts concluded by way of coupons in newspapers,'teleshopping', and of course the Internet. The Regulations impose two main obligations on suppliers of goods or services.The first is to provide certain information to the consumer. The second is to furnish the consumer with a 'cooling off' period of seven working days during which the consumer is able to return the goods to the e-business for a full refund. It is interesting to note that a recent survey of all 235 UK websites listed on Yahoo!, offering goods in the publishing, music and computer hardware sectors, found that 92% of the sites gave incomplete or incorrect advice on the right to withdraw. About half contained key contractual information that was not clear or prominent.

Most of those companies would be shocked to be informed that after each online sale has taken place the customer could contact the business at any time within three months and request the business to collect the goods from them. The e-business would then be required to refund the purchase price to the customer, whether or not it decided to collect the goods.

THE INFORMATION REQUIREMENTS

In most cases the 'information requirements' in the Distance Selling Regulations can be satisfied by posting the appropriate information online. Consumers must be provided with the information shown in the box below in a clear and comprehensible manner.

The consumer must also be informed of any intention by the supplier to provide substitute goods if the goods ordered are not available, and of the fact that the supplier will meet costs of return of such substitute goods by the consumer to the supplier in the event of cancellation.

THE COOLING-OFF PERIOD

The requirement of a 'cooling-off' period for distance contracts puts e-commerce businesses at a disadvantage when compared with their offline competitors. For a consumer to be legally entitled to return goods purchased in the offline world (for example in a shop) for a full refund, they must prove that there is some defect in the goods or that the goods are not of satisfactory quality. The Regulations however allow an online purchaser to return goods within seven working days for a full refund, without obliging the purchaser to furnish any reason for doing so.As far as the cooling off period is concerned, consumers must be given a period of seven working days, from the day after *receipt* of the goods, in which to change their mind. During that period the consumer has the right to return the goods to the e-commerce business for a full refund. Crucially, if consumers are not informed of their right to cancel in this way, then the time period during which they have the right to cancel increases automatically to three months plus seven working days. Businesses should therefore be aware that their failure to inform consumers of the cooling-off period will effectively extend their potential liability to refund the purchase price by three months.

EXCLUDED CONTRACTS

The requirement to provide consumers with the above information, and to give a cooling-off period, does not apply to the following contracts:

- For the sale or other disposition of an interest in land except for a rental agreement
- For the construction of a building
- For financial services
- Contracts concluded by means of an automated vending machine
- Contracts concluded with a telecommunications operator by use of a public payphone
- Contracts concluded at an auction.

It should be remembered that the Distance Selling Regulations apply to contracts with consumers, but not to contracts with corporate and business customers. The information above must be stated clearly and concisely on the Web site — this may mean some changes to existing sites. Additionally, the cooling-off period does not apply to bespoke or tailor-made products. Any attempt to exclude the operation of the Regulations will have no legal effect.

WEB SITE LINKING AGREEMENTS

To date operators of websites have provided links from their own sites to those of third parties with little thought for the legal consequences. Several legal actions in recent months have shown that this carefree attitude to linking is not good business practice. In one case, involving the Web site of a Scottish newspaper, an e-business was sued for providing a link to a page within the site of the newspaper.

This practice, known as deep linking, was challenged on the basis that it allowed users access to the site without being required to travel via the homepage — it was the homepage on which revenue-generating advertising appeared. In a case by Stepstone, the recruitment site, an injunction was obtained in early 2001 that forced OFiR, a Danish media company, to remove links to Stepstone's site.Recently a view has emerged that a link from one Web site to another could infringe the database right in the linked-to site.

In any event, it seems that there is an emerging right for e-commerce businesses to control how users experience their sites, and a growing willingness by the courts to recognise such a right.E-commerce businesses should therefore consider, in appropriate circumstances, putting in place a written contract that sets out the obligations of the parties to a linking agreement.

The contract should deal with the following issues:

- The link — consideration should be given as to how the link should be constructed, any technical requirements and where on the relevant web page the link should appear. If deep linking is to be allowed then the requirements and specifications for this should be set out. The contract should set out those circumstances in which the parties are able to sever the link.

- Intellectual property — even where a copy of part of the site is not made when the link is used (this would raise copyright issues), there may be use of the linked site's trade mark on the link itself. A licence to use all relevant Intellectual Property Rights should appear in the contract.
- Commission — sometimes the motivation for providing a link will be in receiving revenue as a result of users travelling to a third party site via the link. The commission arrangements should be clear in their terms — will commission be paid for example merely upon the site visit by a user or must the user first purchase goods from the site? There should be appropriate provisions for monitoring traffic such that commission can be verified and charged.
- Data protection — if there is to be a sharing of customer information between the linked sites then it must be clear that each site is to obtain the data protection consent of its customers for that transfer to be able to take place
- Database right — the contract should make it clear that the links envisaged by the agreement will not constitute infringement of the database right.

MAIL ORDER RETAILING

Mail order selling arose in a number of ways. Montgomery Ward and Company was founded in 1872 by a former clerk in Chicago who had also worked as a traveling salesman. The Patrons of Husbandry (the Grange) had established a number of cooperative stores and needed a wholesale connection. Mr. Ward saw the opportunity and started the business which still bears his name. The Grange stores were not generally successful so Mr. Ward's business was expanded into a mail order house to take advantage of good will among former members of the cooperative stores.

Sears, Roebuck and Company, the largest mail order firm, grew out of the efforts of Mr. Sears, a small-town station agent in Minnesota, to sell watches which had been shipped to his station on approval but rejected. The success of this venture led to a watch and jewelry mail order house in Minneapolis which was later moved to Chicago. The present large scale enterprise has grown from this small part..

Other general mail order houses had varied beginnings. Many have expanded from ordinary retail stores. Others started as specialty mail order houses and gradually expanded until they handled a more general line of merchandise.Probably the most important reason for the success of the mail order houses in the early stages of their development is to be found in the failure of country merchants to adjust to changing conditions. In the post—Civil War period the country general store was a dominant institution.

Throughout the West and South, farmers and small-town residents raised their standards of living after the period of reconstruction. Cash farm income became larger and farmers became interested in the kinds of things bought by city people. Rural and small-town merchants, however, did not appreciate such changes and continued to stock only staple merchandise which had sold well for many years. Even if such merchants had realized the significance of environmental change, the limitations of their small, local markets would have made it impossible for them to rival the assortments of the evolving mail order institution.Another factor contributing to the development of mail order retailing was the growth of rail transportation. This made it possible to place orders by mail and to deliver merchandise to scattered areas at reasonable cost and at relatively certain dates.

The spectacular and consistent development of mail order retailing began, however, with the establishment of rural free delivery service. Farmers as a class began to subscribe for city daily papers.

They were thus reached by style news and by information on various changing methods of life which before had come to their attention only indirectly. Later, the moving pictures and the rotogravure supplements of the newspapers exercised their effect in creating demand for many articles not previously included in the rural standard of living. Mail order retailing offered an opportunity for the purchase of these goods. Developments in catalog making made it possible to advertise goods effectively and to supply realistic photographs. Establishment of the parcel post system in 1913 made it possible to ship small packages more economically. Another factor in the growth of mail order houses was the recognition that this method of selling could take advantage of the economies of large-scale retailing.

The larger mail order companies engaged in Programmes of diversification as the country became more urbanized and opened many retail establishments of the department store type. Such stores now account for the majority of the business of both Sears' and Ward's, but mail order or catalog retailing continues to be a very large segment of their total sales volume.

PRESENT STATUS OF MAIL ORDER ESTABLISHMENTS

In 1958 there were 2,550 retail mail order establishments, of which 1,502 had paid employees and 1,048 were small units operated exclusively by proprietors and family members.

Aggregate sales volume of these establishments amounted to $20 billions, or about 1 per cent of the sales of all retail establishments. There has been practically no change in the relative sales volume importance of mail order establishments over the period 1929-58

While the 2,550 mail order establishments operated in many lines of trade, more than 75 per cent of their sales was reported by only 35 large establishments handling a complete line of department store merchandise. More than one-half of these establishments are operated by two companies— Sears' and Ward's—thus indicating high concentration in this field.

COMPETITIVE POSITION OF GENERAL CATALOG HOUSES

The general merchandise mail order organizations have, in the main, the advantages and disadvantages of other large-scale retail enterprises. Due to the peculiar nature of their business, certain special conditions affect their competitive situation.

ADVANTAGES

As compared with single-line and general stores in the rural districts, mail order houses offer a more complete and varied line of merchandise. Their location in the larger cities gives a certain amount of prestige to their merchandise, especially in style goods.

Prices, at least for many articles, are somewhat lower than those charged for corresponding articles in the rural communities. Buying from a catalog is perhaps quicker and easier for rural people than going to stores in somewhat distant cities, and such shopping can be done at any time of day or evening that is most convenient. Convenience, moreover, is a strong appeal among urban customers who patronize catalog order offices or telephone order facilities maintained by leading mail order companies in large cities.

Absence of pressure to buy, avoidance of the confusion of crowded stores, informative statements concerning products, guaranties, and a liberal returned-goods policy are other attractions. Because sales are made in all sections of the country and to different classes of consumers, sales are not greatly affected by local industrial depressions, as are those of local merchants.

Some general advantages enjoyed by all mail order vendors grow out of certain operating economies. Warehouses are located in parts of the city where rent is much lower than that which must be paid by the ordinary retailer. Expensive fixtures are unnecessary, for only equipment of the warehouse type is required. It is unnecessary to employ retail salespeople, for the catalog descriptions plus the reputation of the firm and price appeals effect sales. Hence, employees of the clerical and shipping department type are used and their work is scheduled to permit an efficient utilization of time—something difficult to accomplish in retail stores which must be staffed in accordance with daily and hourly variations in consumer traffic.

DISADVANTAGES

Selling by catalogs is limited by the impossibility of examining merchandise in advance of purchase. For shoes, gloves, or clothing, it may be difficult for the buyer to secure the right articles without trying them on for size and fit.

Many consumers hesitate to order products where size, colour, style, or texture are significant in choice making.An important limitation is inflexibility of the merchandising programme. Semi-annual catalogs published by Sears' and Ward's comprise between 1,000 and 2,000 pages. Plans must be made well in advance of the season as to the detailed composition of the line of goods and the manner in which they are to be featured and illustrated. More important, prices must be determined months before catalogs are distributed, and the firm usually must live with its pricing decisions throughout the catalog season.

While the catalogs contain statements that prices are subject to change without notice, and even though special sale catalogs are issued, the companies do not have the pricing flexibility of other forms of retailing. They cannot mark down individual items of merchandise as the rate of sale becomes too slow or as costs decline; neither can they raise prices on individual items as demand increases or as wholesale costs rise. New items can be added or dropped only when new catalogs are prepared.

DYNAMIC ADJUSTMENTS IN CATALOG RETAILING

The inception and period of rapid early development of mail order retailing was associated with the concept of a new merchandising service to the Non-urban population. In modern times, with contemporary conditions of communication, transportation, and urbanization, it is indeed remarkable that catalog retailing has been able to hold a stable share of total retail sales, thus growing at the same rate as all of retailing.

This is attributed to certain dynamic, and in some cases distinctive, methods and policies adopted by the general catalog houses—in large measure for the purpose of capitalizing upon their advantages, minimizing their limitations, and adjusting to changing consumer preferences.

Sales promotion activities are efficiently organized. Mailing lists are prepared with care and efforts are made to keep them up to date. Careful tests are made of the success of different types of copy and appeals. Experienced copy writers know the language and the appeals which are most useful in reaching their clientele. In order to overcome the reluctance of buyers to purchase articles which they cannot see before the order is placed, mail order houses give a very liberal guaranty, covering as a rule both quality and price.

If the purchaser is dissatisfied with the commodity, it may be returned at the expense of the seller, and the purchase price is promptly refunded.

The general catalog houses have a special brand problem. To attract business, as they do in part, on a price-appeal basis, they must purchase from suppliers at lowest prices. For this reason such houses do not generally carry very many nationally advertised, branded articles.

They prefer to sell unbranded commodities or those which carry their own brand. It is usually necessary to brand the specialties which they sell, in order to identify them and give them a certain distinction. Hence it is common for catalog houses to purchase such articles as vacuum sweepers, gasoline engines, washing machines, farm implements, cosmetics and drugs from suppliers who manufacture to the specifications of the catalog firm and who attach to the goods the private brand of the mail order company.

In order to reach a larger number of potential customers, the major firms have opened a large number of catalog order offices which are located in storerooms in hundreds of small cities and in many suburban shopping centers of large cities. No merchandise is available for sale over the counter in these establishments, but selected items and swatch and sample books are displayed for examination.Employees assist customers to make out and transmit orders. Many such order offices have teletype communication with a regional warehouse which services the area. Orders received prior to a certain time each day can be delivered to the customer's home on the following day in most cities, thus rivaling the speed of delivery service available from local stores. Similar catalog departments are also found in the regular retail stores operated by mail order companies. In the typical Sears' store, the catalog order desk is usually the largest sales volume department.Some catalog companies have expanded their customer contact points by establishing order stations in retail establishments operated by other companies. Certain small-town and cross-roads stores have displayed the general merchandise catalogs of some companies for a number of years, and accept and process orders on a commission basis. More recently some variety chains and supermarket organizations have made similar arrangements with mail order firms. For example, in 1960, Ward's established catalog order stations in certain New York state supermarkets of Loblaw, Inc., thus giving Ward's sales outlets in areas where it had no retail stores, and providing the Loblaw organization with a 100,000 item increase in its offering of nonfood merchandise lines.

Another feature is the operation of telephone order offices. While confined to larger cities in which there is a considerable potential volume of daily business, this development is one of increasing significance, accounting in 1960 for more than 30 per cent of all catalog sales volume at Sears'. The catalog customer can sit in her home, order by number from the catalog, have her order dispatched by teletype as explained above in connection with catalog order offices, and receive next-day delivery in many large cities.As a consequence of such innovations, the historic *mail order business* has evolved into a more modern conception of *general catalog retailing*, characterized by efforts to bring to the consumer wanted merchandise at various points of sales contact, using means of communication and delivery which are appropriate to contemporary conditions.

CATALOG SELLING BY STORE RETAILERS AND MANUFACTURERS

Mail order selling is used to some extent by specialty retailers and by certain manufacturers who sell direct to the consumer. It is also used in the direct marketing of some farm products with a special appeal, such as Smoked Virginia Hams, smoked turkeys, and gift packages of fruit.

Such sellers usually do not have elaborate catalogs, but secure orders by advertising in newspapers and magazines, on radio and television broadcasts, and by direct mail addressed to the homes of consumers. Goods so ordered are shipped by parcel post, express, truck, or ordinary freight.

This type of selling brings many kinds of goods to the attention of a broad market. Items so sold are often of a novel or unusual character and are not available in local stores, especially in smaller communities. Some merchandise is sold direct to consumers by manufacturers who stress a price appeal. While specialty mail order retailing is relatively expensive, since it usually involves substantial advertising and handling and shipping costs, many consumers are nevertheless influenced by an appeal which suggests that they save money by purchasing direct rather than from a retail store.

Appeals of "lower prices," "greater values," or "substantial savings," have been used by most of the major book and record club companies that have a membership which is contacted by mail. Such savings are customarily offered in terms of "free" or "bonus" books, awarded when the member actually purchases a predetermined number of books at regular prices, in accordance with a membership agreement. Bonuses offered in this manner are largely due to low purchase prices negotiated with publishers when contracting for large numbers of copies and not to economies of selling and distributing to individual consumers on a mail order basis. Manufacturers and retailers who sell a narrow line of goods by the mail order method are subject to most of the disadvantages enumerated above in connection with general catalog houses. In addition, they usually lack the prestige enjoyed by a large nationally known organization. Hence, such selling is relatively unimportant, and there are no reasons to believe that it will ever be of much significance in other than a very narrow range of merchandise items.

Catalog selling is also an important form of supplementary promotional effort among many regular *store retailers*, especially large department stores and departmentized specialty stores, who have a ready-made mailing list consisting of their regular charge account customers. This is especially significant for the promotion of gift merchandise during the Christmas shopping season.

STORE DESIGN MORE IMPORTANT FOR E-RETAILERS

We have already established that store design is important to both traditional retailers and online retailers. The reader may have already guessed that e-store design is relatively more important for online retailers and might even be considered the most important part of their retail mix. Why?The main reason is that store design has bigger scope with e-retailers. Store design in traditional offline retailing is generally confined to the physical aspects of the store, such as the infrastructure and layout. The online scope of store design is greater because it also includes what used to be covered by interaction with the salesperson. Almost everything has to be covered by what is on the computer screen, so the e-store design is clearly a very important domain. Additionally, areas like customer service and after-sales service that were separate departments in offline retailing, now have to be incorporated into the e-store design. This further increases the scope and importance of e-store design.

MINI CASE STUDY: ONLINE CAR SEARCHES (AUTOS.MSN.COM/HOME/NEW_RESEARCH.ASPX)

This site provides information on new cars and includes data on make, model, dealership, specification, quotes, prices and insurance, as well as a photogallery. It is a typical site in this retail category, but additionally offers a link to multimedia presentations that provide 360-degree views of the exterior and interior of the motor vehicle. The function can be controlled for both speed and vertical views directly by the user.The site is similar to others such as those selling boats, motorcycles, caravans, etc. and includes new and second-hand cars. This is useful for searching for unique or hard-to-find items such as collectables and is convenient for consumers and sellers alike and provides a greater market reach.

START E-STORE DESIGN WITH NAVIGABILITY

Navigability is the most fundamental building block of e-store site design. By navigability we mean the ability of the user to move around the site easily and efficiently, that is, without getting lost. If users have to travel through several topics or layers to find information, they will get frustrated or lost, possibly causing them to exit the site prematurely. Thus a key objective of good navigation design is to minimize travel, depth and redundancy when moving around within a site.Another way of thinking about navigation design is to ask three basic questions in terms of a user at a point in time on an e-site:

- Where am I at the moment?
- Can I get back to where I have been?
- How can I go forward to a particular location?

For well-designed sites, these three questions are readily answered for most users. If a user struggles, then the site is badly designed. Go to an e-retailer site and make a couple of moves around the site. Now answer the three basic questions above. Write down on a piece of paper how well this particular site answers these three basic questions. If the answers are not good, what could the e-retailer do to improve its e-store design? Can you find a site that is really good at this function?

Another study has developed a checklist to assist with evaluating the navigability of a site. Merrilees and Fry (2002) have come up with the following points:

- Is navigation easy?
- Is navigation efficient?
- Is navigation fast?
- Does layout of the site make it easy to use?
- Does the site have a good menu system?
- Overall, is the design simple and user-friendly?

Exercise 6.2: Briefly go back to the site that you used for Exercise 6.1. Now answer the six new questions about site design. Do you get more or less the same answers as to how well the site performs? Would you agree that you need both lists to get the right answer?

Although navigation design might be seen as a technical function, it nonetheless needs to address fundamental requirements that create a user-friendly experience. Two checklists have been presented here to help the reader evaluate existing sites or, alternatively, to guide the development of a new site or a new e-store design for an existing site.

Different devices can be used to facilitate this process, including links that can take the user back to the home page from any page, or have clear menu signposts of how to proceed. The reader can learn from experience of which sites do a good job on this fundamental process. As an example, one site (an online second-hand bookstore used several times by one of the authors) has a good recovery system if a user accidentally double-clicks on the 'order' button. The instructions enable an e-mail to be sent or offer suggestions of another way of proceeding without re-keying in everything again. However, while these suggestions for recovery are good, would it not be better to re-design the site so that it does not collapse if someone does inadvertently double click instead of single click?

PROGRESS TO INTERACTIVITY

Interactivity is another fundamental aspect of e-store design. In simple terms, it refers to the interaction between the user of an e-site and the site itself. Thus this refers to a *person-machine interaction*. However, this relationship has more depth than say the relationship that you have with an ATM or even your home computer doing desktop work. The extra depth comes about because the *machine* in the e-retailer context is an ongoing *entity*, with a capacity to provide service, sell goods, transact money, be cheerful or grumpy, be there tomorrow for you and so on. Such extra depth makes this particular person-machine interaction *virtually* (but not quite fully) that of a person-to-person interaction. Another way of illustrating this is to compare the *user-e-retailer interaction* in the e-world to that of the *consumer-salesperson interaction* in the bricks and mortar world. With a traditional offline retailer, if as a customer you have a question about a product, it is common to ask a salesperson. Salespeople are also important if you want to pay for merchandise or, alternatively, if you want to return goods.

Instead of a salesperson, these functions are handled by a computer interface. Usually the answers are built into the programme, such as a description of the product or a mechanism to order and pay for the merchandise. Discrete questions can be asked, but are usually handled as part of a *frequently asked question (FAQ)* routine. If this does not provide an answer then a separate e-mail might be called for, though most e-retailers do not encourage this option because it is deemed too time-consuming.

Thus the user-e-retailer interaction has to anticipate the sorts of questions that might be normally asked of a salesperson and, where possible, to automate these procedures into the design of the e-store. Obviously it is important to convey the right tone and mood. It is better to have a friendly and helpful 'sales assistant' and this also applies to the user-e-retailer interface. The difference between the online e-retailer and the offline bricks and mortar retailer can be exaggerated. Traditional offline retailers have increasingly become more self-service in their orientation with less personal service from sales assistants. To some extent this trend is even true with normal department stores which used to be very labour-intensive. The move to more reliance on self-service has been achieved through more effective layout of the store and visual merchandising, such as more helpful product tags.

In other words, it has become necessary for offline retailers to improve their skills in selling merchandise with less or no help from salespeople. This is exactly what an e-retailer does, so in a sense it is really an extension of existing offline trends rather than a radically different way of selling. We can take a closer look at interactivity in the e-retail sense by examining how the academic literature views it. Most of the interpretations of interactivity have a strong communication element, which builds on the analogy with the salesperson interaction in the offline world. Five major impressions or dimensions of online interactivity can be highlighted. The most common impression of interactivity from the literature is that it is primarily *communication*-based.

Infrequently, other activities, such as downloading software or making a purchase, are noted as forms of interactivity that seem to have something else other than communication as the driving force. In such cases, we would wish to highlight the communication or information aspects of those activities. Second, interactivity is about *two-way communication*. This spans communication from the viewer to the firm and from the firm to the viewer, as well as simultaneous interaction between the two parties. All three aspects of two-way communication need to be addressed in better understanding the meaning of interactivity. Third, a special feature of Internet interactivity is the ability to *personalize* and possibly customise the situation for an individual. Fourth, a number of writers have emphasized the ability of the individual to *control* the communication and *learn* as a noteworthy feature of the interactive process. Fifth and finally, a broader more holistic role of interactivity has been noted as an important contributor to building up the total *shopping experience* on the Internet.Based on a wide body of Internet-related literature, Merrilees (2002) developed the following checklist of aspects of interactivity:

- Site helps the viewer participate, learn and act;
- Good two-way communication;
- Site facilitates feedback from the viewer to the retailer (directly via the Web and/or e-mail);
- The overall shopping experience is very pleasant and enjoyable;
- The site develops a close, personalized relationship with the viewer;
- Any query or question that you have can be answered quickly and efficiently;
- Site has good interactivity (capstone item).

BUILDING E-RELATIONSHIPS THROUGH INTERACTIVITY

Given the importance of communication in developing *offline* quality relationships, it seems likely that the same may be true in the e-commerce context. Kolesar and Galbraith (2000) suggest that establishing a relationship with customers is harder to achieve in an e-retail context because alienation makes it harder to create the kind of bond that is often enjoyed between other service providers and their customers. They argue that, because the Internet as a medium is less personal than other retail channels, surrogates for direct personal interaction must be provided in an e-retail transaction.

The issue of managing customer relations in e-commerce begs the question as to what the strategic drivers of effective e-relationships are. Some writers (Lindstrom and Anderson 1999; Carpenter 2000) argue that e-relationships are critical for developing strong e-retail sites. One of the few empirical papers demonstrating the importance of interactivity in developing quality e-relationships is by Merrilees (2002), who studied www.amazon.com for books and an Australian online grocer, www.coles.com.au. The relationship between interactivity and higher-quality relationships between users and the e-retailer (as perceived by the user) was very strong

PIONEERING MAJOR ARTICLE ON WEB ATMOSPHERICS

One of the first major journal academic studies of web atmospherics was that of Eroglu et al. (2001). The paper supports the idea that various online cues could influence outcomes like satisfaction, amount purchased and time spent online. Their emphasis is on the process by which these cues work and they begin by adopting two types of atmospheric qualities, namely high task-relevant environment and low task-relevant environment. The high-task cues include product description, price, terms of sale, delivery, product reviews, return policies, product pictures and navigation aids. Low-task cues include unrelated special offers, colours, borders and background patterns, icons, image maps and affiliations. Sites are likely to have a different mix of high-task and lowtask cues, so there is a need to get the balance right. The authors argue that there is a greater need for high-task cues for segments of customers who are either high-involvement or very sensitive to their environment's atmosphere.

ENHANCEMENTS THROUGH WEB ATMOSPHERICS

Web atmospherics have an analogy to traditional offline retailing. Retailers in the latter environment have long added to the atmosphere of the store, in the belief that the feel and look of the store would encourage shoppers to spend more time there and to buy something or something extra. To a certain extent, atmosphere is strongly influenced by visual merchandizing, that is, the way the merchandise is presented to the customer. The patterns of the displays and the use of colour and textures are sometimes offered in a real-life setting, such as a bedroom to sell beds. Such displays can take on various tones, such as sophistication, stylish or economic, depending on the target market of the retailer. Music and other audio can reinforce the mood that the retailer is attempting to create. The same principles apply to e-store design. The visual look of the e-store can change the perception that viewers have of the store. If controlled properly and if they are aligned to the profile of the target market, then web atmospherics can stimulate an increase in sales.

INTERNET FOR MARKETING RESEARCH

In a broad sense, is becoming increasingly central to marketing strategy. Think of the trend towards mass customization, in which customers can specify their exact requirements and the production process is customized accordingly.

Detailed knowledge of customer needs is essential here if the goods are to be produced on an individual basis. Another example concerns permission marketing where specific services are provided to customers based entirely on 'permission' that the customer has given the company. This means that a travel company may be given permission by a customer to send them promotions that relate only to self-catering holidays in Florida in the month of October - and nothing else. The company will need to be able to process and act upon this information (which of course is research data about customer preferences) and not just send the customer a general brochure that includes all of the company's holidays. Loyalty, and hence customer retention, is based upon a thorough understanding of customer needs that can be established and maintained only by research. The economic benefits of customer retention are obvious: revenues and market share grow through repeat business and referrals, while costs fall through economies of scale and the reduced amount of effort that needs to be spent on customer acquisition and the servicing of familiar customers. McDaniel and Gates (2002) describe the example of British Airways, which researched the preferences of first-class passengers and found them to be - sleep. So, as an alternative to receiving a series of intrusive services during the flight, such passengers can now have dinner in the lounge before take-off and then enjoy an uninterrupted flight.

The Internet is becoming an increasingly important *source* of research data (known as secondary data) as well as providing a cost-effective new *medium* for the research process itself, for example as an alternative means of collecting data by completion of an online questionnaire rather than from telephone or face-to-face interviewing (known as primary data).

THE INTERNET AS A SOURCE OF SECONDARY DATA

The best way to find information on the Internet is to key in the unique Uniform Resource Locator (URL) which will take you directly to the page required, without the need to rely upon search engines. Organizations can promote their URL address on company stationery, on the side of vehicles or buildings, or in other increasingly innovative ways.

If you are looking for information without knowing the exact source, then a key word search on one of the many search engines is the best strategy to adopt.

The exponential growth of the Web is making the task of search engines increasingly difficult because of the sheer volume of new sites and information being placed on the Web. McDaniel and Gates (2002) provide a comprehensive table of their book explaining the features of the major search engines, as well as a list of sites that are of specific relevance to market researchers.You might also like to try www.netskills.ac.uk for an online tutorial guide to searching the Internet, or www.researchbuzz.com, which has news on new information sources and search engines, or www.searchenginewatch.com, which explains how search engines work.Information available online is increasingly diverse.

For example, exporters now have the opportunity to resolve historical information gaps when contemplating trading internationally that previously may have dissuaded firms from pursuing such strategies. Details of market access, exchange control regulations, costs of import duties, etc. are now much more transparent on the Web. Some organizations are competing to offer quality content online, thereby enhancing their brand image and encouraging repeat visits and recommendations for research purposes. Many of the traditional sources of market information are now available online, for example annual reports, large-scale market surveys, government reports and economic data. While there are valuable data freely available, care needs to be taken because the Internet also carries vast amounts of poor-quality data. As with traditional market research, appropriate questions to ask are:

- Are the data relevant?
- Are the data accurate?
- Are they up to date?
- What sampling techniques have been used to collect the data?

THE INTERNET AS A MEANS OF COLLECTING PRIMARY DATA

There are a number of primary research tasks that can be effectively carried out online; for example:

- Measuring the effectiveness of a firm's Internet strategy;
- Measuring customer satisfaction levels;
- Obtaining customer feedback on new product/service ideas;
- Polling consumers for information about any subject.

Undertaking primary research to measure the effectiveness of a company's Web site is a critical aspect of the evaluation of online marketing strategy. A brief overview is provided here. The following questions may be asked:

- Are the objectives of the site being met?
- Is the corporate message getting across?
- How effective are the various promotional techniques used to attract visitors to the site?
- What changes need to be made to improve the quality of customer service offered?
- Is the site easy to use?
- How many sales are resulting from online contacts?
- How many visitors are coming back to the site?
- How much new business has resulted from the Web site (as opposed to its merely offering an additional channel to existing customers)?
- How does the site compare with those of competitors?
- Channel promotion measures assess why customers visit a site:
- Which sites have they been referred from? (What was the electronic link?)
- Which offline adverts did they see?

From this analysis it should be possible to measure the percentage of customers whose enquiry was prompted by online and offline means respectively, thereby guiding the nature of future promotional campaigns.

- Channel buyer behaviour measures assess which aspects of the Web site content are visited, the times of day and the duration of the visit. This analysis enables 'stickiness' to be measured, for example the average length of a visit, and the proportion of first-time to repeat visitors. It can also suggest changes to site structure and content.

- Channel satisfaction measures evaluate customers' perception of online service quality issues such as e-mail response times. It is also possible to use services such as Gomez to benchmark service quality against the competition.
- Channel outcome measures compare the number of site visitors to the number of actual purchases made; in other words, how many visitors leave the site without buying anything. For example, if 10 purchases result from 100 visits, the conversion rate is 10 per cent.
- Channel profitability measures are a critical test of success. How much does the online channel contribute to business profit after taking account of the costs incurred?

In addition to evaluating existing marketing strategy, research can also play a more proactive role through identifying changes in the market and customer needs, thereby suggesting future strategic directions for the firm. Asking customers what they expect from a company's site and obtaining feedback on current promotions can provide important information to aid market segmentation and other marketing applications.

For example, Honda now has different sites for male and female customers, following a research exercise that established how men preferred detailed graphics emphasizing different aspects of car performance, while women preferred brief factual information.Company intranets can also be used effectively to gather research data from staff, a key group of stakeholders whose importance is now increasingly recognized by the designation 'internal customers. Staff opinions are a valuable source of research data that can be sought and collated through an online questionnaire.

8

Management in E-commerce

E-COMMERCE POLICY

There are bodies at international, regional and national levels that seek to promote the take-up of e-Commerce. The principal international bodies come under the auspices of the United Nations and include the World Trade Organization (WTO), the World Intellectual Property Organization (WIPO) and the United Nations Committee for International Trade and Law (UNCITRAL).

This latter body has drawn up the UNCITRAL Model Law for Electronic Commerce that supports the commercial use of international contracts in e-Commerce, and offers technical advice to governments on this.

The Model Law creates rules and norms validating the practice of electronic commerce, seeks to make electronic documents and signatures legal and supports the admission of electronic evidence into court proceedings and arbitration.At a European level, the European Union has drawn up a number of directives that aim to provide a legal framework for e-Commerce within the European Union. The member countries are obliged to follow these directives by creating new legislation in order to harmonize the legislative framework across the single market.

These directives include:

- *The Electronic Signatures Directive.* This defines the requirements for electronic signatures and their certification in order to ensure a minimum level of security in e-Commerce dealings. The United Kingdom passed the Electronic Communications Act in 2000 that amended in the region of 300 laws so that any reference to documents, writing and signatures would now include their electronic equivalents. However, to get this Act through Parliament, the UK government was obliged to remove controversial provisions on encryption keys. Public Key Cryptography has both public and private keys that allow the encryption and decryption of data and is seen as critical in the provision of secure e-Commerce transactions.
- *The Conditional Access Services Directive.* This aims to safeguard

against the unauthorized use of conditional access services, and to make illegal, for example, technology that allows decryption of satellite television services when no contract exists with a service provider.

- *The Data Protection Directive.* This seeks to harmonize the rights of individuals and the obligations placed on organizations with regard to the use of 'personal data' gathered in e-Commerce activities. Additionally a prohibition was created on the export of such data to organizations in countries without similar provision. A potential problem that would have seen much of the trade between the European Union and the United States being deemed illegal was averted by use of a 'Safe Harbour Agreement' which sought to bring some level of accommodation in data protection terms between the two bodies. The United States places greater emphasis on the 'freedom of information' in its legislative framework and this comes into conflict with a European focus on the right of an individual to relative privacy. The United Kingdom's 1998 Data Protection Act updated the 1984 Act of the same name in line with this.
- *The Misleading Advertising Directive.* This seeks to prohibit the use of advertising on EU Web sites that is either misleading orlikely to mislead consumers.
- *The Distance Selling Directive.* This seeks to protect those buying products or services on the Internet within the European Union, and to provide seven day 'cooling off periods' during which consumers may choose to withdraw from agreed transactions. The directive does not apply to financial services or a number of product types and services such as auctions or short-life products. In October 2000 this directive was mirrored in the United Kingdom when the Consumer Protection (Distance Selling) Regulations Act was brought into force.

E-COMMERCE DEVELOPMENT

The literature onf *e-service* has by and large followed the commercial thrust of Internet marketing development. Initially, the most common application by firms and use by users was through the Web site itself, often a basic overview of the company and more in keeping with having a public relations 'presence' in the e-commerce world.

The next most common application was to post more detailed information about products, and conversely this was the second most common use by users. The third wave of application is the now dominant interest in e-selling, that is, the use of the Web to sell or buy goods. This takes us to the fourth and emerging wave, one that is still greatly underutilized, namely e-service.

Essentially, e-service offers the potential for some of the more advanced applications of Internet technology. For example, firms could use intelligent agents to provide extraordinary service, by tracking and datamining previous histories through Internet sites and developing known patterns of users' requirements. Customer relationships can be developed, based on prior 'modelled' understanding of which offers a consumer is likely to respond to. This is a special case of market segmentation to a market of one. As another application of work by Brookes *et al.* referred to in Cravens *et al.* (2000, p. 4), a manufacturer of washing machines could include in its warranty agreement the electronic capability of monitoring the ongoing usage of the machine. Suppose that, after the machine has been bought, the household has a new baby. If detergent dosage or load patterns place strain on the motor, the machine could have the built-in communication capability to automatically page the manufacturer's service depot. The depot receives a message for a service representative to visit the household and adjust the washing machine before it becomes a problem. In this way, while both the information technologies and the servicing component are largely unobtrusive to the household, they are nonetheless essential to maintaining customer satisfaction and potential loyalty.

The literature has started to discuss e-service, but it is somewhat unstructured. For this reason, a review of the literature plays a particularly important front-end role and we provide a simple classification of the literature to assist. We have included a separate section debating whether self-service is a myth for e-service. Our own position on this matter is made clear. We follow the literature review with a proposed, more systematic, typology of e-service, which could be useful to readers.

THREE APPROACHES TO E-SERVICE

We have identified three types of e-service literature. The first is what we call the *macro* or *very broad view* of e-service, namely that e-service is effectively synonymous with e-commerce. An *intermediate view* of e-service is that we can study the provision of *specialist services* made available by *specialist service providers* that help service Internet users (both individuals and companies). The third perspective on e-service is what we term a *micro perspective*, namely the provision of particular and varied detailed customer services within a site as *part* of the Web site - user interface.

At the broadest level is the view that e-commerce per se is an electronic service to customers - one that provides greater convenience. This view places e-commerce as an option available to customers, providing another channel of distribution or information. For example, instead of spending, say, an hour to physically access and purchase from a bookstore, the customer has the option to purchase the same electronically. As a further example, a company may use the Web to provide information about the company's offering to assist consumers in their product search, without necessarily enabling the consumer to purchase through the Web.

A related macro view of e-service is the *services marketing* perspective on e-retailing. They argue that e-retail offerings are service offerings and exhibit many of the same characteristics as other non-Internet-based services. They further argue that Internet services can be evaluated by similar criteria, such as responsiveness, empathy and the establishment of trust through courtesy and competency. The principal service provided by e-retailers is a search and evaluation facility that potentially saves time and effort for the consumer. The task of the e-retailer is to provide a Web site design that caters to different shopping styles, provides evidence to reduce risk and also educates the user in a shopping mode that may differ to what they are used to in conventional retail shopping.

There is now a considerable number of papers that have applied the macro perspective of e-service to a specific industry. For example, Muir and Douglas (2001) have studied how service delivery has changed in legal services with the rise of e-commerce. They argue that the quality of service is potentially improved with the Web. A Web presence allows legal practices to be more transparent and to offer greater access to information for customers by way of improving their services. It is suggested that this improved communication may lead to a reduction in complaints against solicitors.An *intermediate perspective* of e-service is the provision of *electronic services* from *specialist providers* to users of the Internet and intranets. Thus we have a market (external or internal) in which key electronic services are similar to products and sold or exchanged in a market to general users of the Web. here is a huge variety of specialist firms that offer their services (products) to Web users.

Web designers form a stereotypical group in this category, but also included are all types of suppliers of a wide range of Internet services, such as portal providers or providers of any specific link in the Internet network. For example, consider the commercial services offered by Compuserve, Prodigy, America Online and e-world. The pages of the national financial newspapers are filled with the advertisements of companies offering such Web-enabling services, some claiming to offer an integrated service.Electronic trust services are specialist e-services that provide reassurance and trust to the financial and privacy security of Internet information flow. There is a number of third-party commercial service providers who guarantee protection of either the financial security or the personal confidentiality of information flows.

A special case of this situation is the role of the electronic signature, an issue discussed by Travers (2001), who is particularly concerned with the status, planning and implementation of electronic signatures, in the context of the UK Electronic Communications Act 2000. He argues that electronic signatures can be considered within a knowledge management framework and proposes a six-part system that incorporates people, clients, knowledge matters, business development and training. Travers notes that the Electronic Communications Act provides:

- An approvals scheme for businesses providing cryptography services such as electronic signature services and confidentiality services;
- For the legal recognition of electronic signatures and the process under which they are verified; and
- For the removal of obstacles in other legislation to the use of electronic communications and storage in place of paper.

A somewhat unusual example of a specialist e-service is the provision of electronic money (Buck, 1997), which could be redefined as a trust-service, but Buck did not do so in his paper. He notes that there is a range of online payment systems, including credit systems (*e.g.* Payflow Pro), debit systems (*e.g.* BankNet), token-based mechanisms (*e.g.* Digicash) and electronic cash schemes (*e.g.* Mondex). Such mechanisms vary considerably in terms of safety, privacy protection and trustworthiness.

An example of a specialist e-service within an internal market is that of an e-mail-mediated help service (Hahn 1998). Hahn analysed 265 help-service responses from service logs and found, among other things, that users and help-service staff held different internal models for ideal e-mail communication. Users desired a fairly simple exchange of communication, that is, a clear question followed by a quick, simple response. Staff, on the other hand, envisaged the need for a more complex interrelationship, over several messages.

This takes us to the third perspective of e-service, namely the *micro* approach. Perhaps the dominant element in this field is the role of information. Some authors see information-based marketing as a potential competitive advantage. Other scholars see the Web as important for tracking and gathering customer feedback (Sampson, 1998; Sen *et al.*, 1998). Still other writers focus on the role of e-information as an aid to facilitating consumer search.

It is particularly in Merrilees (2002) that a broader perspective is given to interactivity. He embraces a more multi-dimensional approach to the concept of interactivity. Included factors are two-way communication between the e-retailer and the user; the ability of each party to communicate with the other including through e-mail; the ability to personalize the situation for the individual user; and the ability of the individual to control the communication and learn from it.Finally, there are numerous other Internet studies that emphasize particular aspects of e-service besides information or interactivity. For example Mols (2000), in his study of Danish retail banking, examined the role of more individualized services for consumers and their need for a close relationship with the bank. As a final example of a difficult-to-classify study of providing services on the Internet see Mathur (1998) who takes a financial accounting approach to the topic.

In summary, we have used our three-part classification of macro, intermediate and micro as an initial way of structuring the literature, as it exists. This is not to say that we endorse all perspectives of the literature. In particular we have reservations about the macro perspective. In a sense, the use of the World Wide Web by a retailer to market its organization as an online e-retailer is no more a services marketing exercise than the use of catalogues makes Lands End a services marketer. The *service component for an e-retailer* is the sum total of the ancillary support mechanisms provided by the retailer and the channel intermediaries to aid the Web prospective buyer to select, pay for and receive the merchandise.

The e-retailer may provide services for the consumption of the prospective buyer through the Web channel, but this still does not make the channel a service unto itself. Thus we prefer the intermediate and micro perspectives of initial classification and our empirical research design is more in keeping with the micro perspective. A more refined taxonomy of e-services is developed below.

BRITISH LIBRARY (WWW.BL.UK)

This is a free service provided by the British Library in London that includes a 'turn the page' function. This technology is new to websites and is only available for three articles at the time of going to press. The home page offers a range of services provided by the library and is easy to use with simple menu selection and navigation.

Of interest is the 'turn the pages' of Leonardo da Vinci's notebook. This technology displays a scanned image of the original notebook and allows the user to turn pages using the cursor in a way similar to a real book. To enter this site, select 'turn the pages' on the home page and follow the instruction. To use this facility a Shockwave driver is required and can be downloaded free in two minutes from the same site. This is an interesting site for those who are interested in history.

A SECOND TAXONOMY OF E-SERVICE

We initially used a three-way classification of the e-service literature, namely macro, intermediate and micro, as a way of sorting the literature in this fragmented domain.Our thinking on this topic has progressed to another proposed taxonomy of e-service. Not all of the aspects covered in this taxonomy are addressed in the empirical part. Taxonomy is put forward as an initial framework that can be debated by interested academics or practitioners.

THE SELF-SERVICE MYTH

Before leaving the literature, it is useful to discuss a crucial issue in the e-service area referred to by Moon and Frei (2000). They give the example of customers visiting a typical airline Web site and being confronted by a self-service search engine. If they know exactly when and where they want to travel, the Web site will generate a list of feasible flights. However, the search process becomes complex if they wish to find the cheapest airfare and are flexible on the dates and destinations. Moon and Frei are sceptical of the usefulness of the self-service approach to e-service and suggest that the customer is likely to have a much more satisfying experience if they call the airline's call centre for handling more complex situations.

Co-production is proposed by Moon and Frei (2000:26) as a better model than self-service for e-commerce. In the co-production model the company undertakes many of the tasks in shopping and buying, relieving the burden on the customer. The new model recognizes that, although customers like having choices, they do not want too many and appreciate pre-screened alternatives geared to their needs. Co-production also understands that customers want to state their preferences only once. Moon and Frei conclude that e-commerce firms should focus on customer service *not* self-service, and give illustrative examples of companies like Dell Computer Corporation. Dell performs a host of back-end transactions that are invisible to customers, such as grouping products by customer segments and displaying only in-stock items.

The current authors tend to endorse the sentiment of Moon and Frei in that we agree that it would be foolish for owners of e-sites to provide a minimalist infrastructure and simply to let users do their own thing. Our only objection is what to call the 'co-production model'. We are content to keep calling it a *self-service model*, but one that is designed appropriately and optimally.

Indeed, we believe that the challenge is for e-commerce firms to strive for an optimal self-service design capability. For a very interesting and relevant study, see Dabholkar (2000). His review of research into what consumers want from technologically-based self-service options suggests that speed, control and privacy are generally required. However, two additional attributes that positively influence the attitude of consumers towards computer technology are ease of use and fun or enjoyment. Web designers searching for the most effective design are advised to consult Dabholkar (2000). We should point out that the same issue has been debated with conventional retailing. Some *weak* retailers have taken the view that *self-service* equals *no service* and have provided very little help to consumers, using the opportunity to reduce their costs (in particular fewer sales staff). This approach will only leave consumers frustrated and unable to find what they want and so they are likely to leave the store very unhappy. In contrast, as Merrilees and Miller (1996) note, for better-performing stores 'self-service' does not mean 'no service'. The best self-service stores, like IKEA, Wal-Mart and many superstores, appreciate that self-service needs to be designed in such a way that it delivers good service, albeit of a kind other than personalized service.

Thus *good self-service design* in *conventional retailing* includes a well-organized store, with good layout, good signage, helpful visual displays and ready access to product information. Merrilees and Miller (2001) have argued that the approach taken by superstores represents a new self-service paradigm of retail service. Broadly speaking, the same good self-service design principles readily transfer from conventional retailing to e-retailing.

E-SERVICE PERFORMANCE

Knowing what is meant by e-service is an important first step in managing an e-retail business. However, it is necessary to take another step, namely the measurement of how well an organization is performing in each e-service activity. At this point it is clear that we only have a limited understanding of which e-service functions are important to consumers and how well e-retailers deliver these services. Some much-needed new research, namely a study of critical incidents in e-service delivery. Our critical incident analysis is followed by an examination of the role of e-service metrics as a management tool. In turn we discuss an alternative measure of e-service performance, namely e-retail service quality.

A CRITICAL INCIDENT APPROACH TO E-SERVICE PERFORMANCE

This section outlines the results of new research initiated especially for this book. A content analysis of 138 e-retail sites was undertaken by four judges in order to assess the nature and effectiveness of e-service across those sites. It was suggested that a good way of getting started might be with book, music, gift and department store sites, because these represent a high share of the e-selling transaction activity. The final discretion as to sites chosen was left to the individual judges. The main criterion for selection as a judge was expertise in analysing e-retailer websites. Notwithstanding each judge's expertise, further controls were built into the evaluation process through careful briefing and training of the judges. This briefing included careful instruction to make sure that all items were fully understood by each judge and that all judges had the same meaning for each. Another instruction was that each judge was to spend about 10 to 15 minutes moving through the site to understand its features and its content before answering the various set questions. Each site was analysed in the same way.

A survey instrument (protocol) was designed for each judge to use with each site. A wide number of site attributes were assessed on a Likert scale of 1 to 7, depending on whether the judge agreed or not that the site performed well on a particular attribute. There was also an open-ended section of the survey instrument where the focus was on the overall level of e-service for the site, based on a 1 to 7 Likert scale. On the same page the judge was asked to describe up to three important critical incidents/areas that positively contributed to their assessment of the overall level of e-service. Additionally, up to three important critical incidents could be listed that detracted from the level of e-service.

POSITIVE CRITICAL INCIDENTS

Initially we present the incidents that positively contributed to e-service. We do this in two ways. First we can note those positive facilitators to e-service across the *total* sample of 138 sites. We also break the results into *high-service sites* and *low-service sites*. High-service sites are those sites that were rated highly on the basis of the perceived overall level of e-service, that is, those sites that scored a 5, 6 or 7 out of 7. Those sites that scored 1 to 4 were called low-service sites. Across the total 138 sites, the three most positive incidents that contributed to e-service were:

- Interactivity and communication (56 per cent of all sites);
- Special offers (33 per cent);
- information (20 per cent).
- The next most important batch included:
- Variety of items for sale (14 per cent);
- Frequently asked questions (FAQs) (a separate type of interactivity) (12 per cent);
- Ease of use (12 per cent).

Other less important facilitators of e-service included security/privacy references (8 per cent), goods delivery (7 per cent) and returns policy (4 per cent). If we compare high-service and low-service sites, we more or less get a similar picture of what is important. One key difference is that the number of positive incidents of good e-service is a lot lower in low-service sites. Thus interactivity and special offers remain the highest two facilitators of good e-service, but the rate of incidence is about twice as much in high-service sites.

For example, in low-service sites there is a 27 per cent incidence of interactivity (compared to 72 per cent in high-service sites) and a 20 per cent incidence of special offers (compared to 39 per cent in high-service sites). A number of key determinants of e-service in high-service sites are downgraded in low-service sites. These include information, FAQ, security/privacy and returns.

NEGATIVE CRITICAL INCIDENTS

Apart from coding those elements of e-service that contribute to the overall level of e-service of a site, we have also analysed those elements that have reduced the overall level of e-service. We have retained the same classification of elements, but now we refer to negative critical incidents. That is, interactivity now refers to a lack of interactivity or a low level of service from this element. The same applies to the other eight elements of e-service.

The pecking order of negative critical incidents that affect overall e-service. The two most important negative incidents are a narrow variety of goods for sale (15 per cent of sites had this problem) and poor delivery service (14 per cent of sites). Other problem areas of e-service included interactivity (11 per cent), information (10 per cent), ease of use (8 per cent) and returns policy (8 per cent). The other three elements, FAQ, security/privacy and special offers, were rarely mentioned as a negative incident.

We have extended this analysis to a comparison of high-service and low-service sites. As we would expect, the number of negative incidents is almost thrice as great in the low-service sites. Variety and delivery were the top biggest problem areas for both types of sites, but had an incidence rate of less than 10 per cent in the high-service sites (compared to more than a quarter of the low-service sites). For the rest of the e-service elements, the most notable difference in the rankings is that of ease of use. It was the equal third highest problem area among low-service sites, but the lowest (and almost non-existent with a 1 per cent incidence) among the high-service sites.

LOGISTIC REGRESSION OF HIGH-LOW SERVICE SITES

We can extend our analysis from an enumeration of the critical incident elements (as a form of Pareto analysis), to a binary logistic regression analysis in which we can predict which sites fall into the high-service or low-service categories. The dependent variable is binary (either one type of site or the other). The independent variables are the nine dummy variables denoting positive critical incidents and the nine dummy variables denoting negative critical incidents.

Overall the degree of explanation is high, with an adjusted coefficient of determination of 0.53. Nine of the dummy variables were significant at the 5 per cent level.

The model predicts very well, with an 88 per cent hit rate. The six major e-service elements that shunt a firm into either a high-service or low-service category were:

- Positive interactivity incidents
- Negative information incidents
- Negative delivery incidents
- Negative interactivity incidents
- Negative ease of use incidents
- Positive FAQ incidents.

In addition, less important influences were positive information incidents, positive special deals and negative variety of items for sale incidents.

Multiple Regression Analysis of Overall Service Rating

Given that we have recorded the actual overall service rating of the site, on a 1 to 7 scale, we can also analyse the data with conventional multiple regression analysis, with the overall service rating as the dependent variable and the same independent variables as before. This is another way of testing the robustness of our results, although the logistic regression and the multiple

Ordinary Least Squares (OLS) are testing slightly different models and therefore we would not expect exactly the same results to be produced. the results. The adjusted coefficient of determination is good, at 0.56. Eight variables were significant. The six most important e-service elements explaining the overall service rating were:

- Positive interactivity incidents
- Negative delivery incidents
- Negative ease of use incidents
- Negative information incidents
- Positive information incidents
- Negative interactivity incidents.

Additionally, positive variety of the offerings had a marginal influence on overall service rating, while positive deals and negative variety of items were not quite significant.If we compare we see that essentially the same elements are at work. However there are slight differences, with some elements appearing in one table only, and the pecking order changing marginally. For example, a positive FAQ service might elevate an e-retailer into the high-service category, but did not have any discernible influence on the overall rating regression.

DETERMINING E-COMMERCE ROLE AND INVESTMENT

Understanding competitive position is necessary but not sufficient to formulate the e-commerce strategy. Companies must also determine the appropriate role for e-commerce inside the company and the level of investment to be made. Thus, the external positioning must be supplemented with an internal analysis of company fit.

The fit may be related to items such as organization structure, product type and mix, customer type and mix, channels, geographical breadth, and financial resources. Thus, every company utilizes e-commerce by directly selling goods or services on the Internet. Some find profitability in supply-chain management, procurement, marketing, and providing general information online.

That decision may become obvious before any significant strategic planning or may be determined after a fuller examination of the facts. But, a full examination of the broad opportunities must be completed and becomes an important input to the investment decision.Among the most important issues is the amount of resources to be committed to e-commerce. As companies examine reports of competitor investments, companies often question whether the size of their commitment is adequate.

Though the late 1990s saw some reckless spending on e-commerce without any justification of an ultimate payoff, current approaches to e-commerce require a carefully determined return on investment, as determined by a methodology.

But, the investment must follow a serious commitment to an e-commerce strategy and should not waver with modest changes in either the technology or the business environment.For companies selling online, the geographic scope of sales efforts is also a consideration.

Selling overseas creates numerous challenges, many of which are known to traditional business but are complicated further by e-commerce. Demographics of Internet users, online payment mechanisms, online marketing, and patterns of online buyer behaviour all vary greatly by country and may present too many permutations for a nascent

Internet venture to handle.A company may be understandably hesitant to begin global e-commerce immediately, even if its traditional business contains a global component. Some companies have chosen to limit the geographic scope of the venture until it has proven feasible and profitable on a domestic scale. The wisdom of such a limitation has been shown clearly in the case of grocery stores such as Tesco.Among the geographic considerations for an e-commerce venture are:

- A Web site can be viewed from anywhere around the world. Companies should be equipped to handle such a change in market size, or be prepared to explain the reasons for necessary geographic limitations.
- Product type is a key factor in any geographic consideration. Customers have far different expectations when using the Internet to order computers than when ordering groceries.

PREPARING IMPLEMENTATION AND ALIGNING COMPANY CULTURE

Most laggard companies do not have the luxury of delaying the implementation of e-commerce until the company culture is sufficiently prepared. Instead, company leaders must constantly reinforce the importance of IT in order to build the appropriate culture for e-commerce. As their personal behaviour and attitudes often send the strongest messages, private behaviour must not undermine or contradict public statements about company commitment to e-commerce ventures. Senior managers must reinforce the message that while technology itself is not a strategy, it remains a tool with strategic implications, and that the introduction of technology does not change the role of every contributor to the success of the company. Leadership must also choose the proper motivational tools, including incentives, coaching, and creating stretch targets.

For an e-commerce venture to be successful in a traditional company, senior managers must also impart a number of clear messages on company strategy and its value proposition. Instead of trying to create a unique culture for units handling the e-commerce venture, the company must create a culture conducive to integrating e-commerce throughout the company. Attitudes of either "the Internet changes everything" or "the Internet changes nothing" should be avoided, and a much more moderate position endorsed. Employees should not feel threatened or overwhelmed by the introduction of e-commerce.

The purpose of the e-commerce venture must also be carefully outlined to all employees, with a focus on the benefits of integration and the notion that e-commerce is typically a new channel for business, not a new business. People in each business unit must be apprised of the way e-commerce interacts with their current work and how best to develop that relationship to maximize integration benefits. At GE, this was achieved in the form of a company-wide initiative called Destroy Your Business, which required business units to analyse the impact and potential pitfalls of e-commerce on their business. Its associated programme, Grow Your Business, required units to formulate solutions to each of these problems. Belief in the value of IT must be instilled throughout the organization, and resistance to IT generally, and to e-commerce specifically, must be handled through education that emphasizes the functionality of these endeavors and their importance to long-term corporate success. Training Programmes must ensure that everyone, especially those employees who directly interact with customers, understands basic e-commerce concepts. Senior management is not immune to these requirements and must lead by example in this area with both public statements and behaviour.

Finally, a sense of urgency must be created throughout the organization, and business decisions should reflect that urgency. The pace of e-commerce is faster than that of traditional commerce, and easing into an e-commerce venture is not a promising strategy. In all areas that impact e-commerce, aggressiveness should be rewarded, and the value of speed should often supplant cost considerations. Many of these considerations must be addressed by specific changes in the company's systems and business processes, but the CEO should be prepared to create this orientation long before strategy implementation begins. Without strong leadership in the early stages, the changes in systems will be too drastic to implement the e-commerce strategy in a timely manner. Thus, to create a proper culture for e-commerce, companies must recognize that:

- Attitudes are as important as company policies regarding e-commerce. Company leaders must not only work to make an e-commerce venture a success, but show that they actually believe in the venture.
- E-commerce should be treated as a new channel for business, not as a revolution for the company. Employees need to be encouraged to embrace e-commerce instead of fearing it.
- The goals of the e-commerce venture need to be clearly outlined for everyone in the company.
- Aggressiveness in e-commerce should be rewarded.

E-commerce represents a major transformation, and the general principles of organizational change management are as applicable as advice specific to e-commerce. John Kotter's organizational change model provided a general framework for the consideration of how to approach significant change in business. As one can see, it can be easily adapted to the challenge of the changes necessary in the implementation of an e-commerce strategy.

PAYOFFS OF E-COMMERCE

We have examined how various organizational inputs and processes can impact the outputs of e-commerce. We have examined leadership, strategy, structure, and systems both in the corporation generally and related specifically to e-commerce. We have also seen how these key factors of success can be successfully managed in a formal process to improve customer acquisitions, customer loyalty, cost savings, channel optimization, and value creation.

Although these outputs are important, the resource allocation decision should rely on understanding the impact of e-commerce decisions and actions on the outcome of improved corporate profitability.

Many researchers and managers have recognized the need to identify and measure the impacts of corporate actions and to provide a better analysis of the return on investment (ROI) of e-commerce expenditures. However, the appropriate metrics have not been well developed. The framework presented here provides the necessary specificity to identify both the causal relationships that lead to e-commerce success, and related measures. In this way, both general managers and IT and e-commerce professionals can more effectively evaluate the success of e-commerce and the potential and actual payoffs of e-commerce investments.

Managers now can also examine the interrelationships among the characteristics of e-commerce success discussed here. The causal linkage analysis illustrates the importance of leadership, strategy, structure, and systems and highlights the specific managerial actions that lead to success.

Some writers have suggested the need for more measurements of the effectiveness of IT. They note that corporations have overlooked economic rationality in justifying IT expenditures and instead have leaned Towards a strategy that resembled an arms race, where firms acquire the best and most recent technologies to outpace others, regardless of the results. To assess the payoffs of e-commerce investments, companies must implement systems that evaluate the impact of e-commerce initiatives on financial performance and the trade-offs that must be made among competing organizational constraints and barriers to implementation.

These systems assist senior executives as they develop an e-commerce strategy and allocate corporate resources to support that strategy. The systems also assist e-commerce managers to evaluate the trade-offs and decide which projects provide the largest net benefit to both short-term financial performance and the long-term success of the firm. The careful identification and measurement of the payoffs also permits e-commerce and IT managers to demonstrate the impact on corporate profitability and value creation.

It also provides information for better corporate resource allocation decisions in the CEO's and CFO's offices, based on a better understanding of the ROI—including a fuller understanding of the benefits and costs of e-commerce. Hence, to implement their e-commerce strategy, companies are faced with a significant challenge: to quantify the link between corporate actions in e-commerce and corporate financial performance.

Indeed, only by making the "business case" for e-commerce expenditures can managers truly integrate potential e-commerce impacts into their business strategies. Yet, many companies have failed to make a case for e-commerce initiatives. Instead, they have often acted because they had a feeling that it was the right thing to do or because their competitors were making the leap into e-commerce ventures. However, projects put into place for these reasons alone are vulnerable to cost overruns and poor ROI, changes in senior management, or shifting corporate or consumer priorities.

To present a clear business case for e-commerce initiatives, senior managers need to identify the metrics of e-commerce performance and how that performance impacts overall long-term corporate profitability. This increased attention to the thorough identification and measurement of the metrics of e-commerce is echoed in popular measurement frameworks such as the popular strategic management system "balanced scorecard."

Frameworks such as balanced scorecard and shareholder value analysis focus on the causal relationships and linkages within organizations and the actions managers can implement to improve both customer and corporate profitability and drive increased value. However, substantial work is required to establish the relationships that relate specifically to e-commerce strategies.

Undeniably, the identification and measurement of the impact of e-commerce strategies is particularly difficult as they are usually linked to long time horizons, a high level of uncertainty, and impacts that are often difficult to quantify. But this analysis is important to improve resource allocation, decision making, and profitability.

In recent years, companies have placed increasing importance on the development of performance metrics to better measure and manage e-commerce performance. Software Programmes and information systems have been developed to provide a broader set of measurement tools to incorporate into new strategic management systems.

Although the need for performance measures for e-commerce has been identified, a large number of specific metrics have not been proposed. E-commerce analysis has typically been operating without measures that permit an effective evaluation of e-commerce benefits, success, or value. This lack of performance metrics has meant a lack of both actual and perceived accountability for firm e-commerce operations to various stakeholders.

It also examines how companies can make a compelling business case for e-commerce Programmes. Senior managers understand how to measure the value of e-commerce and understand the payoffs of e-commerce investments. Its purpose is to answer the question, "Is it worth it?" for companies deciding to start or expand e-commerce projects. This quandary is compounded as senior managers consider the high costs typically associated with e-commerce and the seemingly small percentage of e-commerce or IT projects that succeed. Sometimes the projects are flawed, but often the measures of success are flawed. Examples abound where companies have attempted e-commerce initiatives and have either failed dramatically or have incurred costs that far outweighed the gains. Though some would suggest that those failures occurred when companies were not so well centered on ensuring that IT-related funds were well spent, companies today face similar questions about the value of their e-commerce initiatives.

For most companies, it is not a question of whether or not to invest in e-commerce, but when and how: Should it be a large amount up front, or perhaps a smaller expenditure at a later date? Such decisions are critical and difficult. Key to making these decisions is understanding the causal relationships and identifying and measuring the success of the specific actions that managers can take to drive e-commerce success.

PRACTICES IN E-COMMERCE

Strong measurement practices form one of the cornerstones of good systems, particularly in e-commerce. Performance measures for e-commerce must overcome the uncertainty and unique dynamics associated with the Internet and must be more frequently adjusted in response to real-time information.With these considerations, no company should simply extend its existing performance measures to an e-commerce venture. Still, long-term cost differentials must be balanced with other financial and nonfinancial measures and leading and lagging indicators that are particularly useful for successful e-commerce implementations.

The information systems of the 1990s gave CEOs a new method of accessing, analyzing, and reporting on the accountability of their organization. The systems developed during this time of advancement in information technology helped to create a more streamlined capability for centralized accountability. The variety of data made available to a company at that time ranged from corporate-level results to the small-scale measurements of performance that enabled management to recognize advantages and potential problems in real-time. E-Commerce transforms these capabilities.

Like the root system of a massive tree, IT accountability systems helped management reach and observe every aspect of their business. With the addition of e-commerce to a pre-existing IT accountability system, companies can simplify access to previously collected information for those within the company and for external stakeholders, including partners, customers, and investors. New information could be created and both financial and nonfinancial measures could be integrated into the decision-making process.

The information could also be easily and quickly aggregated and disaggregated to facilitate various decisions. Managers could now measure inputs, processes, outputs, and outcomes in ways never before possible. Cisco's new systems permit outsiders to view on its Web site not only its general business plan but also the company's performance statistics at any given moment.

Seamlessness between internal IT systems and e-commerce gives Cisco the ability to provide such information with relatively little effort. This transparency between internal and external systems also helped Cisco endure many of the pitfalls associated with the technology bust by expanding the role of e-commerce to replace human positions throughout the company.

But e-commerce can be used for more than simply replacing employees. Instead, the information made available through a well-developed e-commerce initiative can empower employees at every level of business. Improved measurement is a key component. Management receives information in a timely manner, which lets it act on up-to-date measures of performance, while lower-level employees can access information at any time and take the initiative based on that information, with or without direct managerial direction.

Among the most important aspects of e-commerce as it applies to system management and measurement is maintaining consistency across all company lines. A company implementing a new e-commerce solution should ensure consistency among accounting systems, information technology systems, and e-commerce systems and related measures. However, the implementation of an e-commerce solution also necessitates working to ensure compatibility between the systems of business partners using unified e-commerce solutions.

The uniquely advantageous relationship between Dell and its suppliers would not be possible without seamless internal and external systems that enable a free flow of information and measures between companies. E-commerce can facilitate consistency of information and measurements by cascading information throughout the organization and then externally to other stakeholders.

In addition to measuring the performance of the business, e-commerce brings added importance to measuring the value and functionality of operations. Most e-commerce strategies will have a strong operational component, including cost savings from value chain management and cuts in labour costs for the online channel. Operational measures should be tracked by some dedicated resource and balanced between financial and nonfinancial assessments of operational performance. This analysis can lead to a better understanding of the payoffs of investment in e-commerce initiatives.

INFORMATION PRACTICES IN E-COMMERCE

For e-commerce to be successful, it is necessary but not sufficient that members of the organization are competent and confident in their use of IT. Strong leadership and investment can bring an organization to that stage, but systems must be created to harness the power of IT for organizational integration. It has recently been emphasized that interactive control systems in traditional business must focus on constantly changing information. These systems provide the sensing and monitoring that is necessary whenever strategic uncertainties are high. In most businesses today, more interactive control systems are needed as strategic uncertainties have been increasing. In e-commerce, these systems become increasingly central to the successful implementation of strategy.

A new policy on information practices must become a central component of the company's systems. Information should be transparent and the sharing of information facilitated. Organizational boundaries must not impede the flow of information. An integration strategy cannot be properly implemented if information about e-commerce stalls within the e-commerce unit and is not disseminated widely.

Ideally, internal processes are developed in-house with substantial consultation and communication; obstacles are easily recognized, understood, and dealt with, internally and quickly. Companies such as Amazon and Office Depot not only have garnered more efficient business practices because of their internal development, but also have been able to expand into other markets such as technology consulting and Web design because of their in-house expertise.

Companies can also use the implementation of an e-commerce strategy as a starting point for proper information practices. Prior to moving online, 3M had a fragmented information system that made it difficult to cross-sell to existing customers. Even having the same customer listed in different systems had additional costs. After moving online, the company created a $20 million data warehouse to store all information, as part of a larger restructuring of information systems.

Senior management must set the example of open information practices and transparency, even when the information is bad news for the company or reflects negatively on an individual or business unit. Problems should be discussed openly, without fear of repercussions. As appropriate, information on the company's goals, measures, and progress should be made available to all employees and the public through the company's Web site.

This information is increasingly available to interested parties, and by making it transparent, a company may build trust with its constituent groups. In addition, it is often beneficial to increase the information flow to the public to ensure that accurate information is communicated, rather than to risk inaccurate information being made public by a third party.Further, many organizational processes should be restructured to fully take advantage of e-commerce. In particular, e-commerce should encourage and facilitate companies to move away from strict hierarchical reporting in some areas and move Towards the use of cross-functional remote teams. By collaborating with other business functions and units, the e-commerce initiative is likely to encounter less resistance in the traditional business. Processes should also be adaptable and flexible enough to respond to changes in real-time information.

Numerous virtual organization techniques serve these purposes, including:

- Cross-functional teams that form themselves
- Teams that may go into and out of existence regularly
- Use of both in-person and remote meetings
- Teams that span organizational boundaries
- Encouragement of innovation through mutual trust
- Self-governance
- Harnessing global resources to solve local problems

An organization that utilizes these processes should then be able to assemble teams to innovate or to resolve challenges associated with e-commerce. Most important, all these techniques should be fully consistent with an integration strategy, eliminating any need for moving e-commerce outside the organization.

By upgrading these information practices, a company positions itself to make significant improvements throughout the value chain. For many companies, value chain management is an integral part of the e-commerce strategy.

But even for those companies that focus primarily on selling online, subtle improvements can be made with minimal extra cost and effort. Thus, improving information practices can create significant benefits for sales, distribution, and procurement, along with various other processes throughout the organization.

Cisco has used its real-time capabilities to create supplier-side processes that vastly improve its supply-chain management. Cisco and its suppliers and manufacturers share extensive information on product quality. This allows Cisco to measure the number of defective products while they are still in the supplier's possession, rather than after they have been delivered. In turn, the supplier can make faster adjustments in its manufacturing process to minimize future quality problems.

Dell has mastered the use of e-commerce in limiting the amount of inventory kept on hand. Many component parts such as monitors and peripherals are never kept in inventory by Dell, and their movement and distribution is entirely handled by e-mail communication. But even for parts retained by Dell, real-time ordering forecasts are sent to suppliers to minimize the inventory and buffer stocks on a cycle as short as two hours. This relationship with suppliers, coupled with its information practices, also permits a *negative* cash conversion cycle. At the delivery end of the supply chain, Tesco spanned traditional organizational boundaries to create the most efficient delivery process. While many in the grocery industry mimicked the Amazon model by attempting to deliver from large, high-tech warehouses, Tesco chose to deliver directly from stock at local physical locations. While this limited the potential delivery zone, it also saved Tesco the effort and resources of building expensive warehouses with uncertain profitability. Delivering from the store meant no separate inventories and no need for entirely new processes.

Nike, Inc. recently implemented a supply-chain system linking the company with its manufacturing partners. Before these system changes, 30 percent of Nike's total volume of shoe orders were based on estimates; now, only 3 percent of the orders are guesswork, because of better forecasting and planning.Whirlpool Corporation has linked every Whirlpool factory and sales site worldwide through e-business software, allowing factories and sales sites to coordinate with suppliers and key retail partners. This has reduced inventories and increased vital communication.

Krispy Kreme Doughnut is another company that has used e-commerce to its advantage by devising an intranet network linking its stores. The Web system tracks doughnut mix, doles out the right colors of sprinkles, monitors managers' decisions, and permits users to fix errors such as damaged goods, by allowing replacements to be sent. The system allows employees to focus more on customer service, reduce problem orders, and increase productivity.

GLOBAL E-COMMERCE

Culture is particularly important for an internationally or globally oriented e-Business, especially in respect to the impact it has on buyer behaviour and all the implications related to the organization and its management.

DEFINITIONS OF CULTURE

Culture has been defined in a multiplicity of ways and because of its diversity, there is no one universally accepted definition.

Anthropologists and sociologists alike have tried hard to produce the perfect definition, which samples their opinions spanning more than a century. In very simple terms, *culture* is defined as 'ways of living, built by a group of human beings that are transmitted from one generation to another'.

ELEMENTS OF CULTURE

In 1999-2001, according to International Data Corporation, roughly 40 per cent of the people visiting the Internet have been seeking sites in languages other than English. Yet, according to the same study, 55 per cent of US companies have done nothing to customise their Web sites for non-English speaking users.

With a total global potential e-Commerce market of $1.6 trillion by 2003, companies worldwide need to become experts fast on the cultural issues that must be met in order to make e-Commerce work. For a successful e-Commerce operation, communication between a diversity of cultures with a multiplicity of languages involves far more than mere text translations. There are a variety of other cultural factors to consider, some of which might appear inconsequential to a globally expanding e-Business but important enough to the consumer, and which could create significant problems if ignored.

LANGUAGE

Today more than 50 per cent of all Internet users have a non-English mother tongue. With the dramatic expansion of the Internet, this number is expected to increase to 70 per cent by 2003. By contrast, more than two-thirds of Web pages are in English, with Japanese and German at a distant joint second position with almost 6 per cent each.

Nevertheless, past research has revealed that Web users are three times more likely to make purchases from Web sites in their own language and two-thirds of surfers will click away from a site in another language. It is expected that a fast increasing proportion of new Web sites will be in languages other than English. Asian languages, mainly Chinese, are poised for especially strong growth, owing to a fast increase in Internet penetration among Asian countries' population.

There is also an increasing trend for companies worldwide to make their current English-language sites available in several other languages. The Internet is at present dominated by English and probably will continue to be for the foreseeable future, although it remains to be seen whether it will be the universally adopted language of the Net.

TRANSLATIONS ON THE WEB

Literal translations of Web sites are a minefield. Machine translations have been an attractive option for some e-Commerce organizations because they are cheap, but they have severe limitations. In circumstances where speed has been the most critical factor, machine translations have been used to understand the general idea of a received message and to send an acknowledgement of its reception with a promise of follow-up. This has been acceptable in the early years of e-Commerce development, as a strategy designed to generate goodwill and buy time. To use it for a permanent Web site is a strategy fraught with danger. Handing the text to computer-aided translators is not enough to ensure that the meaning and scope of the Web site are achieved. Here is an example of machine-translated text which has gone seriously wrong. A news item was taken in 1998 from the German version of MSNBC about the famous round-the-world balloon race, which was about to become an international incident if not properly understood by the Chinese. It was translated with the help of a computer-aided translation service supplied by Systran and sounded like this:

One of the urgent problems of the Weltumrunder in the balloon "global challenge" solve itself now: China gave on Tuesday an overflight/flyover permission to the three balloon drivers on their Weltumseglung the message in Peking, British after information. ' It is clear from this example that human translation and adaptation are required when interfacing with international customers and the correct understanding of critical messages is required.

TONE AND FORMALITY OF THE LANGUAGE

Business culture and etiquette used on the Net, or 'Netiquette', need to be carefully researched and understood in order to avoid embarrassing mistakes. For example in the United States it is common to see Web sites which use informal greetings for their registered users, such as: 'Welcome back, Frank!' To address using first names might be appropriate to Anglo-Saxon cultures, but it would be unacceptable in Japan, where a registered Japanese visitor to the site would take offence at such a casual greeting.

A culturally sensitive business would ensure that it used a significantly more formal greeting such as 'We are honoured by your return visit to our site, Mr Takahashi'. A survey undertaken by Ion Global which focused on the level of formality expected by different cultures in Asian and Pacific countries placed Japan and South Korea at the highest end, whereas Australia and the United States were the least formal.

SYMBOLS AND SYMBOLISM

The use of symbols on Web sites is widespread, owing to space saving requirements. Web designers frequently use icons and images; however, not all of them are exportable. For example, hand gestures could be a minefield to the uninitiated, and as they are natural they are perceived to be universal. In effect, they are culturally transmitted from one generation to another. The commonly used 'A-OK' of a circle formed with the thumb and forefinger, with the other fingers extended, is widely used in the United States, where it is considered a friendly gesture, whereas in Brazil it is considered obscene.

Similarly the 'thumbs up' sign is considered highly offensive in Iran. A palm-forward wave is a nasty gesture in Greece and Nigeria. Some very successful Web sites are designed around a particular theme which has a specific symbolic significance (such as a compass or an animal). Special attention needs to be given to the choice of symbols, as their meanings might have different connotations in other cultures. For example, flowers have a strong symbolic significance in many cultures around the world. The rose is considered almost universally the symbol of love, although a hand holding a red rose is the symbol of socialism in Europe. The white lily is a symbol of purity, although in other cultures it is associated with death.

COLOURS

Similarly, colours must be chosen with care in designing a Web site for global audiences. Colours such as black, white and red have different symbolic or religious meanings throughout the world.

A Web site with a black background can appear 'cool' and 'sophisticated' to an American audience, but black is linked with death and bad luck in Chinese culture. Purple has religious significance in Catholicism, as does green in the Islamic world. User feedback during the design phase is necessary in order to avoid culturally insensitive choices.

INCOMPATIBLE SOFTWARE

Rutherford also mentions a Forrester report entitled *The Multilingual Site Blueprint*, which surveyed twenty-seven US-based multilingual site operators and found that the greatest challenge encountered was adapting software to work with other languages.

She gives the example that, to make Web software work with Asian languages, which contain up to 6,000 characters, site operators must install Unicode, a character coding system that supports written texts in different languages.

CULTURALLY SENSITIVE WEB DESIGN

The way a home page is designed determines whether the user will stay on the site or abandon it out of frustration. There are a number of commonsense Web site development methods which will ensure the building of a loyal and satisfied customer base.

As a matter of practice, the first thing a non-English-speaking Net user will do when reaching a Web home page is to look for navigation leading to the site in a familiar language. According to Hanrahan and Kwok, the presentation of the language selector navigation is one of the key elements of the global user experience.

A popular form of this type of navigation is a pull-down menu with a list of languages and the title such as 'Language selector' or 'Choose a country'. This method might be problematic, as a foreign visitor might not be able to understand the instructions designed to lead to the pull-down menu on a page in English that might be full of information and navigation options. Another commonly used method suggested by Hanrahan and Kwok is to show a selection of country flags representing the different Web site versions. This method is acceptable if the Web sites contain country-specific content as opposed to language-specific content, as flags represent countries and not languages. Sertain languages, such as Spanish for example, are used by majority or minority populations in a number of diverse countries.

Using the flag representing Spain to represent Spanish might confuse users from Mexico, the United States or Argentina, who do not identify with the Spanish flag. The use of flags is appropriate when the target is a specific national market and not all speakers of a specific language.

When the target market is language-specific, one recommended way to address these problems is to design navigational images and buttons showing the name of each language available written in that language and with the appropriate script. This is known as 'good user experience'.

Another aspect related to language specificity is 'text swell', which describes what happens when the translation of a word from one language to another necessitates extended (or contracted) display space. Text swell can have a considerable effect on the layout of a Web page and should be an important consideration in the design of an international Web site.

Both HTML text and text within an image can be affected by text swell, as well as the size of pop-up windows. German tends to take up more horizontal space than English, while Chinese and Japanese take up less, but need taller spaces than languages based on the Latin alphabet.

METHODS OF PAYMENT

Payment preferences vary considerably from country to country. For example, in the United States or the United Kingdom the overwhelmingly preferred method of payment is the credit card, whereas in China cash on delivery (COD) is the prevailing method.In Japan, purchases through the Internet can be dispatched to and paid for at the convenience stores called *conbini*.

From a Web design point of view, it is therefore important to understand what payment options are used in the target market. No matter how appealing the product or service might appear to the consumer, if s/he is not given the right options of payment the purchasing sequence will be aborted.

Along with payment options, the online sales effort should also take into account the variety of currencies and country-linked value-added tax (VAT) systems. Research shows that customers are reluctant to commit to an online transaction in a 'foreign' currency owing to the uncertainty presented by the daily fluctuation of exchange rates.A simple solution is to add an interactive currency calculator to the site, which will give a rough idea of the cost of the product or service and give an indication if it is worth proceeding with the purchase. A better solution includes payment systems that not only perform currency calculations but also calculate VAT (value-added tax or sales tax) by country and product or service category.

The best systems currently available automatically update the currency conversion and tax rates, relieving the e-Commerce Web site operator of a daily burden, and can be used with any payment systems on the market. An example of a multi-currency payment system is WorldPay, launched in the United States, which offers the Web site operator the facility of offering products or services in more than 100 currencies.

With the exchange rate updated daily, customers will have the certainty of seeing the real cost of their purchases, which will give them the ability of meaningful comparison with what they can find in local stores. These customer-sensitive methods are reducing the often painful order cancellations or goods being returned, owing to customers' shocked realization when checking their credit card bills.

For example, having such a system implemented will allow the French or the Italian customer to see in euros exactly what has been charged on their Visa card, whereas the UK-based e-Commerce retailer will receive the equivalent amount in pounds sterling or, if US-based, the equivalent amount in US dollars.Taxware is offering a system solution that calculates the appropriate local sales tax (VAT) for purchases based on geographical location and type of goods or services. It can even supply VAT records to be used by customers for tax return calculations.

The combination of the two system solutions showing prices in the local currency and the local VAT provides the international customer with the complete picture, enabling a rapid and informed purchase decision online. The e-Commerce retailer offering such a facility is showing care towards the target market needs, leading to a satisfied, thus loyal customer base.

HUMAN RESOURCES IN E-COMMERCE

Management of personnel is also central to the implementation of e-commerce strategy. Even in the aftermath of the fallout of the dot.com bust in the stock market, e-commerce is still inexorably linked to the notions of large performance bonuses, stock options, Silicon Valley whiz kids, and new-wave office environments.

It is still necessary to find ways to develop and retain employees who are creative, flexible, and innovative—in addition to competent and diligent. In this light, a company must endeavor to put systems in place that retain key personnel and make strategic new hires throughout the course of an e-commerce venture.

Designing appropriate compensation systems is instrumental both in attaining initial e-commerce success and in retaining the leaders and employees who made that success possible. Above all, compensation systems must be properly aligned with strategy and structure. Symbolically, the CIO's compensation is one of the more important decisions a company dedicated to implementing e-commerce will encounter. CIO compensation should be in line with that of other members of senior management to signal respect for the IT function as a creator of value. Failure to fully and explicitly acknowledge the value of IT and e-commerce contradicts the other messages that must be communicated for e-commerce to succeed.

At lower levels of the company, compensation systems have more practical consequences for alignment. Some companies believe that compensating e-commerce managers the same as managers in traditional commerce fails to create proper incentives for e-commerce and value creation. Differential compensation sometimes creates an incentive to cannibalize from the company's traditional channels as well as more effectively and more quickly to execute an e-commerce strategy.

But, e-commerce compensation should be tied to the overall success of the venture company-wide, rather than rewarding performance within an individual unit. This is particularly true when the company is seeking full integration, because it helps ensure cooperation between departments.

Companies must be prepared to manage the channel conflict that often arises when e-commerce begins to cannibalize the traditional business. Cannibalization is necessary to optimize the use of each channel, and an integration strategy cannot succeed if traditional business units do not accept it. Companies must design compensation systems that gradually shift compensation Towards the creation of value, particularly in businesses heavily dependent on salespersons who work on a commission basis. Traditional business units must be placated not by compensating inefficiencies, but by carving out new roles that optimize the use of each channel and produce a successfully integrated and profitable multi-channel coordinated effort.

At aviation parts distributor Aviall Inc., a few weeks after an upper-management shakeup brought in a new CEO in 1996, a new Web-based order-entry system was introduced. In response, Aviall's 300 sales reps feared their jobs were at stake and told customers not to use it. Despite the benefits to the consumer that were realized through the Web-based system, the role of the sales reps had not been modified to permit them to survive such a drastic change in company strategy.

As companies develop and implement e-commerce strategies, the Internet must be examined and the pre-existing channels must be modified in a way that complements the e-commerce initiative. While compensation systems must often be reevaluated and reconstructed in e-commerce implementations, hiring practices can be improved simply by using the same Web site that showcases other e-commerce activities. Hiring online can significantly reduce advertising costs associated with print and other listings. It can also ensure that potential applicants possess at least some skills in using the Internet and implies a confidence and understanding of the importance of e-commerce. Cisco is one company that greatly improved its hiring process by advertising openings online. Further, special attention should be paid to HR policies covering to those who work in e-commerce and IT.

Companies should recognize the fluidity of the IT labour market and must often create more flexible labour policies than for other employees. To ensure that proper human resources practices are employed in an e-commerce implementation;

- Compensation systems for traditional and e-commerce personnel should be properly aligned with the company's new e-commerce strategy.
- Companies must be prepared for channel conflict due to cannibalization of traditional company segments into an e-commerce venture.
- Hiring practices must fully take advantage of the exposure opportunity and cost savings made available by Internet hiring.

9

E-customer Relationship Management

CUSTOMER RELATIONSHIPS

Under traditional business models, it may be sufficient to offer customer service during normal business hours, either at physical locations or over the phone. E-commerce dramatically changes those expectations both in terms of company strategy and the customer's perspective.

Near-universal and constant customer service availability is expected for almost any viable e-commerce strategy. Companies must re-examine their customer service practices and make numerous key decisions in moving Towards universal availability. Two of the main considerations are the distribution of response tasks between human and automated systems and the operating hours for human responses. Each of these include trade-offs among speed, cost, convenience, and efficiency. Most e-commerce ventures have developed some FAQ (frequently asked questions) function on their Web sites. This function may consist of rudimentary inquiries only or a highly sophisticated taxonomy of nearly every conceivable question. The nature of the offering and the Web site dictates how sophisticated the FAQs should be, but no company can exhaust the list of possible questions.

The challenge then becomes how to provide service to customers who are dissatisfied with the FAQs. A company may choose to provide immediate or delayed e-mail support to customers or may offer a phone line for further inquiries. The company must weigh the value of instant response and satisfaction to the customer against the added costs associated with phone banks or with rapid and 24/7 e-mail response.

Some pure-play companies like Half.com chose to keep the process entirely online and not offer phone service. For traditional companies, however, this strategy is more difficult, as it can inundate the traditional business phone lines with Internet inquiries. Delta Airlines, on the other hand, was able to reduce its phone volume and increase its status among elite customers by moving reservation information online while simultaneously implementing a wireless initiative.

Delta first identified such a programme as "nice to have" but not a necessity, but the company quickly recognized the appeal of wireless capabilities to its elite customers by providing quick access to vast amounts of information. Implementing this programme was not only a cost-saving move, but also a successful effort to appeal to customers who desired this level of functionality.

For companies that do provide phone service in addition to their FAQs and Internet support, a decision must be made on availability. Limiting phone support to normal business hours reduces some of the value added associated with the Web site. On the other hand, labour costs may not justify 24/7 phone service for industries that offer commodity goods. More technical industries, B2B companies, and companies with customized and personalized Internet-related offerings should carefully consider offering a 24/7 service.

Another aspect of customer service practices is the development and implementation of policies on shipping, delivery, and returns.

In particular, companies that use physical branches as part of a bricks-and-clicks strategy must not neglect proper training on the traditional commerce side necessary to facilitate e-commerce developments and service. Customer service representatives in physical branches must be thoroughly familiar with the Web site, its function, and its policies.

While e-commerce requires changes and enhancement to customer service policies, it also affords most companies excellent opportunities to refine marketing strategies, selling practices, pricing, and Web site design by observing customer behaviour.Physical branches have more limited opportunities to collect customer data, particularly data from sites where customers can impart complaints or grievances.When customers shop online, however, their every mouse click is potentially revealing and useful for future improvements in e-commerce service.Although these methods require substantial analysis, companies can draw strong implications and direction about customer behaviour from this data. Unused search results may indicate a problem with the search engine.Aborted purchases may indicate that the checkout procedure is unclear or too time-consuming. Consistent nonpurchase of a product may indicate that more precise information is needed to inspire consumer confidence. Corporations must be willing and able to redesign their Web sites and refine customer processes based on the gathered information as well as direct feedback from the customers. Since convenience is a prime source of competitive advantage, problems with customer service systems must be addressed immediately. Although shutting down the Web site is undesirable, important changes should be made by closing the site for a few hours in nonpeak time and by warning the customers in advance of this downtime.

Thus, to effectively manage and enhance customer service attributes,

- Companies with an Internet presence should provide any information that a customer might need while online.

- Corporate Web sites should incorporate some form of direct contact mechanism, whether it is as simple as a service phone number or as advanced as online chat capabilities.
- Companies should ensure that the Web site easily connects to any other aspect of the company service that a customer might need information about, ranging from traditional brick-and-mortar locations to shipping policies.

CONSUMER BUYING DECISION PROCESS

A potential e-consumers buying decision process will follow the established stages of need recognition, information search, information evaluation, purchase decision and post-purchase behaviour.

NEED RECOGNITION

An e-retail Web site is a combination of the traditional store display window, information desk, stocked display shelving, mood lighting/sound, promotional material that shout out specials, and the time-honoured *barker/spruiker* used to stimulate shopping interest. Such an e-retail site ought to elicit a need recogni tion response from any visitor to the site. A new or returning visitor should be treated to a combination of the four basic marketing elements - *price* (*e.g.* specials, discounts, interest free periods), *product* (*e.g.* new lines, clearance items, seasonal products, fashion and fad limited ranges), *promotion* (*e.g.* sales, seasonal specials, select shopper campaigns) and *distribution* (*e.g.* free delivery, lay-away, home installation) that accentuate the visitor's own need identification.

Technology within the Web site, for example cookie files, captures data about the visitor's responses and what information was accessed. Such information then enables e-retailers to improve the rapport with the online customer by tailoring the site content to consumer demand. One positive application from such data collection is the inclusion of customer loyalty Programmes that encourage return visitation to the e-retailer site and increased purchases.

Information Search

Improved telecommunications technology and general population access to the Internet have transformed user availability to customization of, and digestion of, large information volumes. Unlike the bricks and mortar retailer, an e-retail site has the facilities to make available such large volumes of information in a customized format to meet the immediate and potential queries of site visitors following the need recognition stage. Without personal embarrassment or the self-consciousness of asking a stranger (*e.g.* a shopkeeper) what may be an obvious or foolish product-related question, the e-retail site visitor can access online product brochures, price comparisons, frequently asked questions (FAQs), suggested product applications, cleaning and repair information, and an efficient search engine technology, as well as asking for specialized information via the e-retailer's e-mail system.

Information Evaluation

When seeking to evaluate the collected information on products and services, the potential shopper will often turn to the experiences and advice of family, friends and persons who have already experienced use of such merchandise. Also, e-retailing gives the user added facilities to access evaluative experts and previous users of the merchandise in question to aid in the digestion and customization of all this information. Many consumer groups act as such reference experts through the testing and personal evaluations of retailed products and then make these findings available to others. Experienced e-retailers encourage interactions between previous, current and future shoppers by way of:

- Online discussion groups.
- Suggesting site visitors rate the available merchandise.
- Suggesting site visitors express comments about this merchandise and the service exchange experiences.

Monitoring of the online discussions and visitor comments endows the retailer with invaluable knowledge regarding merchandise features and limitations that may be incorporated into promotional materials. To conclude, apart from all the benefits mentioned above, the e-retailer gains all this free information that would normally require expensive market research.

Purchase Decision

After a visitor to an e-retailer site has determined the merchandise to be appropriate for their needs, it is still not a certainty that this visitor will finalize a purchase. Commonly, an online customer nominates particular merchandise from an e-retail Web site and places those items in the online *shopping cart* (also known as a *shopping trolley*) for the checkout, but later the customer discontinues the purchase process and leaves the e-retailer's site. This action of discontinuing an online purchase is termed 'abandoned cart syndrome;

- A lower level of education.
- Higher frequency of Web purchases.
- Greater concern of online data risk and fraud.
- Greater frequency of Web site service problems.
- The use of shopping as a facility to see family and friends.
- High levels of concern about online retailers' tracking data.
- Younger buying groups.
- Shopping causing little arousal.
- Higher frequency of browsing for a later purchase.
- Higher fashion consciousness.
- Higher frequency of Web search for product information.

Although the e-retailer cannot yet duplicate the human interactions possible in a physical store setting, e-retailers may still empower customers in an attempt to reduce the incidence of online cart abandonment. One positive step to improve the e-retailer's customer interactions is streamlining the order process by:

- Making improvements in the e-retailer's site navigation.
- Incorporation of help links and interactive facilities to stimulate the shopper's arousal and fashion consciousness.
- Supplying the relevant merchandise information as needed.
- Greater use of online help facilities and screen prompts.
- Establishing chat rooms and customer discussion opportunities to share experience with family, friends and new acquaintances.
- Improved guarantees (including deliveries, data security, 30-day trials).
- Offline contact details (phone number, fax number, street address).

Post-purchase behaviour

The key to a retailer's survival and success whether offline or online is to generate repeat purchase behaviour. For a customer to return to a retailer that customer needs to have confidence in the retailer, but e-retailer confidence is often difficult to establish in light of online issues that have caused customers to make complaints and/or never return to the e-retailer. According to Cho *et al*. (2002), the online issues that often alienate customers and lead to complaints are the failure to meet customer *expectations* in relation to:

Merchandise offerings.

The e-retailer's store-front technology (this includes, but is not limited to, the Web site) that integrates:

- Usability of the technology;
- The technology failing to carry out a function.

The e-retailer's information sources (the policies).

Payment/settlement issues;

- Agreed conditions (including delivery timing).

To reduce the chance of customer expectations being unfulfilled, e-retailers will compensate for the lack of a face-to-face exchange by making available more information details than would otherwise be considered in a bricks and mortar environment. Dealing with each of the Cho *et al.* (2002) points, we suggest the following responses:

Merchandise offerings -

- Define all dimensions of the size options, colour variations, and accessories provided. One suggestion is to include the supply of actual colour swatches to reduce the colour errors often attributed to variations on computer colour monitors.

The e-retailer's store-front technology (this includes, but is not limited to the Web site) -

- Provide sufficient technology to cope with peak buying periods such as St Valentine's Day and Mother's Day.
- Keep redundant backup to take over when systems fail.
- Offer facilities to store (file) partial orders for future use should the customer be interrupted and/or wish to continue the shopping process in the near future.
- Provide improved access facilities for the disabled/impaired computer user. Facilities may consist of:
  - Selectable larger display fonts;
  - Voice recognition commands;
  - Spoken responses embedded in the web pages;
  - Written descriptions of displayed images (these can be read out to the non-sighted user even if they can't see the picture).
- Alerts given by the e-retailer's site to advise users:
  - pending specials;
  - replenishment of merchandise that was out of stock;
  - Arrival of special orders.
- Such alerts can reach the user through e-mail, phone short message service (SMS), automated faxing or other communications technologies.

The e-retailer's information sources (the policies) -

- Information is to be detailed (even exhaustive), accurate and timely (not noticeably out of date).
- Information is to be easy to find on the e-retailer site.
- Links to relevant or 'just interesting' sites shall establish the e-retail not only as an appropriate purchasing site but as a point of reference or portal for future enquiries in this area; thereby achieving a great milestone: being bookmarked as a favourite site in the user's Web browsing software.
- A continued customer relationship should be maintained after a purchase by:
  - Continued updates on the relevant and near-relevant issues by e-mail or newsgroup (for example, a customer purchases an electric grill and then receives a monthly recipe; the e-retailer keeps the contact and the customer's satisfaction in the purchase is supported);
  - Space may also be sold to sponsors seeking to promote their products.

Payment/settlement issues -

- Not all customers want to reveal their personal details and movements to online parties. To aid these potential customers, e-retailers can now provide alternatives for the customer in the shopping cycle to minimize risk. In Australia, a purchaser using the Wishlist retailer (www.wishlist.com.au) may opt to have their online purchases delivered to a participating BP petrol service station rather than to their home address. In this way the customer picks up the merchandise at a time that suits and conceals their personal address details while still gaining the advantages of shopping online.

- Most courier organizations (*i.e.* DHL and FedEx) used by e-retailers have facilities for the purchaser to trace and track the merchandise while it is in transit. The e-retailer receives proof the item is 'on its way' and the client achieves the peace of mind of 'seeing' where the item is any time they go online.

THE HYBRID RETAILER: THE MOST LIKELY WINNER IN THE FUTURE OF RETAILING

Retailers today are not restricted to just bricks and mortar, direct and virtual categories of retailing but often opt for a hybrid business model. Hybrid retailers, sometimes referred to as 'multi-channel retailers', appear to be taking the greatest advantage of e-retailing opportunities.

In a study by Haeberle (2003) multi-channel retailers were identified as generating 72 per cent of Web-based sales in 2002, 5 per cent up from 2001, and 18 per cent up from the Web sales of 2000. Using profitability as a success measure, multi-channel retailers and particularly those established in the market as catalogue brands, made the greater impact as e-retailers. The Haeberle (2003) study found that, in 2002, 92 per cent of those retailers for whom catalogue was the primary sales channel were profitable. That compares with 80 per cent of bricks and mortar-based retailers and 50 per cent of Web-based retailers in the study.

When John Lewis bought the UK arm of Buy.com, the takeover gave Buy.com financial credibility while Buy.com gave one of the 'Old Men' of UK retailing street credibility (Editor, 2001). Though the purchase of a virtual retailer by a bricks and mortar retailer was nothing new, it was an early example of a continuing trend as virtual retailers ran out of operating capital. These new players in the retailing arena are faced on one side by the downwards pressure on prices to stay competitive and on the other by fearful investors who remember all too clearly the dot.com crash at the end of the first millennium.

Retailer Adaptation: a Key to Survival and Growth

Long-standing bricks and mortar retailers are not only looking at a Web presence as the means to becoming e-retailers. To improve the relationship with their customers, retailers are adopting new electronic systems that complement their physical store presence. Sears in the US (www.sears.com) uses a system termed 'buy online, pick up at the store', where the customer places and pays for an order with a credit card at the Sears Web site, Sears.com, but, departing from other Web stores' procedures, picks up the merchandise from a local Sears store. An e-mail is then used to advise the customer about stock availability at the time of the order and when the merchandise is ready for store collection.

Misunderstanding or ignoring a market position of strength is a failing that leads to the demise of some retailers. The availability of a new distribution channel is not an automatic indication of future success.

Consider the US retailer Egghead (was www.egghead.com), which in the early 1990s had strong market presence with around 250 stores across the country. The retailer was well respected by its consumer market, had a solid brand image and was profitable. Long before most other retailers, Egghead created an online presence for its technology-minded customers in 1994.

Effectively, this entry into a new distribution channel made Egghead one of the first multi-channel retailers. But, as Lightfoot (2003) described, Egghead did not leverage its unique multi-channel position; rather, it decided to abandon all of its offline stores in 1998 and exclusively sell online, evolving into a virtual retailer.

Regrettably, following a series of problems, *e.g.* much-publicized hacking attacks on Egghead's Web site, technical failures in the e-commerce technology, failing customer loyalty and internal management problems, Egghead went the way of many dot.coms and exhausted its cash reserves and filed for bankruptcy in 2001 (Thornton and Marche, 2003).

On the positive side for customers, the Egghead assets (including brand name and customer base) were sold to Amazon in 2001. To Amazon's credit, the new owner honoured the privacy policy of the previous Egghead clients as noted in the statement:

Please note that if you are a returning Egghead.com customer, Egghead.com will not disclose any existing account information to Amazon.com, so you will need to re-enter all information necessary to complete a transaction. For information about how Amazon.com treats the information you give us, see Amazon.com's Privacy Notice.

WHAT CAN YOU EXPECT TO SEE AND HEAR IN E-RETAILING?

Improved customer education, availability of information and increasing legislation have given rise to a new type of customer for this new millennium. Our new customers are more demanding, have a higher expectation and are increasingly adversarial in their service exchanges with retailers. Part of the retailer response will be to empower the customer to tailor their own service exchange in the physical store and online. Metro, an organization that already markets hardware systems to retailers, has suggested a series of scenarios in a future retail store to provide technologies that make shopping encapsulate greater individualization, reliability and convenience (Metro Group, 2003a).

Greater Individualization

Just as Web browsing technology learns and recalls a user's preferences for colour, fonts and items for inclusion, future stores will match their offering to learned customer experiences.

Once the customer is identified to the store through a loyalty card or personal *radio frequency identification* (RFID) tag, the store's 'electronic personal shopping assistant' (EPSA) technology will record the shopper's preferences for merchandise, delivery (*i.e.* home delivery, parcel pick-up) and method of payment. To save the customer time, the store system would forewarn the customer of difficulties (including stock outages) and then make suggestions for alternative merchandise that is either in stock or pending (*e.g.* new season's stock).

Greater Reliability and Convenience

New store technology will improve reliability for both customer and retailers. When a customer selects an item and adds this to their shopping trolley, the EPSA will read the merchandise's RFID tag and present the details to the shopper via shopping trolley mounted visual display.

No longer will the customer be disadvantaged by the omission of shelf pricing or getting to the checkout only to be told that the product is 'not on the system' and needs a delaying price check.

Through the use of the unique RFID tag being identified by EPSA, the customer will be advised of these details at the point of merchandise access - the shelf or bin stocking the merchandise. Once the price information absence is detected, the retailer's system can search or calculate the price before the checkout is reached.

Aiding the retailer, this technology will indicate low- or out-of-stock situations at the shelf as customers place the item into their trolley, long before the item is removed from the inventory system at the checkouts. Staff will have a perpetual inventory rather than depending upon physical stock updates. Retailers use a *planogram* to determine what merchandise is displayed where and in what quantities throughout a store.

Shoppers become familiar with their favourite stores but what do they do when a new merchandise line is added to the store and they are unsure where it is located? What is needed is a personal guide or in the future an EPSA to direct customers through the store like a global positioning system (GPS) directs a car through traffic.

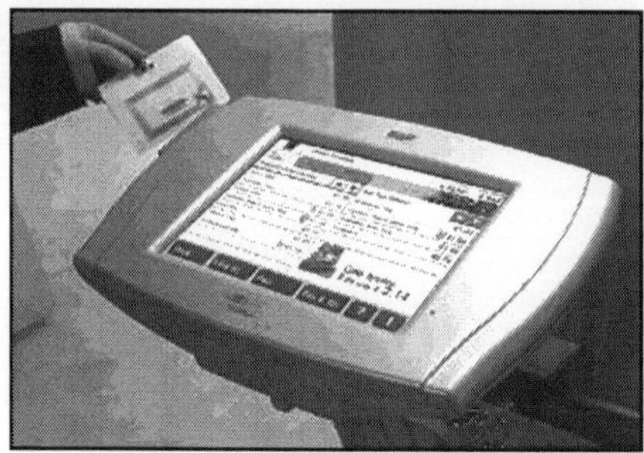

Fig. The new Shopping Trolley will Record the Selected Merchandise and Advise the Customer of the Details, Including Price and Running total Expenditure

Merchandise Tracking

With delivery problems representing one of the main elements holding back the growth of e-shopping, merchandise tracking may be one of the essential development areas for the future. Early developments in bricks retailing followed research by Bernard Silver and Norman Woodland in the early 1950s. As a result, the bar code became a world standard for tracking and recording the movements of retail stock (Anonymous, 2003).

A standard bar code is made up of dark (predominantly black) vertical bars broken up with light (predominantly white) spaces. To read the bar code a beam of light is passed over the code where the dark bars absorb the light and the spaces reflect it. The scanner (also known as a reader or detector) then turns the reflected light into electrical pulses that may be recorded on a data file. While an excellent product identification system, bar codes have a significant and obvious limitation, that is, they need to be scanned to register stock movement. Stock may enter or be removed from the retailer's premises and if the bar code is not scanned with a reading laser, the stock is not identified and recorded so its movement is unknown. The solution is to have the stock *speak* up and identify *itself* to the retailer's electronic inventory management system. The stock speak? How? By adding to, or replacing the bar code with a miniature RFID tag.

Fig. A Sample of a Bar Code

RFID tags are tiny (about one quarter of a square millimetre), carry between 64 and 96 bits of information and have a life of at least ten years. They are inexpensive (as low as one cent per unit) and can be energized and activated by radio waves from a scanner/receiver in close proximity, or can be hooked up to a battery. After being activated by the transmitter's power, the RFID tag then passes the information to the retailer's stock system.

RFID tags have already been trailed and applied in a variety of applications. McDonald's (www.mcdonalds.com) and KFC (kfc.com) are trialling RFID tags; the US Department of Defence will be incorporating RFID tags to improve the management of inventory through hands-off processing; Nokia is incorporating the tags in some of its mobile phones; theme parks are providing them on wristbands to identify the positions of children; and the European Central Bank is considering incorporating the tags on new Euro notes to reduce counterfeiting and track illicit monetary flows.Some bricks retailers have already piloted RFID tags. Privacy concerns have since led to Wal-Mart (www. walmart.com) and Benetton (www.benetton.com) dropping trials and orders of the tags. Privacy becomes an issue when you consider that although the RFID receivers were conceived to detect the movements of the tagged merchandise, they are in effect able to track the movements of the customer carrying the tagged merchandise within a shopping district that contains multiple RFID scanners/ receivers. Consider that, if an organization has more than one member store in the company's group (*e.g.* a supermarket, a bottle shop and a variety store all owned by one organization) in the same shopping mall, radio triangulation by the RFID receivers triggered by the merchandise's RFID radio signal could detect the move of merchandise and, therefore, the shopper from one store to another and so on. The data from these movements could also interpret how long the shopper spent at various spots in the mall and all this data is collected *without* the shopper having given their permission. It is an *ethical* dilemma that will be debated for some time. Despite the debate, bricks retailers such as Tesco are pushing ahead with RFID tags for tracking supply-chain movements and for further trials in-store. As we argue below, the potential benefits are substantial, so we expect the development to diffuse into e-retail tracking as shoppers become more accustomed to it. As the number of applications for RFID tags increases retailers may expect to fulfil management and marketing objectives, including:

- *Reduced retail fraud and theft*- RFID tags will track products for clothing, grocery items, electrical merchandise and recorded music to reduce shrinkage.
- *Asset supply-chain control*- RFID tags will track the movement of goods from one process centre to another, *e.g.* delivery dock and warehouse. This is not limited to the selling inventory but includes organizational assets that have in the past left the premises without authorization or without being entered in a log book, *e.g.* storage pallets and shopping trolleys.

- *Inventory control*- RFID tags will transmit inventory relevant information, *e.g.* batch number, unit code, number of items on the property and consumer-related merchandise information such as product category, size and colour.
- *Intelligent packaging*- RFID tags can be linked to a sensor that recognizes any tampering or deterioration of the merchandise while in transit and when that damage behaviour occurred. This damage may relate to a non-deliberate deterioration error, *e.g.* food storage temperature being outside the recommended range. Equally, the sensor would detect malicious actions of third parties upon the merchandise, *e.g.* when a sealed lid on a container is removed and a subsequent replacement is made to disguise the tampering activity. For customers, the expected benefits from a retailer using RFID tags are:
- *Speedier checkout process*-In combination with intelligent shopping carts/ trolleys, shoppers would have all their purchases totalled automatically as the individual product RFID tags are read by the shopping cart and the totals provided at the checkout point for payment.
- *Security*- Manufacturers will introduce RFID tags into the components of final products so that if the components are removed they can be tracked. Consider the theft of car parts from a whole vehicle; in the past the panels would be almost impossible to detect and trace once removed from the original car.
- *Tracking*- 'Where are the b—y car keys?' Consumer RFID tag readers will become available to learn the tag codes of products that the consumer wishes to inventory. An immediate benefit is being able to locate the proximity of individual RFID tagged items, such as the ever-elusive car keys.
- *Preparation and care*- RFID tags provide the opportunity to include preparation and care information that will be understood by future appliances. Potential applications in this vein are:
- For allergens - home health systems that are programmed for the individual's health requirements will 'listen' to the RFID tags of grocery items. The tags may contain all the ingredients of the grocery items, even the complicated chemical codes, and notify the home health system of potential allergens that could be harmful to the customer/householder.
- For clothing - RFID tags would alert the washing machine that the fabric is not machine washable or should be dry cleaned only.
- For frozen foods - RFID tags would alert the freezer display panel that the food is near or at its expiration date.
- For frozen foods - RFID tags would pass cooking instructions to the microwave or convection oven to avoid over- or under-cooking.

In-store interactive electronic kiosks

Multi-channel e-retailers are not restricted to the sale of physical merchandise in bricks and mortar establishments, but may also market digital products and services that were previously limited to virtual retailers. Through the use of interactive kiosks, retailers will be able to offer such services as:

- Detailed product information;
- Price checks;
- Recipes and product application suggestions;
- Tickets for events;
- Reservations for events and activities;
- Self-checkout to make purchases;
- Personalized and targeted promotions;
- Photo-finishing - this is a growing segment as customers bring in their digital camera cards and have the kiosks transfer the images to final photos;
- Internet access;
- Customer loyalty programmes;
- Banking and financial services;
- Maps and direction services;
- Human resource services, *e.g.* recruitment.

Interactive kiosks generate extra revenue and, because the customer is self-servicing, the variety of service exchanges is increased without added staff and subsequent drains on profits.

Greater use of Electronic Payments

The advent of the cheque made it possible for consumers to make purchases for items that cost more than the cash funds they carried on their person. A cheque could only be written up to the amount of funds the customer had in, or could deposit into, the financial institution issuing the cheque prior to the cheque being cashed by the retailer.

To improve on the flexibility of the cheque and to make purchases using the financial institution's funds (up to a predetermined limit) the store and bank credit card became a popular alternative to the cheque.

Fig. Interactive Kiosks Come in a Variety of Styles

To make a payment by credit card necessitates the retailer obtaining a payment authorization from a financial clearance centre and the customer's identification being validated by a signature or personal identification number (PIN). All this takes time and depends upon the retailer's authorization equipment being operational. Now that consumers are carrying their own mobile technology, *e.g.* cellular mobile phones, there is an opportunity for the consumer to contribute to the transaction verification process.

The consumer may pay for the goods by sending an SMS message to a specific phone number that verifies that a payment should be made to the retailer for the specific merchandise. Other mobile phones permit the transmission of an inferred (IR) transmission to the retailer's equipment to again verify that this payment is to be passed to the customer's charge or mobile phone account.Widening the application of wireless device payments, Royal Philips Electronics and Visa announced an alliance to encourage and develop chip technology that does not require any physical contact with other devices. With this technology consumers will be able to pay for merchandise by waving the new smart card in front of a sensor in the retailer's store (Shim, 2003). For both retailer and customer it means reduced payment delays and improved customer satisfaction.A further development in progress by the major credit card companies at the time of writing is 'pay-as-you-go', which should enable consumers who do not have access to credit to e-shop.

Audio Visual Shopping Trolley

As seen in the section Greater reliability and convenience, the electronic personal shopping assistant will increasingly support shoppers as they negotiate a bricks store, and we argue below that the development should lead to future benefits for e-retailers and e-shoppers. Linked to a future shopping trolleymounted touch screen, an EPSA will provide shoppers information on current store merchandise, in-store events, specialized product demonstrations/taste testing and, of course, store specials.The audio visual shopping trolley will act as a two-way shopping data vehicle presenting benefits to customers and retailers. Benefits to customers from using the EPSA-linked shopping trolleys are:

- A quicker shopping trip for those customers who do *not* enjoy the shopping experience.
- Personalization of the product offering and related information.
- Recall of frequently purchased items to reduce the chance of forgetting items.
- Reduced embarrassment in asking for item locations.
- Reduced delays by transmitting special orders to specific departments before arriving at those sections, *e.g.* special cuts of meat from the meat department.
- Suggested recipes for a grocery item on special or in bulk.

Management equally receives benefits from EPSA-linked shopping trolleys through greater control over their operations resulting from improved knowledge and awareness of stock issues. Advantages to the future e-retailer will be:

- Real time inventory levels.
- Better understanding of customer shopping habits and profiling.
- Promotion of specialized or seasonal merchandise direct to the customers with the greater likelihood of making a purchase.
- Shelving that recommends cross-sells and up-sells to increase sales volumes.
- Improved feedback to suppliers on what sells and daily traffic patterns for demonstrations and gondola-end displays.
- Alerts for corrective action being needed in dramatic situations, *e.g.* staffing issues with long queues of customers at checkouts or other sections of the store.

The future of e-retailing is, as is the case for most estimates of the future, encouraging, but the format is uncertain. What can be said with certainty is that success and profitability will revolve around an historical truism: when the retailer knows the customer, the customer will continue to know the retailer and that translates into repeat sales and profits. The solution is in adopting the appropriate technology to meet the needs of customers.

CASE STUDY: METRO AG EXTRA FUTURE STORE

In April 2003 the Dusseldorf-based Metro Group opened what they called the 'Extra Future Store' to test a range of retail technologies. Metro is the fifth largest retailer in the world, with 2,300 stores in 26 countries and sales of □51.5bn in 2002. The systems include radio frequency identification, smart shelves, intelligent scales, electronic shelf labels, kiosks, personal shopping assistants, anti-theft portals, portable self-scanning and self-checkout lanes.

The 33,000-square-foot Extra Future Store is covered by a wireless LAN (WLAN) based on the Wi-Fi 802.11b standard to link this new shopping technology. Attending the grand opening of the Extra Future Store were officials from the German Government and retailing industry, with German model Claudia Schiffer dubbed the first customer. Metro's partners in the initiative incorporated 40 separate partners including Chep, Cisco, Coca-Cola, Gillette, Hewlett Packard, Kraft Foods, IBM, Intel, Mettler Toledo, NCR, Oracle, Procter and Gamble, Symbol technologies and Wincor Nixdorf.

According to Zygmunt Mierdorf of the Metro Group, the expected outcome of the retailing technology adoption would be higher sales levels and lower costs following improved customer satisfaction from goods being more readily available, the service becoming more individualized and the increase in shopping convenience. The RFID applications in the Extra Future Store represent an ambitious test of the technology developed by the Auto-ID Centre at MIT, Cambridge, Massachusetts. This Auto-ID technology uses the EPC (electronic product code) - a 96-bit chip identifier of an individual item or packaged group of items.

'Anti-theft portals' linked to the RFID tags were set up at Extra Future Store exits and 'checkout lanes' were equipped with RFID readers. Checkouts also use bar code scanners for merchandise not yet RFID tagged. As part of the 'smart-shelf application', RFID tag readers recognize the removal of the tagged merchandise from the shelf. An alert may then be passed by Wi-Fi to the store's distribution centre and to store staff via PDAs advising that a shelf is low in stock and requires replenishment before embarrassing and loss-causing out-of-stock situations. Through the WLAN-linked PDAs, employees are able to check the inventory and, if necessary, reorder goods by directly linking into Metro's merchandise management system from any area in the store. A future extension of the PDA functionality will be to add telephony features that will allow staff to make calls, send messages or download data.

The next significant Extra Future Store device is the personal shopping assistant, a mini-computer with a touch-screen video display attached to a shopping cart. Manufactured by Wincor Nixdorf International, a PSA enables the customer to enter their shopping list or download it to the screen from the Internet. PSA computer software then directs the customer to the store positions that hold the merchandise on the shopping list. As an information support to the customer or as an advertising medium, the PSA screen has the facility to display a video about merchandise taken off a shelf or for merchandise in proximity to the PSA shopping cart. Linked to the store checkout system, the PSA empowers the customer to scan bar coded and/or RFID-tagged merchandise prior to arriving at the checkouts and wirelessly transmit the merchandise details and price data to the checkouts and so reduce the payment stage of the shopping experience. Should the customer choose, they have the option of self-checkout machines that avoid the need to interact with checkout staff.

For customers not choosing to look at their PSA or wanting additional information about merchandise taken from the shelves, the Extra Future Store utilizes electronic kiosk applications at various points around the store. The kiosks display video footage on the merchandise with such information as the supplier, ingredients, preparation, storage, etc. Metro's electronic shelf labelling and advertising displays permit store personnel to wirelessly update merchandise prices and any promotions from a central merchandise management system. Providing information back to the store personnel are the smart shelves with shelf-mounted RFID readers to impart updates on stocks that are running low or nearing their expiration dates.The Boston Consulting Group has studied the Extra Future Store and found the new technologies are readily accepted by most of the customers. Dr Gerd Wolfram, Project Manager of the METRO Group Future Store

Initiative explained, 'customers are really enthusiastic about some of the innovations. The study also bears evidence to the fact that the technologies deployed in the store have prompted a higher customer frequency' Metro Group, 2003b).Of the specialized Extra Future Store technologies, especially popular with two-thirds of the customers was the Intelligent Scale containing the so-called VeggieVision camera, which automatically recognizes the fruit or vegetable being weighed and then prints out the appropriate price labels.

Dispelling the long-held view that technology adoption is inversely related to age, elderly people using the Extra Future Store also made regular use of the new technologies offered. As an example, 56 per cent of the customers over 60 years old were using the Intelligent ScaleAlthough it is a working experiment in future retailing and customer interactions, the Metro Extra Future Store is a strong indicator of how e-retailing will look in the near future and traditional retailers had better take note.

CUSTOMER CARE AND SERVICE

To test the service, we ordered a long, complex list of equipment and fittings at 4.00 p.m. on a Sunday. The complete, correct order was delivered by 8.00 a.m. on Monday.

C6 Customer Franchise

The most successful bricks retailers have invested heavily in quality and customer care and service in order to raise their standing in the assessments of customers. Some authors refer to the accumulated value of image, trust and branding as the retailer's 'customer franchise'. Consumers' lack of trust has been one of the main factors inhibiting the growth of e-retail. As McGoldrick (2002) pointed out, with greater choice consumers choose the brands that they trust.

Many bricks retailers have high-quality brands with clear personalities backed by long-term corporate promotion. These strong brands give bricks and clicks retailers a head start over 'pureplay' dot.coms. *Start-up* brands must work hard on trust. For example, one of the few pure plays to prosper, the auction site eBay, includes five levels of safeguards, including fraud protection and dispute resolution.

C7 Customer Care and Service

According to McGoldrick (2002), retailing has traditionally been classified as a 'service industry' but, for most retailers, the preoccupation with service quality and services offered is of more recent origin. At the broadest level, most of a retailer's activities deliver a form of service to the consumer, creating assortments at competitive prices in accessible locations. These activities, therefore, all play major roles in creating customer satisfaction. More specifically for the e-retailer, good service means, for example, reasonably fast and reliable deliveries at times convenient to the shopper; the availability of telephone help; and return and refund facilities. These are aspects in which the early e-retailers have been lamentably poor, with the big majority of e-shoppers still having a sorry tale to tell. For the bricks retailer, even in self-service settings, store personnel play a crucial role in forming retail images and patronage intentions. The e-retailer is at a disadvantage, but elements such as *click-through* telephone help, bulletin boards and chat rooms can help to make the e-shopping experience more interactive. In general, the successful (e-)retailer sets out to make shopping more enjoyable, more convenient and/or less worrying for the customers. When buying high-priced items and those with a high 'personal' content such as cars, shoppers particularly value personal service. Retailers such as Virgin attempt to overcome this drawback with a pop-up window with a phone number to reach a sales consultant and the working hours in which they are available.

SALE THE 7CS - THE (E-)RETAIL MIX

C1 Convenience for the Customer ('Place' from the 4Ps)

- Physical location
- Multi-channel options: browse the Web, buy in-store or vice versa - or buy on the Web, return to the store for a refund
- Virtual location and ease of finding the Web site: registration with search engines, location in e-malls and links from associates
- Web site design: connectivity, navigation, 'shelf' space allocation and ease of purchase
- Layout: 'free-flow', 'grid' or 'free-grid'

C2 Customer Value and Benefits ('Product')

- Satisfactions wanted by customers
- Solutions to problems or good feelings
- Specification (sometimes design) of products reflecting closeness to the customer and benefits that customers want
- Selection of the range of products offered for sale, assembled for target markets from diverse sources
- Wide and/or deep range, where the clicks e-retailer can score relative to the bricks retailer
- Content: describing a compelling offer of products clearly in customer value and benefits terms
- Customization of products to match the wants of customer segments as closely as possible

C3 Cost to the Customer ('Price')

- The real cost that customers will pay, including transport, carriage and taxes

- Costs of Internet telephone access
- Customers' perceptions that prices should be cheaper online than in-store

C4 Communication and Customer Relationships ('Promotion')

Communication is a two-way process also involving feedback from customers to suppliers, including:

- Marketing research surveys
- Public relations (PR)
- Direct mail
- e-Mail
- Internet
- Offline advertising such as magazines and 'click here' sections of newspapers
- Online methods such as banner ads and pop-ups (often incentivized); paid-for listings in search engines and directories; and affiliate programmes
- Atmospherics and web atmospherics: visual (decor, colour management, video clips, 3-D), olfactory (perfume and samples), tactile (smooth and cool or soft and cuddly - communicated by visuals or samples) and aural (music).

Customer Relationships

- In-store sales representatives use verbal and non-verbal (body language) communication
- Marketing database and loyalty schemes
- The e-retailer can enhance product value using Customer Relationship Management (CRM) and data mining to tailor products specifically to individual customers

C5 Computing and Category Management Issues

- Supplying the products that customers want, in the right sizes and quantities, at the right time and in the right place
- Efficient supply chains with computer network links between suppliers and retailers
- Minimizing stocks and speed of response: Efficient Customer Response (ECR - the retailers' equivalent of Just in Time or JIT)
- Cooperation between suppliers and (e-)retailers aiming to improve the efficiency of satisfying customers while minimizing stocks and costs. On the larger scale, this is 'category management' (CM), the retailer/supplier process of managing categories as strategic business units
- Efficient logistics systems - an important component of customer care and service

C6 Customer Franchise

- Image, trust and branding - long-term investment in quality, corporate communications, and customer care and service
- Safeguards, including fraud protection and dispute resolution
- Safe shopping icons, *e.g.* Which? Webtrader

C7 Customer Care and Service

- Creating assortments at competitive prices in an accessible format
- Fast and reliable deliveries at times convenient to the shopper
- Availability of help; return and refund facilities
- For the bricks retailer store personnel are crucial
- For the e-retailer click-through telephone help, bulletin boards and chat rooms make the experience more interactive and add a feeling of community
- Addressing customer concerns, particularly for credit card security, *e.g.* displaying the 'padlock' secure site logo

The extra 3Cs of the (e-)retail mix (in addition to the 4Ps or 4Cs of the marketing mix) can therefore be seen to be particularly critical for e-retailers. The computing, category management, supply chain and delivery systems are areas in which the early e-retailers, particularly pureplay dot.coms, have been sadly lacking, affecting trust, image, and customer care and service. The stronger brands with greater customer franchise have higher sales and potentially higher profit - for example, Tesco and Next. With few exceptions, it is already strongly branded bricks retailers with established computer and supply chain systems who are making the running in e-retailing. Notable exceptions include Amazon and Dell, both well known for efficient systems, quality, service, communications and interaction.

GROWTH AND PROSPECTS FOR E-RETAILING

Online shopping is growing in the UK with sales having reached £3.3 billion by 2003. This was only 2 per cent of all retail sales but is predicted to rise to 5 per cent within a year or two and to 10 per cent by 2009. Other researchers estimate the market to be even larger and growing faster. For example, IMRG (2003) estimated e-retail sales to have already reached 7 per cent of all retail sales. 'Most people' will buy groceries, books, CDs and even clothes by e-shopping. Books, movies and software, high on 'factual search', are natural for e-retailing, but electronic products, groceries and clothing are also increasing. Ninety-four per cent will be at the expense of existing channels and only 6 per cent from extra growth. According to the industry body, the Interactive Media in Retail Group, there are about 4 million people in the UK who spend an average of £3,000 to £5,000 per year online.

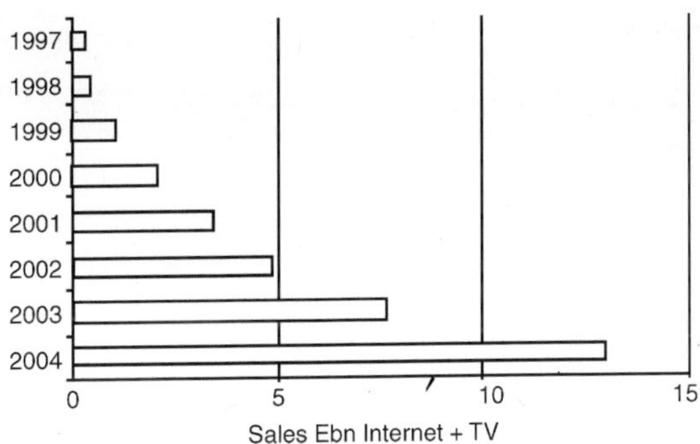

Fig. The Growth of online Shopping: Surveys, 1997 to 2003, Forecast 2004

Shoppers have long used the Internet to browse for products before buying offline, but US e-shoppers at least are reversing that trend, with 45 per cent of e-shoppers buying online after researching in stores and catalogues, according to a survey of 1,252 e-shoppers and over 80 e-retailers . This must be a worrying trend for bricks retailers, but also helps to strengthen the competitive position of multi-channel bricks and clicks retailers.

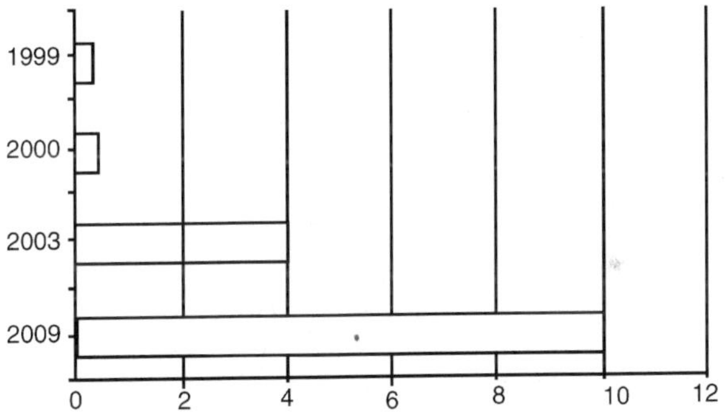

Fig. E-Retailing as Percentage of UK Shopping

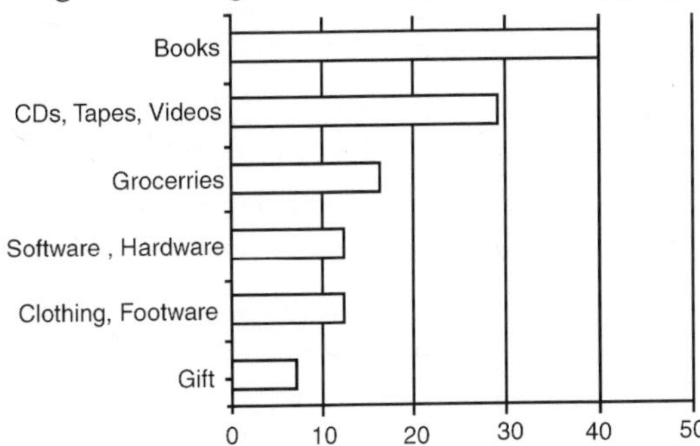

Fig. What E-shoppers Buy

According to Verdict, in 2001 grocery accounted for half of all UK e-retailing - £1.3 billion - which sounds massive but represents only 5.6 per cent of groceries. The market leaders in their sectors were Amazon (books, plus CDs and DVD movies), Tesco (groceries), Dell (computers), Next (clothing) and Comet (electrical and electronic hardware). Though perhaps not actually an e-retailer, eBay is the leader for auctions and is the most visited of all UK websites.

Average spend has risen faster for men (+15 per cent) than women (+5 per cent), leading Verdict to comment that 'the proliferation of female-orientated sites... [has] failed to motivate women to shop significantly more'.

The proportion of e-shoppers preferring to shop from e-sites run by high street retailers rather than Internet-only is soaring. The main service is travel and the main virtual product is sex (pictures, stories and video) - often absent from published statistics, but accounting for around 10 per cent of e-retailing. In the words of *The Virgin Internet Shopping Guide*: 'However much you may despise the sex industry, it has been almost solely responsible for driving forward the revolution in online

Bibliography

Adam Musgrave: *Forces and Fueling of E-Commerce and E-Business*, Global Vision, Delhi, 2012.

Alan Davidson: *The Law of Electronic Commerce*, Cambridge University Press, Delhi, 2011.

Anil Passi: *Oracle E-Business Suite Development & Extensibility Handbook*, Tata McGraw-Hill, Delhi, 2009.

Bastin Gerald: *Oracle: E-Business Suite Manufacturing & Supply Chain Management*, Tata McGraw-Hill, Delhi, 2003.

Bharat Bhaskar: *Recommender System in Electronic Commerce*, McGraw Hill, Delhi, 2010.

BRAHM CANZER: *E-Business and Commerce: Strategic Thinking and Practice*, Wiley, Delhi, 2004.

Debasis Mukherjee: *Customer Relationship Management*, Adhyayan Publication, Delhi, 2011.

Ekta Rastogi: *Customer Relationship Management*, Excel Books, Delhi, 2001.

Geoffrey Sampson: *Electronic Business*, Viva Books, Delhi, 2009.

J. Christopher Westland and Theodore H.K. Clark: *Global Electronic Commerce: Theory and Case Studies*, Universities Press, Delhi, 2001.

Nandan Kamath: *Law Relating to Computers Internet and E-Commerce*, Universal Law Publishers, Delhi, 2012.

Navin K. Sinha: *Electronic Commerce*, Shree Publication, Delhi, 2006.

Nina Verma: *E-Commerce Taxation : Prospects and Challenges*, Global Vision Publication, Delhi, 2012.

Paul Phillips: *E-Business Strategy*, Tata McGraw-Hill, Delhi, 2011.

Pravin Kumar Tayal and Sugan C. Jain: *E-Commerce and Marketing*, RBSA Publication, Jaipur, 2008.

R K Uppal: *Customer Relationship Management in Indian Banking Industry*, New Century Publication, Delhi, 2008.

R. Ramachandran: *Customer Relationship Management*, Serials Publications, Delhi, 2011.

R.K. Mohanty: *E-Commerce Models : Modern Methods and Techniques*, Yking Books, Delih, 2012.

Rahul Gupta: *Cyber Rules : Strategies for Excelling at E-Business*, Global India Publications, Delhi, 2010.

Rajesh Talwar: *Indian Laws of e-Business*, Vision Books, Delhi, 1999.

Ravindra Kumar and Manish Deshpande: *Electronic Business*, Pacific Books International, Delhi, 2012.

S B Verma; R K Shrivastawa and S K Singh: *Dynamics of Electronic Commerce*, Deep and Deep Publication, Delhi, 2007.

S.K. Bansal: *E-Business Fundamentals*, APH Publication, Delhi, 2004.

S.R. Sharma: *Laws on E-Commerce*, Anmol Publication, Delhi, 2004.

Shankaran Iyer: *Oracle E-Business Suite Financials Administration*, Tata McGraw-Hill, Delhi, 2004.

T Vetrivel: *Customer Relationship Management*, Discovery Publishing House, Delhi, 2011.

U. S. Pandey and Rahul Srivastava: *E-Commerce and Mobile Commerce Technologies*, S. Chand Publisher, Delhi, 2007.

V P Gupta: *E-Business*, Researchco Book Centre, Delhi, 2006.

Index